Economic Challenges in the Gulf Cooperation Council Countries

THE ECONOMIES OF THE MIDDLE EAST

Series Editors: Jalal Qanas, *Assistant Professor of Economics, Department of Finance and Economics, Qatar University, Qatar* and Malcolm C. Sawyer, *Emeritus Professor of Economics, University of Leeds, UK*

The Middle East is a region of immense economic diversity and complexity, characterized by a unique blend of historical legacies, resource endowments, geopolitical realities, and ongoing transformations. This series seeks to capture this multifaceted nature by offering a comprehensive and nuanced exploration of the economic landscapes across the Middle East. It aims to move beyond simplistic narratives and delve into the intricacies of economic development, challenges, and opportunities in the region. The volumes in this series will serve as essential resources for scholars, policymakers, practitioners, and anyone interested in understanding the economic dynamics of the Middle East.

For a full list of Edward Elgar published titles, including the titles in this series, visit our website at www.e-elgar.com.

Economic Challenges in the Gulf Cooperation Council Countries

Moving Toward Economic Diversification and Sustainability

Edited by

Jalal Qanas

Assistant Professor of Economics, Department of Finance and Economics, Qatar University, Qatar

Malcolm C. Sawyer

Emeritus Professor of Economics, University of Leeds, UK

THE ECONOMIES OF THE MIDDLE EAST

Edward Elgar
PUBLISHING

Cheltenham, UK • Northampton, MA, USA

Published by

Edward Elgar Publishing Limited
The Lypiatts
15 Lansdown Road
Cheltenham
Glos GL50 2JA
UK

Edward Elgar Publishing, Inc.
William Pratt House
9 Dewey Court
Northampton
Massachusetts 01060
USA

Authorised representative in the EU for GPSR queries only: Easy Access System Europe – Mustamäe tee 50, 10621 Tallinn, Estonia, gpsr.requests@easproject.com

A catalogue record for this book is available from the British Library

Library of Congress Control Number: 2026932105

This book is available electronically in the **Elgar**online
Economics subject collection
https://doi.org/10.4337/9781035358441

MIX
Paper | Supporting responsible forestry
FSC® C013604

ISBN 978 1 0353 5843 4 (cased)
ISBN 978 1 0353 5844 1 (eBook)
ISBN 978 1 0353 9318 3 (ePub)

Printed and bound by CPI Group (UK) Ltd, Croydon, CR0 4YY

Contents

List of contributors

Quosay Awad Ahmed, ENERQA Consultancy, Qatar.

Zaheer Ahmed, Iqra University, Karachi, Pakistan.

Ahmad Alawadhi, Kuwait Institute for Scientific Research (KISR), Kuwait.

Shaikha Al-Fulaij, Kuwait Institute for Scientific Research (KISR), Kuwait.

Adnan Aljawareen, College of Administration and Economics, Qurna, University of Basrah, Iraq.

Maha Alshebani, Qatar Museums, Qatar.

Husam Arman, Kuwait Institute for Scientific Research (KISR), Kuwait.

Omar Bortolazzi, American University in Dubai, Dubai.

Joel Foyth, Rosario Institute for Studies of the Arab and Islamic World (IREMAI – UNR), Philippines.

Nazar Hilal, College of Arts and Sciences, Qatar University, Qatar.

Islam Mohamed Mahmoud, School of Management Studies, University of Khartoum, Sudan.

Duncan Mayall, chief economist at a government advisory firm.

Umara Noreen, College of Business Administration, Prince Sultan University, Saudi Arabia.

Jalal Qanas, Department of Finance and Economics, Qatar University, Qatar.

Malcolm C. Sawyer, Emeritus Professor of Economics, University of Leeds, UK.

Attayah Shafique, Department of Communication and Management Sciences, Institute of Engineering and Applied Sciences, Pakistan.

Zariyah Zein, Qatar Museums, Qatar.

Preface

The economies of the Gulf Cooperation Council (GCC) stand at a critical juncture in their developmental history. For decades, the region has been defined by its immense hydrocarbon wealth, which has fueled unprecedented economic growth, financed rapid modernization, and provided its citizens with a high standard of living. This reliance on oil and gas, however, has created a unique economic structure—often characterized by the dynamics of the rentier state—that presents profound and complex challenges for long-term sustainability. The global energy transition, coupled with the inherent volatility of commodity markets and the demographic pressures of a young and growing population, has made the imperative for economic diversification more urgent than ever. The core question is no longer *whether* to diversify, but *how* to successfully navigate the structural transformation toward a post-oil future.

This book, E*conomic Challenges in the Gulf Cooperation Council Copuntries: Moving toward Economic Diversification and Sustainability*,, confronts this question directly. It moves beyond generalized policy prescriptions to offer a multifaceted and in-depth examination of the specific obstacles and opportunities that define the region's path forward. The central premise of this book is that meaningful diversification is not merely an exercise in launching new industrial sectors; it requires a fundamental rewiring of the region's economic, institutional, and social fabric. It involves addressing deep-seated structural challenges, from the dominant role of the state and the nature of its sovereign wealth funds to the development of a dynamic private sector, the cultivation of human capital, and the redefinition of the social contract.

The challenge is multifaceted. It involves managing the transition away from an economic model where the state is the primary engine of growth and employment, toward one where a competitive, innovation-driven private sector takes the lead. It requires fostering new comparative advantages in non-oil sectors, a task complicated by labor markets often segmented between expatriate and national workforces. Furthermore, sustainability in the GCC context is a dual concept: it refers not only to environmental stewardship in a climate-vulnerable region but also to the creation of an economic model that is fiscally sustainable and can provide prosperity long after the oil and gas reserves have dwindled. This book brings together a diverse range of scholarly perspectives to dissect these challenges from various angles, providing a comprehensive and nuanced understanding of the task at hand.

To navigate this complex terrain, this book is structured to guide the reader from the macroeconomic and institutional framework to specific sectoral strategies and innovative policy approaches. We begin with a foundational analysis of the state's role, with Qanas and Sawyer exploring the potential for an 'entrepreneurial state' to actively shape and direct a new development paradigm. This is followed by a broad overview of regional trends, with Nazar Hilal mapping the opportunities and challenges in the current diversification landscape, while Adnan Aljawareen provides a rigorous empirical analysis of the determinants of diversification over the past two decades.

The subsequent chapters delve into the key instruments and enablers of structural change. Duncan Mayall examines the evolving role of the region's powerful sovereign wealth funds, assessing their potential to act as catalysts for transformation rather than as simple managers of foreign assets. Umara Noreen, Attayah Shafique, and Zaheer Ahmed investigate the pivotal role of information technology and digitalization as a cross-cutting enabler of sustainability and economic diversification across all sectors. Then the critical importance of fostering a vibrant ecosystem for small and medium-sized enterprises (SMEs) as a cornerstone of a diversified economy is expertly detailed by Husam Arman, Ahmad Alawadhi, and Shaikha Al-Fulaij.

The focus then narrows to specific, innovative strategies being deployed within the region. Islam Mohamed Mahmoud and Quosay Awad Ahmed provide a timely case study on the development of green credit lines in Qatar, evaluating their impact on the crucial energy transition. Moving from finance to identity, Omar Bortolazzi analyzes how the UAE is leveraging nation-branding and public diplomacy to move beyond its rentier identity on the global stage. Broadening the definition of diversification, Joel Foyth examines the strategic importance of food security, highlighting opportunities for international cooperation between the Gulf and nations like Argentina. Finally, Maha Alshebani and Zariyah Zein explore the untapped potential of cultural and creative industries as a source of sustainable economic diversification in Qatar.

Collectively, these chapters offer a rich tapestry of analysis that underscores the complexity of the GCC's economic transition. They highlight that the path to a sustainable and diversified future is not singular; it requires a portfolio of coordinated strategies that are tailored to the unique context of each member state. It is our hope that this book will serve as an essential resource for academics, policymakers, and all those interested in the future of the Gulf, providing not just a sober assessment of the challenges, but also a clear-eyed view of the opportunities that lie ahead.

Acknowledgments

The completion of this edited book owes a great deal to the intellectual contributions and collaborative spirit of many individuals and institutions. As editors, our first and most profound gratitude goes to the distinguished group of scholars who authored the chapters of this book. Their expertise, rigorous research, and insightful analyses form the very foundation of this work. They have tackled a complex and multifaceted subject with the nuance and depth it deserves, and we are honored to have brought their work together in this collection.

A special acknowledgment is owed to the Gulf Research Centre (GRC) for their invaluable support. Many of the chapters in this book were first presented and discussed at the Gulf Research Meeting (GRM) held at the University of Cambridge from July 9–11, 2024. Specifically, we are grateful for the platform provided by Workshop 4, titled "The Structural Economic Challenges that GCC Economies Face to Move Toward Economic Diversification and Sustainability," which we had the privilege to direct. The insightful discussions and feedback from the workshop participants were instrumental in shaping the direction and quality of this book.

We are indebted to our respective institutions, the Gulf Research Centre (GRC), Qatar University, and the University of Leeds, for providing the intellectual environment and support that made this project possible. The vibrant academic communities at both universities have been a source of constant inspiration and critical feedback.

We would also like to extend our sincere thanks to the anonymous peer reviewers whose constructive comments and suggestions were invaluable in strengthening the arguments and refining the focus of each chapter. Their scholarly diligence has significantly enhanced the quality and coherence of the final manuscript.

A special note of appreciation is due to our publisher, whose team has guided this project with professionalism and patience from its conception to its conclusion. Their belief in the importance of this topic has been a driving force throughout the publication process.

Finally, this book is dedicated to the policymakers, business leaders, students, and citizens of the GCC region. It is our hope that this book will contribute to the ongoing dialogue about the region's economic future and provide a valuable resource for those working to build more diversified, sustainable, and resilient economies for the generations to come.

Jalal Qanas
Malcolm C. Sawyer

1. The role of entrepreneurial state in GCC economies in building a long-term sustainable development

Jalal Qanas and Malcolm C. Sawyer

1.1 INTRODUCTION

The economies of the Gulf Cooperation Council (GCC) stand at a critical historical juncture. For over half a century, the region's development trajectory was defined by a single commodity: oil and natural gas. The immense revenues (external rents) generated from hydrocarbon exports fueled a period of extraordinary growth, enabling the construction of modern metropolises from the desert sands and funding extensive cradle-to-grave welfare systems for citizens. This rentier state model, however, has revealed its inherent fragility. The accelerating global transition away from fossil fuels, coupled with the endemic volatility of energy prices and pressing demographic pressures from a burgeoning youth population, has rendered the old development paradigm unsustainable. The imperative to diversify is no longer a matter of long-term planning but of urgent economic survival. This transition represents a fundamental strategic pivot from leveraging a natural comparative advantage in hydrocarbons to building a durable competitive advantage in knowledge-intensive global industries.

In response, GCC governments have launched a series of bold and ambitious national visions. Notable among these are Saudi Arabia's Vision 2030, the UAE Centennial 2071, Oman Vision 2040, and Qatar National Vision 2030. These are not merely policy adjustments but represent a fundamental effort to re-engineer the very foundations of their political economies. At the core of this effort is a profound redefinition of the role of the state itself. Moving beyond its historical function as a passive distributor of oil wealth, the GCC state is actively recasting itself as a strategic, risk-taking investor and market-maker. This new posture aligns closely with the concept of the "entrepreneurial state" popularized by Mariana Mazzucato (2021), where the state does not simply regulate existing markets but actively creates and shapes new ones through mission-oriented public investment in strategic sectors like renewable energy, artificial intelligence, biotechnology, and tourism.

This transformative ambition can be understood through the lens of Karl Polanyi's (1944) concept of the "double movement." Polanyi argued that the expansion of the self-regulating market (the first movement) inevitably provokes a societal counter-movement demanding social protection from the market's disruptive effects. The GCC's initial development path represented a complete integration into the global energy market, exposing its fortunes to external volatility. The current diversification drive can thus be seen as a protective counter-movement, a deliberate state-led attempt to re-embed the economy within a more stable and diversified domestic structure, thereby shielding society from the instabilities of a single global commodity market. It is, in essence, a grand project of national economic self-preservation.

This chapter explores the immense potential and inherent contradictions of this state-led transformation. It puts forward a central argument that while GCC nations are impressively adopting the policies, investments, and rhetoric of the entrepreneurial state, their progress is fundamentally constrained and shaped by the enduring structural legacies of their rentier past. We contend that a deep-seated tension exists between the forward-looking aspiration to foster a dynamic, innovative, and private-sector-led economy and the deep-rooted realities of an economic system built on oil rents. This clash manifests in several critical arenas that will be explored in detail, viz. a private sector historically conditioned for dependency on state patronage, a bifurcated labor market that disincentivizes citizen participation in productive and globally competitive industries, and a persistent gap in the indigenous research and innovation ecosystem required for a genuine knowledge-based economy.

The analysis will proceed in four parts. Section 2 will establish the chapter's theoretical foundations, defining and contrasting the rentier state model with the classic East Asian developmental state and the entrepreneurial state. Section 3 will examine the GCC's diversification drive in practice. Section 4 will provide a critical analysis of the key structural impediments hindering this transition. Finally, Section 5 will conclude by assessing the future prospects of the GCC's unique state-led development model.

1.2 THEORETICAL FRAMEWORK: STATE, MARKET, AND DEVELOPMENT IN THE GCC CONTEXT

To critically evaluate the GCC's ambitious economic transformation, it is essential to establish a robust theoretical framework that can account for the region's unique starting point and its declared destination. The journey from a rentier economy to a diversified, sustainable one involves a fundamental shift in the nature of the state and its relationship with the market and society. This section defines and contrasts the key conceptual models, that is, the rentier state, the developmental state, and the entrepreneurial state, and situates them within a broader understanding of industrial policy and the state's role in economic development.

1.2.1 Conceptualizing the State: a Spectrum of Roles

The state is not a monolithic entity but a concept that has been realized in vastly different forms across history and geography. Political economy offers a spectrum of "ideal types" (in the Weberian sense) to understand the state's role, particularly its relationship with the market and society. At one end of this spectrum lies the night-watchman state, a minimalist model whose functions are limited to enforcing contracts, protecting property rights, and defending national borders. In this view, the market is the primary mechanism for coordinating economic activity, and the state's role is simply to provide a stable and secure environment for it to function.

Moving along the spectrum, the regulatory state assumes a more active role. It goes beyond the minimalist functions to correct perceived market failures, such as monopolies, negative externalities (e.g., pollution), and information asymmetries. This state formulates and enforces the rules of the economic game through antitrust laws, environmental regulations, and consumer protection agencies, aiming to make markets not just possible but also efficient and fair. Further still, the welfare state, most prominently developed in post-war Europe, adds a powerful redistributive function. It seeks to protect citizens from the inherent insecurities of the market through comprehensive social insurance, public healthcare, and state-funded education, creating a social safety net funded primarily by taxing the productive activities of its citizens and firms.

These models provide a crucial backdrop for understanding the unique case of the GCC. The region's historical development did not neatly follow any of these Western-centric trajectories. Instead, the influx of hydrocarbon revenues allowed for the creation of a unique state form, the rentier state, which combines elements of a cradle-to-grave welfare system with a fundamentally different economic logic. Analyzing this specific model, and the GCC's ambitious effort to transition towards an entrepreneurial one, requires moving beyond these traditional archetypes to appreciate the distinctive path the region has forged and the one it now seeks to navigate.

1.2.2 The Rentier State and its Social Contract

A major characteristic of each of the GCC countries for the past half-century has been their status as rentier states. A rentier state is one that derives a substantial portion of its national revenue from external rents, which are generated by selling indigenous natural resources (in this case, oil and gas) to foreign actors (Gray, 2020). This economic foundation is profoundly different from that of a production-based economy, where state revenue is primarily derived from taxing the productive activities of its citizens and domestic firms. This distinction is not merely economic but shapes the entire political and social fabric of a nation. This fosters what Beblawi (1987) termed a "rentier mentality," a cultural outlook that decouples reward from productive work, creating economic distortions and a passive private sector. While classic rentierism is evolving into what some scholars call "late rentierism," where states invest in diversification while maintaining rentier structures, the core dependencies remain (Gray, 2011).

The most significant consequence of rentierism is the formation of a particular form of social contract. Because the state does not depend on its citizens for its revenues, it is not bound by the traditional logic of "no taxation without representation." Instead, a different bargain is struck in which the state distributes a portion of the oil and gas rents to the populace in the form of secure public sector employment, free or heavily subsidized services (healthcare, education, housing, utilities), and a general absence of personal income or significant consumption taxes. In return, the state expects political loyalty and a general depoliticization of public life. This system effectively creates a unique form of welfare state, one funded by external rents rather than by the collective contributions of a productive society. This rent-funded welfare system, while providing high living standards, creates powerful economic distortions, particularly in the labor market, by establishing the state as the employer of first resort for nationals and artificially inflating wage expectations.

1.2.3 Models of State-led Development: Developmental and Entrepreneurial

As GCC countries seek to move beyond rentierism, they are implicitly or explicitly drawing on established models of state-led development. Two are particularly relevant: the developmental state and the entrepreneurial state.

The developmental state model is classically associated with the post-war economic miracles of East Asian nations like Japan, South Korea, and Taiwan (Amsden, 1989; Marquand, 1988). These resource-poor states pursued a "catch-up" industrialization strategy characterized by several key features:

- A strong, autonomous bureaucracy: insulated from political pressures, a skilled cadre of bureaucrats guided economic policy.

- Strategic industrial policy: the state actively nurtured "winner" industries, often in the manufacturing and export sectors, through subsidies, preferential loans, and protection from foreign competition.
- State–business cooperation: a close, symbiotic relationship existed between the state and large private conglomerates, disciplined by export performance targets.
- Emphasis on production and exports: the ultimate goal was to build internationally competitive industries that could drive sustainable growth.

While the GCC's current approach shares the emphasis on state guidance, it differs in a crucial respect. The East Asian developmental states were capital-scarce and labor-abundant. The GCC states, on the other hand, are capital-abundant and (in terms of national labor) relatively labor-scarce. Their challenge is not accumulating capital but deploying it effectively without falling into the traps of inefficiency and patronage that immense wealth can engender.

This is where the entrepreneurial state model, as articulated by Mariana Mazzucato (2021), offers a more contemporary and relevant lens. The model fundamentally challenges the conventional view of the state's role in the economy, which is often limited to that of a market facilitator or a fixer of market failures. In traditional economic theory, the state should only intervene to address problems like public goods provision, externalities, or information asymmetries, after which the private sector, seen as the true engine of innovation and value creation, should take the lead.

The entrepreneurial state theory posits a far more proactive and central role. It argues that historically, the state has not been a passive observer but a lead investor and risk-taker in the creation of new technological paradigms. From the internet and GPS (originally defense projects) to biotechnology and renewable energy, the state has often acted as the "investor of first resort," providing the patient, long-term, and high-risk capital that the private sector is typically unwilling to commit, especially in the early stages of a technology's development. This is because private venture capital, often driven by short-term exit strategies, tends to be risk-averse when faced with the radical uncertainty of foundational scientific breakthroughs. The state, by contrast, can and does invest in the entire innovation chain, from basic research to applied R&D and eventual commercialization.

Crucially, the entrepreneurial state does not merely "level the playing field," it actively tilts it in the direction of bold, societal missions. These missions, such as tackling climate change, achieving public health goals, or bridging the digital divide, provide a clear direction for innovation and help to coordinate public and private investment towards a common purpose. In doing so, the state is not "picking winners" in the traditional industrial policy sense, but rather "picking the willing" by creating new technological and industrial landscapes that incentivize private firms to co-invest and innovate. The state's role, therefore, is to create and shape new markets, not just fix existing ones. By making these strategic, mission-oriented investments, the state de-risks new sectors and creates opportunities that "crowd in" subsequent waves of private sector investment, which often reaps the rewards of these early-stage public expenditures.

However, the effective implementation of an entrepreneurial state model is contingent on several critical preconditions. It requires public sector organizations with dynamic capabilities, an ability to embrace experimentation, and the institutional resilience to learn from inevitable failures. Furthermore, as critics of the model argue, a successful entrepreneurial state cannot exist without a vibrant "entrepreneurial society" (Sanders et al., 2024). The state can create opportunities, but a dynamic private sector, a skilled workforce, and a risk-taking culture are needed to seize them. Without this symbiotic relationship, state-led initiatives risk becoming isolated public projects with limited economic spillovers. This raises the critical challenge for the GCC where its immense capital reserves allow it to fund the ambitious missions and patient investments characteristic of an entrepreneurial state, yet its rentier legacy may have constrained the development of the very entrepreneurial society needed to make those investments truly transformative. The GCC's focus on giga-projects like NEOM, investments in renewable energy, and the creation of new technology hubs thus represents a high-stakes test of this model in a unique and challenging context.

1.2.4 Industrial Policy and the Nature of State Intervention

The strategies employed by both developmental and entrepreneurial states fall under the umbrella of industrial policy. This term, often viewed with suspicion in neoliberal economics, simply refers to government efforts to shape the structure of the economy. However, as recent analysis from institutions like the IMF highlights, industrial policy is not a monolith. It has varied objectives and takes many forms (Cherif & Hasanov, 2019). It can range from broad, "horizontal" policies that improve the overall business environment (e.g., education, infrastructure) to targeted, "vertical" policies that support specific firms or sectors.

To better understand the nature of state intervention in the GCC, we draw on Ronald Dore's (1986) analysis of Japanese industrial policy to distinguish four broad types of state intervention:

1. Regulatory intervention: actions to make markets work better, such as enforcing contracts, preventing fraud, and ensuring competition. This is the baseline role of the state in any market economy.
2. Domestic developmentalism: interventions to promote general growth where social benefits exceed private benefits, such as investing in R&D, education, and infrastructure.
3. Competitive developmentalism: actions explicitly aimed at improving the international competitiveness of the nation's firms. This includes classic industrial policy tools like infant industry protection, export subsidies, and promoting national champions.
4. "Pork-barrel" intervention: the use of state power and funds to benefit politically connected sectional interests, often leading to corruption and inefficiency.

The challenge for the GCC countries is to ensure that its state-led initiatives align with developmental or competitive goals (2 and 3) and avoid degenerating into pork-barrel politics (4), a significant risk in economies where the lines between public and private wealth can be blurred. As Best (1990) argues, a successful industrial policy does not seek to replace the market with a central plan but rather, its purpose is "not to substitute the plan for the market but to shape and use markets" (p. 20). This requires a creative and strategic approach to statecraft, mapping out future directions for the economy and building a competitive advantage, rather than simply relying on the comparative advantage of natural resource endowments. The GCC's journey is a high-stakes test of whether rentier wealth can be transformed into a tool for shaping markets and building a truly sustainable and diversified economic future.

1.3 THE ENTREPRENEURIAL STATE IN ACTION: NATIONAL VISIONS AND STRATEGIC INVESTMENTS

Across the Gulf, a clear and concerted effort is underway to operationalize the principles of the entrepreneurial state. This is most evident in two interconnected domains: first, the articulation of ambitious, long-term national visions that serve as "missions" to guide economic and social development; and second, the direct deployment of state capital through powerful investment vehicles to create new markets and strategic industries from the ground up.

1.3.1 National Visions as Mission-setting Frameworks

The national visions adopted by GCC countries are more than just policy documents; they are comprehensive blueprints designed to mobilize state and society towards a post-oil future. They function as the "missions" described by Mazzucato (2021), setting a clear direction of travel and defining success in terms of concrete, long-term targets.

Saudi Arabia: The Kingdom's Vision 2030 is the most prominent and far-reaching of these missions. It aims to increase non-oil government revenue from $43 billion in 2021 to $266 billion by 2030 and increase the private sector's contribution to GDP from 40% to 65% (Alqahtani, 2023). Its goals are cross-sectoral, encompassing economic diversification, social liberalization (such as increasing female labor force participation from 19% in 2016 to 36% in 2022), and enhancing quality of life (Relocate MENA, 2023). This mission is operationalized through giga-projects like NEOM, a $500 billion futuristic city intended to be a hub for advanced industries like biotechnology and robotics, and the development of tourism around cultural and religious heritage sites.

United Arab Emirates: The UAE has a multi-layered strategy, including "Operation 300bn," which aims to increase the industrial sector's GDP contribution from $100 billion to approximately $300 billion by 2031 (UAE, 2024). This mission focuses on moving up the value chain from labor-intensive industries to a knowledge-based economy driven by technology and R&D. The development of Masdar City in Abu Dhabi as a pioneering hub for renewable energy and clean technology is a prime example of the state creating a living laboratory to catalyze a new industry. A report by Ramadan and Uppal (2024) highlighted that the UAE's non-oil revenue had already hit a record $953 billion, underscoring the tangible progress of its diversification efforts.

Qatar, Oman, and Kuwait: Other GCC nations have adopted similarly mission-oriented visions. Qatar's National Vision 2030 focuses on building a diversified economy with competitive advantages in logistics, tourism, and petrochemicals, an effort significantly boosted by the state-led investment in infrastructure for the FIFA 2022 World Cup. Its Third National Development Strategy (2024–2030) targets a 4% annual economic growth rate through investments in technology and education (Invest Qatar, 2024). Oman's Vision 2040 aims to reduce the contribution of oil to GDP to less than 10%, focusing on developing sectors like fisheries, manufacturing, tourism, and logistics (Raza, 2023). Kuwait's Vision 2035, while facing more implementation challenges, aims to increase its non-oil revenue from 5% to 40% by 2035, targeting financial services and healthcare as key growth areas.

1.3.2 The State as a Strategic Investor and Market Creator

The engine rooms of this transformation are the region's powerful and increasingly sophisticated sovereign wealth funds (SWFs) and state investment vehicles. These entities are not acting as passive portfolio investors but as the primary agents of the entrepreneurial state, deploying patient, long-term capital to de-risk and develop strategic sectors.

> Bahrain: Having successfully reduced its oil dependence over the last decade, Bahrain provides a compelling case study. In 2010, oil exports accounted for around 70% of total budget revenue; this is projected to fall to just 15% by 2030. This was achieved through a concerted state-led push into financial services and fintech, which now represent the largest non-oil sector, contributing 17.4% to GDP (HKTDC, 2023). By creating a favorable regulatory environment and providing initial support, the state effectively nurtured a new, high-value industry.
>
> Oman: The state's strategic investments are yielding clear results in diversifying Oman's export base. The trend in the country's non-oil exports demonstrates this success, showing a consistent and sharp increase between 2018 and 2022 (Trade Finance Global, 2024). Non-oil exports increased by a remarkable 54.6% in 2022, driven by growth in chemicals, mineral products, and base metals, which collectively now account for nearly 70% of total non-oil exports (Trade Finance Global, 2024). This illustrates a successful state-guided shift in productive capacity away from traditional reliance on oil.
>
> Saudi Arabia and Qatar: The state's role as market creator is perhaps most visible here. The Public Investment Fund (PIF) of Saudi Arabia has become one of the world's most active investors, tasked with funding Vision 2030 projects and building national champions in sectors from electric vehicles (Lucid Motors) to tourism and entertainment. In Qatar, state investment has successfully positioned the country as a global logistics and aviation hub through Qatar Airways and Hamad International Airport. This state-led investment has reshaped the economy's composition, as illustrated by the dramatic growth of the services sector to comprise over 65% of GDP by 2022, a significant increase from just over 53% in 2016 (O'Neill, 2025).

In each of these cases, the state is not merely "leveling the playing field"; it is actively tilting it towards strategic, long-term objectives. It is building the infrastructure, providing the capital, setting the direction, and absorbing the initial risk in a manner that is fundamentally entrepreneurial. The tangible progress in growing non-oil sectors across the region is a direct testament to the power and intent of this state-led model. However, the sustainability of this model depends critically on whether it can overcome the deep-seated structural challenges inherited from its rentier past.

1.4 STRUCTURAL IMPEDIMENTS: THE ENDURING LEGACY OF THE RENTIER STATE

While the ambition and capital deployment of the GCC's entrepreneurial state project are impressive, its path is fraught with formidable structural challenges. These are not merely technical or policy-related obstacles; they are deep-seated impediments rooted in the very fabric of the rentier political economy that the region is trying to transcend. The success of the diversification drive hinges on the ability to overcome these legacies, which manifest in four critical areas: the persistent gravity of oil dependence, a nascent and dependent private sector, a distorted labor market, and a significant deficit in indigenous innovation capacity.

1.4.1 The Unbroken Gravity of Oil Dependence

The foundational challenge is that the diversification project is almost entirely funded by the proceeds of the old economy based on oil and gas. This creates a powerful paradox: the mission to reduce oil dependence is itself dependent on high oil prices. Analysis shows the fiscal breakeven oil price, that is, the price per barrel required to balance the government's budget, remains precariously high for several GCC nations. For instance, in 2020, this price was estimated to be around $96 for Saudi Arabia and $96 for Bahrain, compared to a lower $40 for Qatar, highlighting different levels of vulnerability across the region (Kabbani, 2020). This reliance exposes long-term diversification plans to short-term market volatility. A sustained period of low oil prices would not only strain state finances but could directly threaten the funding for the very giga-projects and industrial subsidies designed to wean the economy off oil.

Furthermore, the continued profitability of the hydrocarbon sector creates powerful institutional inertia. State-owned oil companies remain the crown jewels of the economy, and there is a strong incentive to continue expanding hydrocarbon production capacity to maximize revenue. This dual strategy of investing in both green energy and expanded oil and gas production sends mixed signals to markets and can dilute the focus and resources required for a genuine green transition. As a Moody's report highlighted, despite heavy investment in non-oil sectors, progress in reducing fundamental dependence remains limited, with plans to further expand hydrocarbon capacity acting as a significant counterweight to diversification aims (Al Jazeera, 2021).

1.4.2 A Nascent and Dependent Private Sector

A core objective of the entrepreneurial state is to "crowd in" private investment and foster a vibrant, competitive ecosystem of firms. In the GCC, however, the private sector has been historically conditioned for dependence, not independence. For decades, the most profitable private enterprises have been those with close ties to the state, operating as agents for foreign companies, contractors for government projects, or beneficiaries of state subsidies and protectionist regulations (Salim, 2023). This has fostered a culture of "rent-seeking" rather than true entrepreneurship, where success often depends more on political connections (*wasta*) than on innovation or efficiency.

The current state-led investment boom risks perpetuating this dynamic. With the state acting as the primary investor, planner, and customer for new industries, private firms are incentivized to align with state priorities rather than to chart their own course. This can lead to the emergence of a "quasi-public" private sector, dominated by large, state-affiliated conglomerates that can easily out-compete smaller, more agile startups for capital and contracts. A recent S&P Global report noted that while the sale of minority stakes in state-related entities can deepen capital markets, it also intensifies funding competition for truly private firms, which already struggle with resource constraints (S&P, 2022). The challenge, as articulated by Callen (2023) in the context of Saudi Arabia, is that developing new, capital-intensive sectors will inevitably require massive public support, which can potentially stymie the organic development of an independent private sector.

1.4.3 The Labor Market Conundrum and the *Kafala* System

Perhaps the most complex and deeply entrenched challenge lies in the region's unique labor market structure, a direct product of the rentier social contract. This market is fundamentally bifurcated:

1. A National labor market: Dominated by the public sector, which provides citizens with high wages, job security, and generous benefits. This has created wage and productivity expectations that are often misaligned with the demands of a globally competitive private sector.
2. An expatriate labor market: Comprising the vast majority (around 75%) of the private sector workforce, historically regulated by the *kafala* (sponsorship) system. This system tied a foreign worker's legal status directly to their employer, granting the employer significant control and keeping labor costs low and flexible (PwC, 2024).

This dualism creates a formidable barrier to building a knowledge-based economy. The new, high-value industries envisioned by diversification plans require a highly skilled, motivated, and productive workforce. However, the existing incentive structure pulls national talent towards the public sector. A PwC Middle East report (PwC, 2023) revealed that two-thirds of Emiratis in the private sector would prefer a public sector job, citing concerns over job stability and compensation.

While recent reforms to the *kafala* system in countries like the UAE and Saudi Arabia have increased labor mobility for expatriates, the fundamental challenge remains. "Nationalization" policies (like Saudi's *Nitaqat*) that mandate private sector hiring quotas for citizens can help address unemployment but do not solve the underlying skills and productivity gap. Moreover, as South Asian economies grow more prosperous and the cost of living in the Gulf rises, the region's ability to attract and retain highly skilled foreign talent is facing new pressures (Oxford Analytica, 2022). Without resolving this structural imbalance, the GCC risks building advanced industries that its own citizens are either unable or unwilling to power.

1.4.4 The Research and Development and Innovation Gap

The final critical impediment is the region's relative deficit in indigenous innovation capacity. The entrepreneurial state model is predicated on a strong foundation of Research and Development (R&D) to generate the scientific and technological breakthroughs that fuel new industries. The GCC, having historically been a net importer of technology and expertise, is only now beginning to build this foundation.

R&D expenditure, while increasing, remains low by global standards. In 2021, the UAE, a regional leader, spent 1.5% of its GDP on R&D (Knoema, 2021). While a significant increase, this is still well below the levels of innovation-driven economies like South Korea (4.8%), the US (3.5%), or Germany (3.1%). Across the region, the total R&D spend is dwarfed by that of major global tech firms (Ubaydli, 2020). This gap is a result of several factors: a limited number of world-class research universities, a private sector with little incentive to conduct its own R&D, and a historical reliance on purchasing ready-made solutions from abroad. This deficit forces the GCC to rely on foreign partners and consultants for the intellectual capital behind its most ambitious projects, limiting the potential for knowledge spillovers and the development of a self-sustaining innovation ecosystem. Until the GCC transitions from being a consumer of global innovation to a significant producer of it, the long-term sustainability of its knowledge-based economic ambitions will remain in question.

1.5 CONCLUSION: A NEW MODEL OR RENTIERISM REIMAGINED?

The Gulf Cooperation Council is engaged in a monumental effort to architect a post-oil future. By deploying immense capital, articulating bold national missions, and directly intervening to create new industrial ecosystems, the GCC states are vigorously embracing the role of the "entrepreneurial state." The tangible progress is undeniable: non-oil sectors are expanding, new industries are taking root, and the economic landscape of the region is visibly diversifying. This state-led push represents a rational and necessary response to the existential threat of hydrocarbon dependency, a determined counter-movement to secure a more stable and prosperous future.

However, as this chapter has argued, this forward-looking project is unfolding on a terrain shaped by the deep-seated legacies of a rentier past. The ambitions of the entrepreneurial state are in constant tension with the structural realities of the rentier state. The analysis has shown that this is not a simple transition from one model to another, but a complex and often contradictory process. The very oil revenues that fund the diversification drive also create dependencies and institutional inertia that resist change. The state's dominant role as an investor, while necessary to catalyze new sectors, risks stifling the emergence of a truly independent and innovative private sector. Most critically, the social contract forged in the era of oil wealth has created a distorted labor market and a deficit in homegrown innovation capacity, the very human and intellectual capital upon which a knowledge-based economy must be built.

The central question, therefore, remains open: is the GCC successfully building a new, sustainable development model, or is it primarily engaged in "rentierism reimagined"? Is this a genuine transformation into a productive, diversified economy, or a more sophisticated form of state-led rent distribution, where oil wealth is channeled into new, state-controlled assets and giga-projects without fundamentally altering the underlying economic logic? The answer will be determined by the willingness and ability of GCC governments to move beyond large-scale investment and confront these foundational structural challenges head-on.

Based on the analysis presented, we offer the following policy recommendations to help navigate this complex transition:

1. Cultivate Private Sector Independence through "Crowding-In" Policies: The state must shift its focus from being the primary economic actor to being a strategic enabler. This involves:

- Reforming procurement: Designing public tenders and contracts to favor consortia of smaller, innovative firms rather than single, large incumbents.
- Developing "patient" venture capital: Creating state-backed but independently managed venture capital funds to provide early-stage financing for startups that are not directly aligned with state megaprojects, fostering organic growth.
- Enforcing pro-competition regulations: Establishing strong, independent antitrust and regulatory bodies to ensure that new markets do not become the domain of state-affiliated monopolies.

2. Undertake Comprehensive Labor Market and Education Reform: Closing the gap between the national workforce and the needs of the new economy is paramount. This requires a multi-pronged strategy:
   - Aligning education with future jobs: Radically reforming national education curricula from K–12 to university level to emphasize critical thinking, STEM skills, and entrepreneurship over rote learning for public sector careers.
   - Rebalancing public/private sector incentives: Making private sector work more attractive for nationals through targeted training programs, performance-based wage subsidies, and gradually reducing the wage and benefit gap with the public sector.
   - Strategic talent immigration: Moving beyond a general reliance on low-cost labor to creating fast-track visa and residency programs specifically for highly skilled global talent—scientists, engineers, entrepreneurs—who can contribute to knowledge transfer.
3. Commit to a National R&D "Moonshot": Building indigenous innovation capacity is a long-term project that requires sustained commitment. GCC states should:
   - Triple R&D spending: Set an ambitious target to raise R&D expenditure to at least 3% of GDP over the next decade, with a significant portion allocated to basic and applied research at universities.
   - Incentivize private R&D: Introduce generous R&D tax credits and co-funding schemes to encourage both domestic firms and multinational corporations to establish R&D centers within the region.
   - Foster university–industry linkages: Create dedicated technology transfer offices at universities and science parks to facilitate the commercialization of academic research.
4. Embrace a "Green Industrial Policy" as a Core Mission: The transition to renewable energy offers the single greatest opportunity to build a new, globally competitive industrial ecosystem. The state should:

- Phase out energy subsidies: Systematically dismantle the remaining energy subsidies to encourage conservation and make renewable energy sources more commercially viable.
- Build local supply chains: Use the massive investment in solar and wind projects to mandate and support the creation of local manufacturing and service industries for renewable energy components (e.g., solar panels, turbine maintenance), creating a durable new productive sector.

The road ahead for the GCC is long and challenging. Future research should move towards more granular, comparative case studies. For instance, do different governance models within the SWFs (e.g., PIF vs. Mubadala) lead to different outcomes in fostering private enterprise? How are recent reforms to the *kafala* system impacting skill levels and innovation in specific sectors? Longitudinal studies tracking the economic impact and sustainability of the giga-projects will be crucial. Ultimately, the success of the GCC's historic pivot will be measured not by the height of its new skyscrapers, but by its ability to cultivate a dynamic, resilient, and innovative economy that can thrive long after the last barrel of oil has been sold.

REFERENCES

Al Jazeera. (2021). Gulf states show "limited" progress kicking oil and gas dependency. Available at: https://www.aljazeera.com/economy/2021/6/21/gulf-states-show-limited-progress-kicking-oil-gas-dependancy.

Alqahtani, T. (2023). *The Persuasive Use of Public Relations in Saudi Arabia 2030 Vision* (Doctoral dissertation, Duquesne University).

Amsden, A. (1989). *Asia's Next Giant; South Korea and Lute Industrialization.* Oxford University Press.

Beblawi, H. (1987). The rentier state in the Arab world. *Arab Studies Quarterly*, *9*(4), 383–398. http://www.jstor.org/stable/41857943

Best, M. H. (1990). *The New Competition: Institutions of Industrial Restructuring.* Harvard University Press.

Callen, T. (2023). *Signs that Economic Diversification is Working in Saudi Arabia.* The Arab Gulf States. Available at: https://agsiw.org/signs-that-economic-diversification-is-working-in-saudi-arabia/.

Cherif, R., & Hasanov, F. (2019). The return of the policy that shall not be named: Principles of industrial policy. International Monetary Fund.

Dore, R. (1986). Industrial policy and how the Japanese do it. *Catalyst*, *2*(2), 45–58.

Gray, M. (2011). A theory of "late rentierism" in the Arab states of the Gulf. *CIRS Occasional Papers.*

Gray, M. (2020). Rentierism's siblings: On the linkages between rents, neopatrimonialism, and entrepreneurial state capitalism in the Persian Gulf monarchies. In M. Kamrava (ed.), *The "Resource Curse" in the Persian Gulf* (pp. 29–45). Routledge.

HKTDC. (2023). Bahrain: Market profile. Available at: https://research.hktdc.com/en/article/MzU3ODA3Njg1.

Invest Qatar. (2024). Qatar's third national development strategy: The road ahead. Available at: https://www.linkedin.com/pulse/qatars-third-national-development-strategy-road-ahead-investqatar-dgcvf/.

Kabbani, N. (2020). BDC Snapshots: GCC countries must redouble their efforts to reduce oil dependence. Available at: https://www.brookings.edu/articles/bdc-snapshots-gcc-countries-must-redouble-their-efforts-to-reduce-oil-dependence/.

Knoema. (2021). United Arab Emirates: R&D expenditure as a share of GDP. Available at: https://knoema.com/atlas/United-Arab-Emirates/topics/Research-and-Development/RandD-Expenditure/RandD-expenditure-as-a-share-of-GDP#:~:text=In%202021%2C%20R&D%20expenditure%20as%20a%20share,is%20composed%20by%20our%20digital%20data%20assistant.

Marquand, D. (1988). *The Unprincipled Society*. Fontana Press.

Mazzucato, M. (2021). *Mission Economy: A Moonshot Guide to Changing Capitalism*. Penguin UK.

O'Neill, A. (2025). Distribution of gross domestic product (GDP) across economic sectors Qatar 2022. Statista. Available at: https://www.statista.com/statistics/379940/qatar-gdp-distribution-across-economic-sectors/#:~:text=In%202022%2C%20agriculture%20contributed%20around,percent%20from%20the%20services%20sector.

Oxford Analytica. (2022). The Gulf states will face new labour force challenges. *Emerald Expert Briefings* (oxan-db).

Polanyi, K. (1944). *The Great Transformation*. Foreword by Robert M. MacIver. Farrar & Rinehart.

PwC. (2023). The retention riddle: How to keep Emirati talent in the private sector. PwC Middle East—Emiratisation Survey 2023. Available at: https://www.pwc.com/m1/en/publications/emiratisation-survey-2023-the-retention-riddle.html.

PwC (2024). *Population Trends*. Available at: https://www.pwc.com/m1/en/publications/middle-east-economy-watch/population-trends.html.

Ramadan, T., & Uppal, R. (2024). UAE's non-oil trade hits record $953 billion in 2023. Reuters. Available at: https://www.reuters.com/world/middle-east/uaes-pm-says-countrys-non-oil-sector-hit-record-35-trillion-dirhams-2023-2024-02-18/#:~:text=Expanding%20services%20sectors%20in%20UAE,copper%20wire%20and%20ethylene%20polymers.

Raza, A. (2023). GCC countries: Diversifying sources of revenue and reducing oil dependence. Available at: https://www.linkedin.com/pulse/gcc-countries-diversifying-sources-revenue-reducing-ali-raza-waxvf/.

Relocate MENA. (2023). Breaking down barriers: How women are driving economic growth in Saudi Arabia. LinkedIn. Available at: https://www.linkedin.com/pulse/breaking-down-barriers-how-women-driving-economic-growth/.

S&P. (2022). GCC asset sales will increase transparency, broaden funding sources, and support capital market development. Available at: https://www.spglobal.com/ratings/en/research/articles/220321-gcc-asset-sales-will-increase-transparency-broaden-funding-sources-and-support-capital-market-development-12275959.

Salim, A. (2023). The Gulf's twin failings: Innovation and private sector employment for nationals. Middle East Institute. Available at: https://www.mei.edu/publications/gulfs-twin-failings-innovation-and-private-sector-employment-nationals.

Sanders, M., Stam, E., & Thurik, R. (2024). The entrepreneurial state cannot deliver without an entrepreneurial society. In M. Henrekson, C. Sandström, & M. Stenkula (eds), *Moonshots and the New Industrial Policy: Questioning the Mission Economy* (pp. 259–270). Springer.

Trade Finance Global. (2024). Oman's economic diversification: A closer look at non-oil exports and trade partnerships in 2022. Available at: https://www.tradefinanceglobal.com/posts/omans-economic-diversification-a-closer-look-at-non-oil-exports-and-trade-partnerships-in-2022/.

UAE. (2024). Operation 300bn, the UAE's industrial strategy. Available at: https://u.ae/en/about-the-uae/strategies-initiatives-and-awards/strategies-plans-and-visions/industry-science-and-technology/the-uae-industrial-strategy.

Ubaydli, O. (2020). Why R&D activities are limited in GCC countries? Available at: https://www.derasat.org.bh/why-rd-activities-are-limited-in-gcc-countries/.

2. Economic diversification trends in the Gulf Cooperation Council (GCC) countries: opportunities and challenges

Nazar Hilal

2.1 INTRODUCTION

The objective of this study is to identify the diversification trends in the Gulf Cooperation Council (GCC) countries and the challenges they face, with a particular focus on the Kingdom of Saudi Arabia (KSA) and Qatar as a case study. This study analyses the factors that have limited success of diversification initiatives in the context of the GCC. Following the decrease in oil prices in 2014 and the resulting instability in oil markets, there has been a renewed focus on economic diversification agendas. GCC countries have documented collections of economic reforms and adjustments characterized as visions to diversify the economy (Karolak, 2018; Mishrif and Al Balushi, 2018; Tsai, 2018). As Siegel, Johnson and Alwang (1995) assert, economic diversification denotes the reformation and reorganization of an economy by the reallocation of resources from primary sectors reliant on natural resources such as oil, to manufacturing and services sectors. The core concept of economic diversification is to progressively diminish the relative significance of the oil and associated industries, while shifting focus towards other sectors, namely the industrial, service, agricultural, financial, technological and knowledge-based production sectors. Moreover, economic diversification is crucial for promoting balanced growth, fostering sustainable development and playing a pivotal role in establishing global economic resilience (Prasad et al., 2024). Therefore, the primary aims of economic diversification are to transform the economy by utilizing several income sources across all sectors (Ngarava, 2021). First, diversification would facilitate the generation of employment opportunities in the private sector, which is crucial for accommodating the expanding labour force in the region. In addition, diversification among commodity producers results in enhanced macroeconomic stability, more sustainable growth patterns, facilitates a gradual transition towards higher value-added economic activities (reducing reliance on primary commodities) and reduces trade concentration (i.e. increases a country's capacity to export a broader range of products to a larger group of trading partners) (Prasad et al., 2024).

Economic diversification is crucial for achieving sustainable development because it improves macroeconomic stability and facilitates structural and long-term transformation in various areas, including the economy, social institutions and dimensions of development (Jolo, Ari and Koç, 2022; Prasad et al., 2024). Effectively, economic diversification is a policy aimed at decreasing dependency on a single commodity or industry, such as oil, which contributes significantly to a country's domestic gross product (GDP), earnings and revenues (Mishrif, 2018; Prasad et al., 2024). However, the primary concern regarding the GCC countries is whether economic diversification has the potential for generating employment prospects for nationals or expatriates. In summary, despite numerous and current economic diversification measures in the GCC countries, can these efforts rely on local labour, foreign labour, or a combination of both in the foreseeable future?

The economies of GCC countries are experiencing significant transformations in terms of distribution of population, information accessibility and employment, as compared to the preceding generation (Ewers, 2015). Globalization has facilitated their interconnectivity with the rest of the world. As a result, after the oil boom in the 1970s, GCC countries became closely associated with the emerging global power structure and emerged as major hubs for energy production and financial accumulation (Hanieh, 2011). GCC countries have comprehensive strategic economic plans to diversify their economies by reducing their dependence on oil and expanding into various sectors (Mishrif, 2018). It is essential to underscore that the state as political entity and primary enabler, rather than the government as executive structure and secondary agent, possesses the capacity and capability to implement these goals. This includes strengthening trade relationships with non-traditional partners with whom GCC countries have had little or no trade in the past and focusing on education and knowledge-based economies (Hossain, 2013; Mishrif, 2018). The non-traditional partners are emerging or advanced countries that have effectively implemented economic diversification strategies, like Singapore, Norway and South Korea. For instance, trade with these economies occurs through many avenues, such as bilateral agreements or participation in regional trade or economic groups that include these countries. Nonetheless, education and knowledge-driven economies, together with their experiences and endeavours, are vital components of trade with these countries. Directing economies towards knowledge-based and innovation-driven initiatives has the potential to empower and enable the GCC countries to use these experiences for economic diversification (Conference Proceedings, 2024).

Although GCC countries possess substantial investment funds from oil and gas revenues, they have seen poor success in achieving economic diversification (Ewers, 2015). Even in the more affluent countries within the GCC region, there are significant challenges when it comes to deciding how to distribute resources and determining the direction of diversification initiatives. These countries want to explore private sector prospects to create employment opportunities for their citizens, a role that has traditionally been fulfilled by the government (Hertog, 2013). However, it is important to consider whether the government will prioritize the interests of business elites and the private sector, which are the main providers of jobs for non-nationals. Employment is crucial to improving productivity across industries and significantly contributes to individual economic production (Conference Proceedings, 2024), but it is worth noting that higher employment does not in itself bring higher productivity. Therefore, the GCC countries exhibit a strong commitment to achieving economic diversification, with a specific focus on the ruling elites who wield significant power in decision making and emphasize these strategies as top-down policies. However, challenges and complexities arise when it comes to implementation.

This study analyses the strategies employed by GCC countries to diversify their economies, along with the barriers they encounter in performing these strategies. Specifically, it examines policies established by the KSA and Qatar as a case study. It argues that diversification in GCC countries has various patterns but is limited in extent and faces challenges. It examines the variables that have hindered the success of diversification efforts in the context of the GCC. What is the level of sustainability of the current diversification projects? What are the barriers facing diversification efforts in these countries? To investigate these study topics, it is imperative to meticulously analyse the socio-economic elements that shape and impact the acceptance of diversification as a feasible and essential approach in GCC countries. These elements emphasize the urgent necessity of pursuing an economic diversification strategy, as it provides economic prospects and fosters growth in the region. As the literature shows, there is a correlation between economic growth, economic diversification and structural transformation, especially during the early stages of development (Jolo, Ari and Koç, 2022). As shown in Figure 2.1, the Global Economic Diversification Index (EDI), released in 2024, encompassed territories from 2000 to 2022 and had core pillars comprising measurements associated with trade diversification, production, and government income. The EDI relies exclusively on quantitative data, without qualitative surveys or perception metrics, therefore offering a quantitative baseline and assessment of countries' economic diversity. The Global EDI seeks to comprehend the essence of

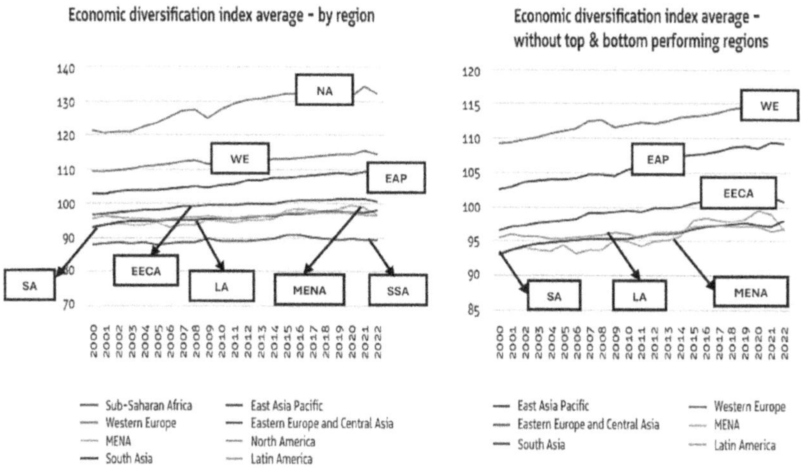

Note: The econometric setting for the EDI is a panel with a significant number of cross-sections: this consists of a large number of indicator series and relatively short time series. The objective is to design a weighting scheme such that the large number of indicators can be reduced to a smaller number of diversification indices: potentially three (output, trade and government revenue), and/or one (diversification). Principal Components Analysis (PCA) (n indicator produced using PCA is the linear combination of the indicators that accounts for the maximum possible proportion of the total variance in the set of underlying indicators), a standard dimensionality-reduction technique, was used to generate the results. The strategy for applying PCA to the detailed indicators relied on two steps. The first was to use PCA to produce the three sub-indices: output, trade, and revenue (indices are produced using the standard sum of squares approach and are converted from variables with mean zero and unit standard deviation to variables with mean 100 and standard deviation 10). The second step was then to aggregate the three sub-indices into an overall EDI by taking the arithmetic (simple) mean.
Source: Performance of the Economic Diversification Index across regions, 2000–2022 (EDI, 2022; Prasad et al., 2024, 27).

Figure 2.1 *Performance of the Economic Diversification Index across regions, 2000–2022*

economic diversification and the elements that directly or indirectly influence a country's total degree of diversification (Prasad et al., 2024). The Economic Diversification Index consists of three components: the diversification of economic activities, which includes indicators such as real GDP, resource rents as a percentage of GDP and manufacturing value added per capita; the diversification of international trade, encompassing products, services and countries, with indicators like total value of exports, total value of imports, total value of services exports, import product concentration index and export product concentration index; the diversification of government revenues to mitigate dependence on natural resource or commodity income, represented by indicators such as excise tax revenue as a percentage of GDP, total revenue as a percentage of GDP and trade revenue as a percentage of GDP (Prasad et al., 2024).

Figure 2.2 depicts the average performance of diversification of the GCC countries depending on their factors of production, government revenue and trade from 2000 to 2022. The measure relies exclusively on quantitative data that assesses diversification across three dimensions: output (production), trade and government revenue for more than 100 countries from 2000 to 2022. The foundation of assessment comprises around 25 quantitative indicators, yielding a replicable quantitative benchmark. The economic diversification assessment and score for a country is determined by first calculating the scores of three principal sub-indices: the output sub-index, the trade sub-index and the revenue sub-index. Each sub-index comprises many underlying indicators. Utilizing Principal Components Analysis (PCA), a dimensionality reduction approach, yields a sub-index score for each of the three dimensions. This generates a singular value for each of the three sub-indices. The calculation of these three values—through their simple arithmetic mean—yields the final overall EDI score for the country. The primary indicators under this pillar are the sectors of economic activity: agriculture, industry/manufacturing, and services. The proportion of each sector's value added to GDP has been utilized to facilitate comparisons between nations and temporal periods. The trade diversification pillar comprises many measures, including the total value of exports, total value of imports and total value of services exports. The government revenue diversification indicators encompass income tax revenue as a proportion of GDP, total tax revenue as a percentage of GDP, and trade revenue as a percentage of GDP.

This study makes three fundamental statements concerning economic diversification trends and challenges in the GCC countries context. First, the GCC countries gain tremendous financial resources and influence as a result of the substantial revenues obtained from exporting natural resources, particularly oil and natural gas. The presence of plentiful natural resources is associated with negative phenomena called the 'resource curse' and 'Dutch disease'. The resource curse, also known as the resource trap or the paradox of plenty, refers to a paradoxical situation in which a country that possesses abundant valued natural resources experiences economic underperformance (Jolo, Ari and Koç, 2022). The concept of 'Dutch disease' is a paradoxical scenario, which occurs when positive improvements in one sector of the economy, such as the discovery of natural resources, negatively impact the country's overall economic performance. This is evident in the significant increase in

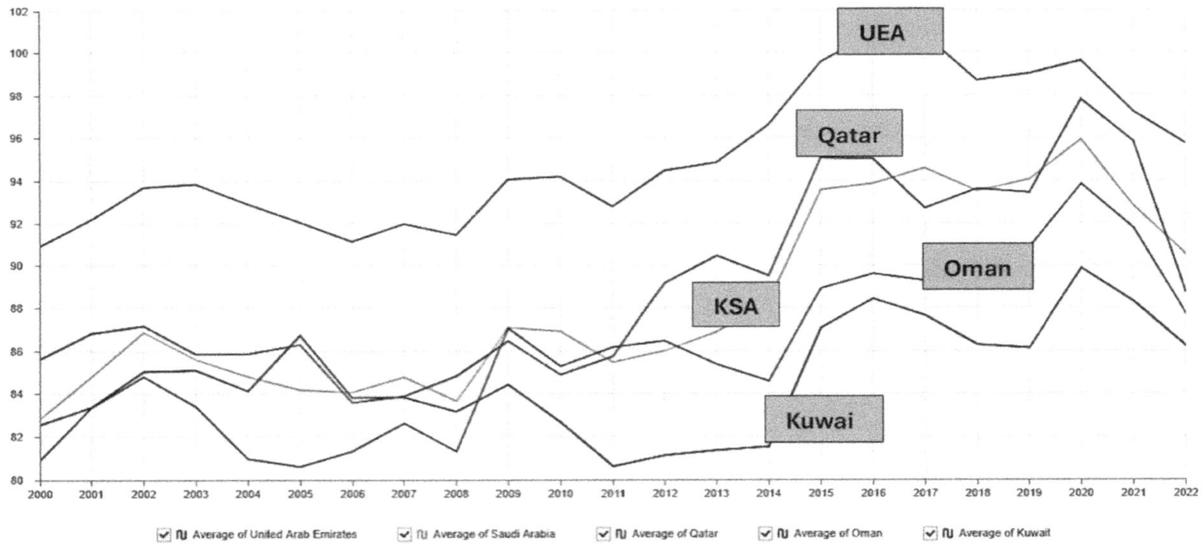

Note: There exist improvements in GCC scores that have arisen from the execution of changes at a significantly accelerated rate following the epidemic of COVID-19 in 2020. These include incentives for investment in emerging technological industries, strategies to expand tax bases, trade liberalization via free trade agreements, enhancements to the regulatory and corporate environment and facilitation of establishment rights and labour mobility.
Source: Global Economic Diversification Index (EDI, 2022; Prasad et al., 2024).

Figure 2.2 *Visualization of a country's average performance (GCC Countries) on each measure of diversification (production, government revenue, trade) from 2000–2022*

the national currency's value, which has led to higher unemployment rates and a decline in the manufacturing industry (Mishrif, 2018). However, these phenomena lead to poor long-term economic performance, as well as corruption, and an economic model based on a rentierism system. Moreover, in a comparative advantage framework for international trade, industries or sectors exhibiting comparative disadvantage shrink while those demonstrating comparative advantage expand. The corruption and rentier dependency associated with substantial natural resources may diminish these industries or sectors with comparative disadvantages in the GCC setting. Corruption is an evident reality in these countries, characterized by a heavy reliance on abundant natural resources that foster a rentier economy, so obstructing development towards a real productive economy (Conference Proceedings, 2024).

The second is that GCC countries are currently confronted with some inherent economic challenges that impede their progress towards achieving economic diversification and sustainability. These challenges include a substantial dependence on oil and gas revenues (rentier state model) and the pronounced influence of residents on the public sector in GCC countries (dual labour market problem) as the GCC citizens dominate the public sector and the foreign workers dominate the private sector. In addition, there are the issues pertaining to the social contract: labour segmentation across various dimensions such as national versus non-national, public sector versus private sector, male versus female, and blue-collar versus white-collar distinctions, as well as the lack of transparency and accountability in the administration of sovereign wealth funds; the issue of unemployment; the sluggishness and stagnation of the private sector; and the segregation of women in the workforce. Moreover, concerns exist regarding economic diversification itself: its societal roles and values; the inability to transition to a real economy due to the failure to alter the mentality surrounding economic structuring, including the necessity to grant greater rights to expatriates and integrate them into productivity and economic diversification; and the constraints of human capital (both national and non-national). There is also the failure to connect the non-oil economy with the oil economy; the insufficient regulation of Foreign Direct Investment (FDI) in GCC countries; and the neglect of private entrepreneurship's role, as inventions cannot be transformed into innovations without it. Likewise, the insufficiency of financing for research and education hinders economic diversification progress; nonetheless, investments in these areas improve conditions for entrepreneurship, while they do not directly create entrepreneurial ventures. Accordingly, the substantial engagement of GCC governments in entrepreneurship further exacerbates the issue, perhaps resulting in the marginalization of independent entrepreneurs. Still, the limitation of the state's role in economics by the GCC countries constitutes a substantial barrier as the state must act as an external facilitator/enabler of entrepreneurship rather than being the principal agent; and eventually the issue of corruption in the GCC countries (Conference Proceedings, 2024).

Third, the national visions developed by the GCC countries present an opportunity to implement systematic policies for economic diversification, albeit with limited achievements. Based on these premises, this study is structured as follows. The first section provides an analysis of the variables that motivate economic diversification strategies. The second section examines the policies of GCC countries, specifically the KSA and Qatar, in terms of exploring methods and trends in economic diversification. The final section highlights the difficulties that GCC countries face in implementing economic diversification strategies. In addition, it outlines recommendations for maximizing advantages to promote economic diversification and an agenda for future research.

2.2 METHODOLOGY

The primary aim of this research is to explore the patterns and difficulties of economic diversification in the GCC region, focusing specifically on economic diversification trends in the KSA and Qatar as case studies. Moreover, this chapter analyses the development of various strategies for economic diversification and explains the issues that have impeded their progress. This study is categorized as qualitative analytical research, in which I utilized pre-existing secondary data obtained from different sources to thoroughly assess the selected research problem. Further, this study is based on an examination of scholarly literature and authoritative reports.

2.3 CATALYSTS FOR ECONOMIC DIVERSIFICATION

The GCC region has achieved significant wealth as a result of its abundant hydrocarbon resources. This is particularly remarkable, given the comparatively small size of the region's national populations. The oil, natural gas and petrochemical industries continue to be the primary sources of national income and government revenues in GCC countries (Ben Hassen, 2022; Elbargathi and Sweidan, 2023). Given the prevailing economic circumstances and the ongoing decrease in oil prices, diversification has become a necessary and urgent policy for GCC countries (see Figure 2.3). Due to factors such as volatile international oil prices, reduced demand for oil, technological advancements and concerns about climate change (conventional energy sources, referred to as 'black' energy sources, are being substituted with more environmentally friendly alternatives, known as 'greener' sources, specifically in the transportation industry), all GCC countries are increasingly prioritizing diversification as an essential strategy to minimize the adverse effects on their

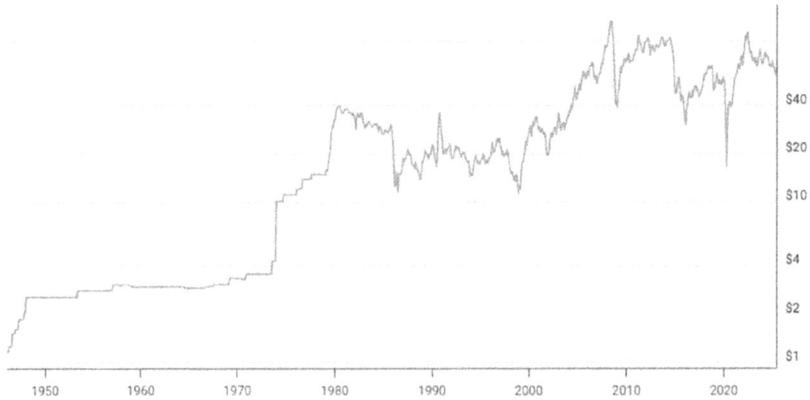

Source: https://www.macrotrends.net/1369/crude-oil-price-history-chart (Macrotrends, 2024).

Figure 2.3 *Global oil price fluctuations between 1950 and 2024 – all years historical chart*

economies (Mishrif, 2018; Ben Hassen, 2022). Nevertheless, the crucial matter at hand is the significance and enduring viability of transitioning away from an economy dependent on oil. Hence, GCC countries have initiated a process of reconsideration and reassessment of the existing significance of oil in the global context, particularly in light of climate change and the increasing prevalence of electric vehicles and batteries, as well as the growing importance of renewable energy sources (IRENA, 2019). In addition, these countries are facing vigorous global campaigns led by renewable energy advocates that question the future role and importance of oil and its societal value. This is further compounded by the escalating production of shale oil and gas (cheaper oil and gas supplies from unconventional sources) in the United States in recent times (Agheli, 2018; Ben Hassen, 2022; IRENA, 2019). Likewise, factors such as population increase, the inability of the oil and gas industry to generate employment opportunities, political instability in the region and volatility in oil prices contribute to the pressing need for economic diversification (Ewers, 2015; Hvidt, 2013; Mansfeld and Winckler, 2007).

Energy is the primary sector that dominates exports and revenues in the GCC region. As a result, oil continues to account for the majority of export revenues and government budgets in most GCC countries. Tsai (2018) confirmed that these countries represent a small portion of the world's population (0.73%) but contribute significantly to the worldwide GDP (1.80%). Additionally, they possess a substantial share of global oil reserves (33.3%) and produce a significant amount of oil (23.8%). Furthermore, they have a considerable portion of global natural gas deposits (20.7%) and contribute to global natural gas production (11.2%). In addition, it is projected that, in four out of the six GCC countries, hydrocarbon reserves will be depleted over the lifetimes of individuals born in the present generation (Hvidt, 2013; Tsai, 2018). Therefore, the decrease in global oil prices during the COVID-19 era emphasizes these concerns.

However, the market and economic indicators for energy earnings and prices are consistently unstable, and there has been a general decrease in global oil prices since 2014. Mishrif (2018) asserted that diversification strategies offer effective ways to mitigate the impact of declining international oil prices and the subsequent reduction in oil export revenues in volatile and unpredictable energy markets. In the GCC countries, with the exception of the UAE and Qatar, which have notably small populations, the degree of urgency and timeframe for addressing these economic difficulties differ across countries. Oman and Bahrain, the countries with the lowest oil export levels, experienced the most significant social and political instability during the 2011 Arab uprisings. Hence, the primary driving force behind the adoption of economic diversification as a policy among GCC countries is the risk element in having an unproductive economy. Additional reasons contributing to the situation are the sluggish rate of long-term economic growth, insufficient motivation for individuals and organizations to acquire knowledge and skills, efforts to prevent sudden economic disruptions, and a significant drop in commodity prices and its adverse impact on the economy (Elbargathi and Sweidan, 2023; Due-Gundersen and Suwaidi, 2024). Furthermore, the consequences of energy subsidies in the GCC region are compounded by population expansion, which contributes to the already significant proportion of public sector wages in these countries' GDP (Fattouh and El-Katiri, 2013; Tsai, 2018).

The economies of GCC countries and the relationships between citizens and states have been shaped by the oil economy, as observed from a political economy perspective. Hence, the countries in the GCC region are widely recognized as 'rentier states' due to their substantial wealth and income derived from the export of oil and gas. The concept of 'rentier states' is adequately explained by the rentier state theory (RST), which is identified as a political economy theory that aims to explain the relationship between the state and society in states where a significant amount of income is derived from rents, which are unproductively produced payments obtained from external sources. Rents primarily consist of royalties or other payments received from oil and gas exports. However, other forms of income, such as fees and aid, are also generally classified as rents (Gray, 2011), given that these GCC countries were established under a system of patronage, primarily dependent on the provision of financial support. Accordingly, subsidies such as social transfers and the like serve as the main method for distributing rent to the general citizens in return for protection and political influence (Kabbani, 2021; Tsai, 2018). Post-independent governments and their relationships with their people were significantly influenced by the oil boom of the 1970s and their ability to provide generous benefits. However, in the medium to long term, the revenues from energy resources are insufficient to maintain the current political and economic agreement, despite recent efforts to diversify the economy (Hertog, 2013; Mishrif, 2018; Prasad et al., 2024). The combination of expanding populations and more complex and expensive societies to govern, along with stagnant or declining oil income, poses challenges in maintaining the previously successful economic growth model, referred to as the rentier state model (Ben Hassen, 2022). These changes indicate political shifts that have occurred at the governmental level in recent years, but more needs to be achieved (Khodr, 2014).

However, there are two significant drawbacks associated with the current economic strategies espoused by the rentier state model. The first is the lack of a comparable strategic analysis of the political consequences of significant shifts in the role of states (Khodr, 2014). Changes in energy markets could lead to regular disruptions for GCC countries. This is because these governments depend on oil earnings to maintain their political legitimacy (Gray, 2011; Hvidt, 2013; Khodr, 2014). Furthermore, GCC countries, which are currently in the process of establishing their statehood, have not adequately addressed the political risks and costs associated with their plans. In times of potential social unrest, such as the 2011 Arab Uprising, also known as the Arab Spring, these countries have tended to postpone or disregard these plans. The complexity of the economic and political relationship between citizens and the state in the GCC hinders diversification and political decision making, as revealed by Khodr (2014) and Kabbani (2021) in their studies on the problem of social contracts. These states have the opportunity to create their policies without involving their citizens due to their income from hydrocarbons. As a result, they have distinct political obstacles. Hence, the process of economic diversification indirectly presents a problem for the ruling elites in GCC countries. The GCC region and the rest of the Middle East rarely witnesses the continuation of effective economic policies because these policies are closely intertwined with competent politics. This poses a challenge for the ruling elites in the region (Agheli, 2018; Malik, 2015).

There are several instances of good economic strategies which are impeded by incompetent political practices in the GCC countries, including neglect of revenue from taxes, excessive government expenditure, and ineffective decisions about money allocation embedded in the political economy of rentier economic model. Furthermore, the impediment of funds for research and development (R&D) in the private sector is due to elite control (Thafer, 2023). Hvidt (2013) characterizes the GCC countries as 'allocation states', wherein they dispense favours, public goods and services as rents. Furthermore, the institutional quality (which is political decision-making entity) in the GCC countries is inadequate, and there is uncertainty regarding its nature, whether external or indigenous, which might hinder the implementation of successful economic strategies (Thafer, 2023).

According to Malik (2015), economic diversification requires structural changes that involve producing higher-value goods. In addition, the establishment of a new, comprehensive and long-lasting social contract, which may serve as the basis for the modern Arab state, requires cooperation and partnership between citizens and the government (Kabbani, 2021).

2.4 TRENDS IN ECONOMIC DIVERSIFICATION

GCC countries are seeking to diversify their economies across several sectors with the capacity to facilitate the export of industries and services that are not reliant on oil exports. Additionally, these countries are striving to export these businesses and services to markets beyond the GCC region (Due-Gundersen and Suwaidi, 2024; Elbargathi and Sweidan, 2023). The sectors encompassed are tourism, transportation, knowledge-based sectors and financial services. Thus, tourism is a significant industry in GCC countries that is being focused on as part of diversification strategies. The tourism industry has the capacity to redistribute wealth, promote economic diversification as a priority, utilize existing economic resources, such as renowned natural and historical sites, and stimulate the growth of other local economies, such as agriculture and transportation (Alhowaish, 2016; Hilal, 2020; Lejárraga and Walkenhorst, 2013; Sharpley, 2002). Tourism is a labour-intensive sector that mostly focuses on employment and job generation. Alhowaish (2016) asserted that tourism and the influx of tourists into a country impact its economic growth, as well as labour, capital, and exports, a notion based on the tourism-led growth hypothesis. Moreover, tourism leverages and improves existing economic resources, since it is emblematic of a labour-intensive industry.

Tourism in the KSA is a key sector that is prioritized for the purpose of diversification. Saudi Arabia has made significant investments in the fast-expanding religious tourism sector, specifically targeting the Hajj market (Kalin, 2019). The market segment known as 'faith travel', 'religious tourism', or 'pilgrimage' holds significant importance because it is widely thought that this sort of tourism is among the earliest to have existed (Abuhjeeleh, 2019). The Saudi Commission for Tourism and Antiquities (SCTA) was founded in April 2000 with the purpose of fostering and advancing tourism in the Kingdom (Mansour and Mumuni, 2019). As a result, the KSA has achieved a remarkable feat by attracting more than 100 million tourists, a significant milestone recognized and acknowledged by the World Tourism Organization (UNWTO, 2024). This significant achievement, characterized by the arrival of more than 27 million international tourists and over 79 million domestic tourists, who collectively spent over USD67 billion, not only highlights the strong tourism industry in the Kingdom but also emphasizes the Saudi Ministry of Tourism's dedication to collecting and analysing data in a sophisticated manner, a priority shared by UN Tourism (UNWTO, 2024). What is noteworthy is the rise in both local and foreign visitors in the tourism industry.

Nonetheless, the tourism industry in the Kingdom is now in its nascent phase and has the potential for growth. However, the key factor is to evaluate the quality of job opportunities that can be created to involve Saudi citizens. Furthermore, Vision 2030 has allocated $64 billion for investment in cultural, recreational and entertainment projects over the next ten years. This substantial funding will greatly enhance the appeal of the country as a tourism destination (Mansour and Mumuni, 2019). Furthermore, the KSA has initiated extensive tourism investment initiatives and has loosened numerous prohibitions on social and cultural activities, while also facilitating the entry of tourists (Yap, Saha and Alsowaidi, 2022). Additionally, the Kingdom has the greatest percentage of unemployment among young people compared to other countries in the GCC (Mishrif, 2018). The Saudi government's predictions indicate that over 50% of the population is expected to be below the age of 25. The tourism industry has the capacity to employ young individuals due to its labour-intensive nature. By 2030, there is a potential for an influx of 4.5 million Saudi individuals of working age to enter the labour force. Nevertheless, the public sector lacks the capacity to manage this abrupt surge unaided. Most young adults who are in the age range suitable for employment need to actively seek employment opportunities in the private sector (Ben Hassen, 2022). The Kingdom's 2030 strategy prioritizes improving the business climate through the reformation of regulations and policies that hinder investment in several industries, including tourism (Abuhjeeleh, 2019; Hvidt, 2013; Kingdom of Saudi Arabia 2030 Vision, n.d.).

The tourism sector's strategy for diversification still depends on oil revenue, as it serves as the primary source of funding and salaries for the workforce in the sector (Hvidt, 2013). Nonetheless, a detrimental cycle exists in linking funding and expenditure in tourism among individuals who provide financial resources to this sector, some of whom may be working in the oil business while others are not. Besides, the revenue generated from oil plays a crucial role in the financing of this industry, both in the short and long term, either directly or indirectly. In addition, the tourism industry is susceptible to fluctuations in oil prices, making it closely linked to the oil and gas sector, although these countries are not entirely dependent on it. In addition, in order for a country to succeed in a highly competitive business climate, policymakers must assess its relative and competitive strengths. Simply put, comparative advantage is defined as the combination of a destination's natural and developed resources, whereas competitive advantages refer to the efficient utilization of these resources (Crouch and Ritchie, 1999). Moreover, consider competitive advantage as a construct that must be developed. For instance, Japan's prosperity from the 1950s to the 1970s was predicated on establishing competitive advantages, particularly in the automotive sector. Still, continued investment in the tourism sector is crucial for stimulating economic growth, promoting development and reducing dependence on the energy sector (Ozturk and Al-Kuwari, 2021).

Qatar covers an area of 4,416 square miles and is located on a peninsula that stretches 350 miles along the sandy coastline of the Arabian Gulf (Henderson, 2015). Qatar has the highest gross domestic product (GDP) per capita in the world, primarily due to its reliance on oil and gas as the main source of economic generation (Prasad, Nair and Purohit, 2019). Qatar has developed numerous appealing tourism locations, along with significant advancements in telecommunications and infrastructure, to establish itself as a prominent player in the tourism business. The Islamic Museum, Qatar National Library, Banana Island, Falcon Market, the Arab Museum of Modern Art, eight new stadiums, the newly developed National Museum of Qatar and Katara Cultural Village are all significant representations of cultural heritage. In 2013, the Al Zubarah Archaeological Site was added to the World Heritage List (Henderson, 2015; Yap, Saha and Alsowaidi, 2022). In addition, Qatar has made significant investments in upscale tourism projects, including the Lusail planned city, Qatar Entertainment City and the Pearl Project, which has a budget of 20 billion US dollars. Nevertheless, Qatar faces intense rivalry from neighbouring countries, such as Egypt, Saudi Arabia, the United Arab Emirates and Turkey (Yap, Saha and Alsowaidi, 2022). Therefore, Qatar's tourism strength encompasses the fact that the public health system is highly ranked, indicating its excellence. The financial system is reliable and efficient, ensuring stability. In addition, there is significant competition in terms of infrastructure, information and communication technology (ICT) adoption and corporate dynamism, indicating a strong and thriving business environment and, finally, emphasizing cultural and sports tourism (Yap, Saha and Alsowaidi, 2022).

However, the tourist business in Qatar has a few drawbacks, including being an expensive location for both visiting and staying, and a lack of diversity in tourism products. Furthermore, there is a significant focus on specifically targeting areas that cater to Arab culture and fans of sports. As most sports enthusiasts disapprove of the limited availability of alcoholic beverages, nonetheless, the 2022 World Cup for football, hosted in Qatar, showed that limits may be enforced for visiting sports enthusiasts.

Although Qatar may encounter various opportunities, it can derive benefits by promoting itself as a global financial centre for investors and diversifying its tourism offerings, such as health-related tourism and ecotourism (Henderson, 2015; Yap, Saha and Alsowaidi, 2022).

Concerning the diversification sector of Qatar's knowledge-based economy, according to the economic vision outlined in Qatar National Vision 2008, "[Qatar] ... If attained, these achievements would in turn provide a broader platform for the diversification of Qatar's economy and its positioning as a regional hub for knowledge and for high value industrial and service activities" (Qatar National Vision, 2008). Qatar prioritizes the development of a dynamic knowledge-based economy as part of its strategy to diversify its economy. For instance, the 'Education City' in Doha accommodates educational and research establishments comprising some American and European university campuses, most of which are financially funded by the 'Qatar Foundation', a semi-governmental organization that funds education and scientific endeavours (Henderson, 2015). A significant drawback of the knowledge-based economy in GCC countries is the scarcity of human capital in technology-related domains, specifically in the disciplines of engineering and other crucial STEM (science, technology, engineering and mathematics) sectors (Ben Hassen, 2022).

In order to promote the transition of GCC member countries' economies towards the knowledge economy, a specific factor is required (Wirba, 2017). This aspect pertains to the importance of research and development in the transformation process towards the knowledge economy. Therefore, generating knowledge is crucial, and this necessitates substantial financial support from both the government and the private sector. In a globalized world, the ability of national economies to generate and utilize knowledge is increasingly crucial for their competitiveness (Ben Hassen, 2022). Similarly, knowledge, education and innovation are the key factors that determine economic development. It is imperative that knowledge and innovation originate from inside the GCC countries rather than being imported. Moreover, entrepreneurship is necessary among the inhabitants of the GCC, and it is also important to collaborate with prominent research institutions throughout the region. These institutions should be willing to establish research and development centres or universities within the GCC countries (Wirba, 2017). According to Wirba (2017), the key to enhancing global competitiveness lies in the achievement of a knowledge-based economy. Education is undeniably the most influential component among all other economic and structural variables (Jolo, Ari and Koç, 2022). The KSA attained the 16th position in the 2024 World Competitiveness Ranking (WCR).[1] The methodology employed by the IMD (International Institute for Management Development) World Competitiveness Center to construct the IMD World Competitiveness Ranking (WCR) is similarly applied to the IMD World Digital Competitiveness Ranking and the IMD World Talent Report, but with specific distinctions. In 2024, the empirical data was analysed to establish 164 criteria. All criteria are grouped into four factors: economic performance, government efficiency, business efficiency and infrastructure (IMD, 2024). Nevertheless, as a member of the G-20 economy, it should strive to secure a place among the top ten globally. The primary factor contributing to this issue is the GCC countries' insufficient allocation of their economic and financial resources to research and development (R&D). Specifically, GCC countries invest less than 1% of their GDP in R&D (mainly in universities and industries in the private sector) (Al Naimi, 2022; Mishrif and Al Balushi, 2018). As a result, oil continues to be the primary driver of the Saudi economy.

However, the process of transitioning a state into a knowledge-based economy is not simple, as the success of a knowledge-based economy relies on complex interconnections between entrepreneurship, motivation, supportive economic policies and institutional frameworks (Ben Hassen, 2022).

2.5 CHALLENGES OF ECONOMIC DIVERSIFICATION

Figure 2.4 indicates that the GCC countries have several challenges in their efforts to attain economic diversification. Concerning the challenges in labour markets, GCC countries have labour markets that are different and

	2000	2004	2008	2012	2016	2019	2020-22
North America	121.5	122.3	127.4	130.3	132.2	135.0	132.8
Western Europe	109.2	110.6	112.6	112.0	113.4	114.4	114.8
East Asia Pacific	102.6	104.0	104.8	106.7	107.8	108.9	109.0
Eastern Europe & Central Asia	96.5	97.9	99.1	99.8	100.8	101.2	101.2
MENA	93.1	93.5	93.7	95.0	98.5	98.3	98.4
South Asia	92.9	94.8	95.3	96.0	97.1	97.6	97.5
Latin America & the Carribean	95.6	95.4	95.9	96.2	97.3	97.2	96.8
Sub-Saharan Africa	87.7	88.5	88.7	88.9	90.7	89.5	89.3

Least Improvement — Most Improvement

Source: Global Economic Diversification Index 2024 (Prasad et al., 2024, 25).

Figure 2.4 *Top ten average and lowest ten average Economic Diversification Index (EDI) scores, by region and over time (2000–2019 and 2020–2022)*

characterized by segmentation along multiple lines. These differences persist in various forms, such as national versus non-national, public sector versus private sector, male versus female, blue collar versus white-collar, 1960s generation versus millennials generation, and even along tribal and sectarian affiliations (Mohamed, 2020).

According to Mishrif and Kapetanovic (2018), public sector employment policies have a detrimental impact on labour productivity, leading to a waste of resources. In addition, similar to other countries in the Middle East, the GCC countries have predominantly young populations, with the majority under the age of 30. Consequently, the problem of unemployment is a significant and urgent concern. The unemployment rates among these youths are notably high, especially in the KSA and Bahrain (Hvidt, 2013; Mishrif, 2018). Nonetheless, diversification does not necessarily create employment, since it is contingent upon whether the expanded sectors are capital-intensive or labour-intensive. In addition, the presence of appealing public sector packages as a means of revenue distribution in the social contract between rulers and the local population hinders diversification attempts.

GCC countries have the potential to invest in the private sector as part of their economic diversification. The current rentier economic model in the GCC is no longer suitable due to its reliance on oil, lack of worker diversity and skills, increasing demand for public services and inadequate innovation (Ghazaly et al., 2017; Hertog, 2013). Accordingly, an effective approach involves the private sector, sometimes known as private-sector participation (PSP). GCC countries can tackle these difficulties by implementing two types of public–private partnerships (PPPs) and privatization (Ghazaly et al., 2017). PPPs encompass a range of contractual agreements that allow a public institution and a private-sector partner to collaborate in the provision of infrastructure, products or services by sharing expertise, resources and risks. Privatization is the process of transferring complete or partial ownership of a property, product or service, along with its associated risks and benefits, to a privately owned firm (Ghazaly et al., 2017). For this reason, the private sector plays a vital part in the economic development and diversification of GCC countries. However, the GCC countries have utilized it strategically, and on a case-by-case basis. In the GCC region, the majority of jobs are held by non-natives, while just a small number of nationals are employed in the private sector (Hertog, 2013). This is because the oil and gas business requires a large amount of capital investment and has a limited capacity to generate employment opportunities (Hvidt, 2013). Therefore, this scenario presents a challenging atmosphere for the private sector to thrive (Hertog, 2013; Mishrif, 2018). Hertog (2013) confirmed that the functioning and performance of the GCC private sector, despite significant progress since the initial oil boom, primarily include sophisticated rent recycling rather than independent diversification. Accordingly, the private sector is experiencing moderate performance, primarily because of a shortage of qualified individuals to fill high-skilled positions in the sector. Other contributing factors include the regulatory environment, which is influenced by the state, the segregation of women in the workplace and social contracts. According to Mishrif (2018), it is significantly challenging for GCC nationals to obtain employment in the private sector. The high percentage of education participation among women in the GCC region does not translate into equal success in securing jobs in the private sector, despite their higher qualifications compared to men. This discrepancy can be attributed to the influence of cultural, traditional, societal and legal factors on the diversification process in labour, the private sector and the political economy of the region.

2.6 CONCLUSION AND DISCUSSION

Diversification plans and trends are imperative strategies, not discretionary choices, that have arisen as a consequence of tangible considerations for oil producers in the GCC region. The purpose of these strategies is to generate employment, reduce the potential impact of fluctuating oil prices and foster prospects for private sector growth. In addition, the GCC countries have implemented such diversification strategies to promote the growth of several sectors, including financial services, tourism, free zones, transportation, education and research centres associated with the formation of a knowledge-based economy, as well as diversification through urbanization, trade and light industries. Due to the nearly exhausted and unstable supply of oil, the decreasing demand for it, the impact of climate change, expensive internal subsidies for electricity, water and fuels, high unemployment rates and the uncertainties surrounding its role and value in society, the diversification plans in the GCC countries are progressing slowly, and they are in their initial stages. Mishrif (2018) indicated that, despite the substantial financial surplus and significant investment in infrastructure, the outcomes of GCC government policies have not met the targets outlined in their national visions, and the difficulties of economic diversification continue to exist. This is due to the ambiguity surrounding the implementation of concrete modifications in the rentier system entrenched in GCC countries. Economic diversification is a crucial strategy for ensuring long-term economic viability. It is imperative to have political will and plan in order to effectively handle the consequences of socio-economic transformations. For example, collaboration between citizens and the state is necessary to create a new, all-encompassing and enduring social contract (a new political economy) that may serve as the foundation of the contemporary Arab state, including GCC countries (Kabbani, 2021).

GCC countries should recognize the significance of an entrepreneurial state and its institutions in attaining their national visions and aspirations.

An entrepreneurial state is based on the concept that the government can take a more aggressive role in promoting industrial innovation at the cutting edge of knowledge, which is not fully recognized by policymakers at present (Mazzucato, 2011). In practical terms, this entails establishing markets that are conducive to venture capital, implementing regulations that are favourable to venture capitalists, creating funding channels, fostering a dynamic culture and providing various support systems (Ben Hassen, 2022).

Furthermore, the realization of GCC countries' claims of having a tradition of consultation necessitates the effective functioning of institutions. Nevertheless, it is important to create strong institutions to achieve significant diversity (Mohamed, 2020). In addition, the GCC governments' unmistakable dedication to diversifying the economy and fostering dynamic, knowledge-based and tourism industries support a new stage in rentier state theory, known as 'late rentierism', as postulated by Gray (2011) (Ben Hassen, 2022). Ultimately, the crucial enquiry revolves around the potential for GCC countries' economic diversification trends to be sustainable in the long run.

The current level of diversification in the GCC region can be attributed to the creation of an unproductive rentier political economy. The insufficient allocation of resources towards innovation and research and development (R&D) in universities, industries, and particularly in the private sector, which is influenced by the business elites, is another significant cause. Furthermore, there is a substantial proportion of youth unemployment. For diversification to succeed, it is crucial for GCC governments to recognize the significance of creating and developing new markets, as well as the advantages of participating in high-risk projects. Furthermore, establishing decisions on consensus fosters transparency and openness, so facilitating the growth of attractive investments, markets, firms, service sectors and industries that contribute to a functioning economy. Furthermore, human capital is essential in the process of diversification. Therefore, it is crucial for the GCC countries to pursue their national visions strategies such as building state-of-the-art educational institutions that can efficiently provide individuals with the essential skills and knowledge commanded by the public and private sectors. It is worth mentioning that the private sectors in the GCC countries necessitate additional government support and regulation to generate employment opportunities. Similarly, the strategy involves gradually decreasing or eliminating subsidies to stimulate a more productive economy.

This study is subject to two main limitations. Currently, investigations into the effects of diversification strategies are in their nascent stages. This study focuses especially on analysing the immediate and intermediate impacts of these strategies. There is a pressing need for thorough evaluations to analyse the lasting impacts of diversification strategies on the expansion of the knowledge-based economy and tourism in the GCC region.

Future studies should prioritize conducting a full analysis of different diversification strategies and thoroughly examining their characteristics. In addition, future studies should examine the impact of political instability, market and economic disruptions or unforeseen biological and ecological disasters on these strategies and their fundamental principles.

ACKNOWLEDGEMENT

This chapter is an outcome of GRM 2024 Workshop No. 4 GRC.

NOTE

1. This version of the World Competitiveness Ranking (WCR) evaluates 67 global economies. The ultimate score for each economy is calculated by integrating executive impressions with statistical data. This is meant to utilize several data kinds to independently assess measurable and qualitative concerns. Statistical indicators are obtained from international, national and regional organizations, corporate entities and our partner institutes. These statistics are sometimes termed 'hard data'. The empirical data constitute two-thirds of the overall rankings. Five sub-factors are created within each. These sub-factors do not necessarily include the same number of criteria because, let's say, it takes more criteria to assess the Education sub-factor than it does to evaluate the Prices one. Sub-factors, irrespective of the number of criteria they contain, have the same weight in the overall consolidation of results: the weight of each sub-factor is 5% $(20x5 = 100)$.

BIBLIOGRAPHY

Abuhjeeleh, Mohammad. 2019. "Rethinking Tourism in Saudi Arabia: Royal Vision 2030 Perspective." *African Journal of Hospitality, Tourism and Leisure* 8 (5): 1–16.

Agheli, Lotfali. 2018. "Oil Depletion and Quality of Democracy in Selected Middle East Countries." *Acta Oeconomica* 68 (1): 101–14. https://doi.org/10.1556/032.2018.68.1.5

Alhowaish, Abdulkarim. 2016. "Is Tourism Development a Sustainable Economic Growth Strategy in the Long Run? Evidence from GCC Countries." *Sustainability* 8 (7): 1–10. https://doi.org/10.3390/su8070605

Al Naimi, Sarah Muhanna. 2022. "Economic Diversification Trends in the Gulf: The Case of Saudi Arabia." *Circular Economy and Sustainability* 2 (1): 221–30. https://doi.org/10.1007/s43615-021-00106-0

Ben Hassen, Tarek. 2022. "The GCC Economies in the Wake of COVID-19: Toward Post-Oil Sustainable Knowledge-Based Economies?" *Sustainability* 14 (18): 11251. https://doi.org/10.3390/su141811251

Conference Proceedings. 2024. In *Workshop # 4 (The Structural Economic Challenges That GCC Economies Face to Move Toward Economic Diversification and Sustainability)*. Cambridge, United Kingdom.

Crouch, Geoffrey I., and J. R. Brent Ritchie. 1999. "Tourism, Competitiveness and Societal Prosperity." *Journal of Business Research* 44 (3): 137–52. https://doi.org/10.1016/S0148-2963(97)00196-3

Cummings, Veronika. 2018. "Economic Diversification and Empowerment of Local Human Resources: Could Singapore be a Model for the GCC Countries?" In *Economic Diversification in the Gulf Region*, Volume II, edited by Ashraf Mishrif and Yousuf Al Balushi (pp. 241–60). Singapore: Springer Singapore. https://doi.org/10.1007/978-981-10-5786-1_10

Due-Gundersen, Nicolai, and Khalifa Al Suwaidi. 2024. "Potential for the UAE as a Model for Coordinating GCC-Wide Economic Diversification." Economic Diplomacy. Agda Insight. UAE: Anwar Gargash Diplomatic Academy.

EDI. 2022. "Global Economic Diversification Index (EDI)." Country Comparisons. UAE: The Mohammed Bin Rashid School of Government (MBRSG). https://economicdiversification.com/countries-compare/?ctr=4296,4302,4305,4306,4307,4310

Elbargathi, Khadiga, and Osama D. Sweidan. 2023. "Economic Diversification in Saudi Arabia: Comparing the Impact of Oil Prices, Geopolitical Risk, and Government Expenditures." *International Economics* 175 (October): 13–24. https://doi.org/10.1016/j.inteco.2023.05.003

Ewers, Michael C. 2015. "Oil, Human Capital and Diversification: The Challenge of Transition in the UAE and the Arab Gulf States." *The Geographical Journal* 182 (3): 236–50. https://doi.org/10.1111/geoj.12138

Fattouh, Bassam, and Laura El-Katiri. 2013. "Energy Subsidies in the Middle East and North Africa." *Energy Strategy Reviews* 2 (1): 108–15. https://doi.org/10.1016/j.esr.2012.11.004

Ghazaly, Salim, Rawia Abdel Samad, Karim Aly, and Hilal Halaoui. 2017. "Private-Sector Participation in the GCC: Building Foundations for Success." Ideation Center Insight. PwC Network. https://www.strategyand.pwc.com/m1/en/ideation-center/media/private-sector-participation-in-the-gcc.pdf

Gray, Matthew. 2011. "A Theory of 'Late Rentierism' in the Arab States of the Gulf." Occasional Paper No. 7. Georgetown University School of Foreign Service in Qatar: Center for International and Regional Studies. https://doi.org/10.2139/ssrn.2825905

Hanieh, Adam. 2011. *Capitalism and Class in the Gulf Arab States*. 1st ed. New York: Palgrave Macmillan. https://link.springer.com/book/10.1057/9780230119604

Henderson, Joan C. 2015. "The Development of Tourist Destinations in the Gulf: Oman and Qatar Compared." *Tourism Planning & Development* 12 (3): 350–61. https://doi.org/10.1080/21568316.2014.947439

Hertog, Steffen. 2013. "State and Private Sector in the GCC after the Arab Uprisings." *Journal of Arabian Studies* 3 (2): 174–95. https://doi.org/10.1080/21534764.2013.863678

Hilal, Nazar. 2020. "Tourism in the Gulf Cooperation Council Countries as a Priority for Economic Prospects and Diversification." *Journal of Tourism and Hospitality* 9 (7): 451.

Hossain, Amzad. 2013. "Evolution of Mutual Knowledge-Based Economy in Regional Integration: An Experience from the Cooperation Council of Arab States of the Gulf." *Journal of the Knowledge* Economy 6 (4): 790–817. https://doi.org/10.1007/s13132-013-0148-5

Hvidt, Martin. 2013. "Economic Diversification in Gulf Cooperation Council (GCC) Countries: Past Record and Future Trends." Kuwait Programme on Development, Governance and Globalisation in the Gulf States 27. London School of Economics and Political Science.

IMD. 2024. "World Competitiveness Ranking." Lausanne, Switzerland: International Institute for Management Development (IMD). https://www.imd.org/centers/wcc/world-competitiveness-center/rankings/world-competitiveness-ranking/

IRENA. 2019. "Renewable Energy Market Analysis: GCC 2019." Abu Dhabi: International Renewable Energy Agency (IRENA).

Jolo, Abdulrahman M., Ibrahim Ari, and Muammer Koç. 2022. "Driving Factors of Economic Diversification in Resource-Rich Countries via Panel Data Evidence." *Sustainability* 14 (5): 2797. https://doi.org/10.3390/su14052797

Kabbani, Nader. 2021. "Economic Dimensions of the Social Contract and How to Address Them." In *The Modern Arab State: A Decade of Uprising in the Middle East and North Africa*, edited by Youssef Cherif (pp. 117–47). Tunisia: Konrad-Adenauer-Stiftung.

Kalin, Stephen. 2019. "Saudi Arabia Opens to Foreign Holidaymakers, Chases Tourism Investment." Reuters, September 27. https://www.reuters.com/article/us-saudi-tourism/saudi-arabia-opens-to-foreign-holidaymakers-chases-tourism-investment-idUSKBN1WB2VV

Karolak, Magdalena. 2018. "Destination Place Identity, Touristic Diversity and Diversification in the Arabia Gulf." In *Economic Diversification in the Gulf Region*, Volume I, edited by Ashraf Mishrif and Yousuf Al Balushi (pp. 183–208). Singapore: Springer Singapore. https://doi.org/10.1007/978-981-10-5783-0_9

Khodr, Hiba. 2014. "A Preliminary Comparative Study of Policy Making in Two GCC Countries – Qatar and Kuwait: Processes, Politics, and Participants: Policy Making in Qatar and Kuwait." *Politics & Policy* 42 (2): 271–310. https://doi.org/10.1111/polp.12068

Kingdom of Saudi Arabia 2030 Vision. n.d. *Document: Vision 2030 Pillars*. Kingdom of Saudia Arabia.

Lejárraga, Iza, and Peter Walkenhorst. 2013. "Economic Policy, Tourism Trade and Productive Diversification." *International Economics* 135–136 (October): 1–12. https://doi.org/10.1016/j.inteco.2013.09.001

Macrotrends. 2024. Macrotrends. https://www.macrotrends.net/1369/crude-oil-price-history-chart

Malik, Aded. 2015. "The Gulf Economies' Coming Meltdown?" *Foreign Affairs*. https://www.foreignaffairs.com/articles/persian-gulf/2015-11-05/gulf-economies-coming-meltrdown

Mansfeld, Yoel, and Onn Winckler. 2007. "The Tourism Industry as an Alternative for the GCC Oil-Based Rentier Economies." *Tourism Economics* 13 (3): 333–60. https://doi.org/10.5367/000000007781497728

Mansour, Mourad, and Alhassan G. Mumuni. "Motivations and Attitudes toward Domestic Tourism in Saudi Arabia." *European Journal of Tourism, Hospitality and Recreation* 9 (1) (May 1, 2019): 27–37. https://doi.org/10.2478/ejthr-2019-0004

Mazzucato, Mariana, 2011. *The Entrepreneurial State*. London: DEMOS.

Mishrif, Ashraf. 2018. "Challenges of Economic Diversification in the GCC Countries." In *Economic Diversification in the Gulf Region*, Volume II, edited by Ashraf Mishrif and Yousuf Al Balushi (pp. 241–60). Singapore: Springer Singapore. https://doi.org/10.1007/978-981-10-5786-1_10

Mishrif, Ashraf, and Yousuf Al Balushi (eds.). 2018. *Economic Diversification in the Gulf Region, Volume I: The Private Sector as an Engine of Growth*. Singapore: Palgrave MacMillan. https://doi.org/10.1007/978-981-10-5783-0

Mishrif, Ashraf, and Harun Kapetanovic. 2018. "Dubai's Model of Economic Diversification." In *Economic Diversification in the Gulf Region*, Volume II, edited by Ashraf Mishrif and Yousuf Al Balushi (pp. 89–111). Singapore: Springer Singapore. https://doi.org/10.1007/978-981-10-5786-1_5

Mohamed, Sufian. 2020. "Challenges and Potentality of GCC Countries towards Achieving Sustainable Economic Growth: Analytical Framework." *European Journal of Business and Innovation Research* 8 (5): 23–37. https://doi.org/10.37745/ejbir/vol8no5.pp23-37.2020

Morakabati, Yeganeh. 2013. "Tourism in the Middle East: Conflicts, Crises and Economic Diversification, Some Critical Issues: Middle East Tourism." *International Journal of Tourism Research* 15 (4): 375–87. https://doi.org/10.1002/jtr.1882

Ngarava, Saul. 2021. "Relationship between Economic Diversification and CO_2 Emissions: ARDL-EC Modeling in South Africa." *Development Studies Research* 8 (1): 264–79.

Ozturk, Ozcan, and Maryam Al-Kuwari. 2021. "The Contribution of Tourism to Economic Growth: The Case of Qatar." *Journal of Environmental Management and Tourism* 12 (2): 598–60. https://doi.org/10.14505//jemt.v12.2(50).29

Prasad, Keertana Subramani, Salma Refass, Nasser Saidi, Fadi Salem, and Ben Shepherd. 2024. "Global Economic Diversification Index 2024." UAE: The Mohammed bin Rashid School of Government (MBRSG). https://economicdiversification.com/app/uploads/2024/02/Global-Economic-Diversification-Index-2024_Full-report.pdf

Prasad, Swati, Girish K. Nair, and Harsh Purohit. 2019. "Tourist Satisfaction: An Analysis of Push and Pull Factors – A Case of Qatar." *Journal of Management* 6 (2): 187–99. https://doi.org/10.34218/JOM.6.2.2019.022

Qatar National Vision. 2008. *Qatar: General Secretariat for Development Planning.* https://www.psa.gov.qa/en/qnv1/Documents/QNV2030_English_v2.pdf

Sharpley, Richard. 2002. "The Challenges of Economic Diversification Through Tourism: The Case of Abu Dhabi." *International Journal of Tourism Research* 4 (3): 221–35. https://doi.org/10.1002/jtr.378

Siegel, Paul B., Thomas G. Johnson, and Jeffrey Alwang. 1995. "Regional Economic Diversity and Diversification." *Growth and Change* 26 (2): 261–84. https://doi.org/10.1111/j.1468-2257.1995.tb00171.x

Thafer, Dania. 2023. *Creative Insecurity: Institutional Inertia and Youth Potential in the GCC.* London: Hurst Publishers.

Tsai, I-Tsung. 2018. "Political Economy of Energy Policy Reforms in the Gulf Cooperation Council: Implications of Paradigm Change in the Rentier Social Contract." *Energy Research & Social Science* 41 (July): 89–96. https://doi.org/10.1016/j.erss.2018.04.028

UNWTO. 2024. "UN Tourism Applauds Saudi Arabia's Historic Milestone of 100 Million Tourists." Madrid, Spain: United Nations World Tourism Organization. https://www.unwto.org/news/un-tourism-applauds-saudi-arabia-s-historic-milestone-of-100-million-tourist-arrivals

Wirba, Dr Asan Vernyuy. 2017. "The Role of Research in Knowledge Economy within GCC Countries." *European Journal of Business and Management* 9 (3): 166–84.

Yap, Ghialy, Shrabani Saha, and Saif S. Alsowaidi. 2022. "The Competitiveness of Qatari Tourism: A Comparative and SWOT Analysis." *Advances in Social Sciences Research Journal* 9 (7): 187210. https://doi.org/10.14738/assrj.97.12536

3. Determinants of economic diversification in GCC countries: empirical study for the period (2000–2022)

Adnan Aljawareen

3.1 INTRODUCTION

For many years, the Gulf Cooperation Council (GCC) countries have been worried about the long-term viability of their hydrocarbon earnings. Oil and gas supplies will inevitably run out in the long run. The two most vulnerable countries are Bahrain and Oman, whose reserves are predicted to run out in the next ten years for Bahrain and twenty five years for Oman. Oil revenues are anticipated to diminish by 2040, if not earlier, due to a decrease in global demand (Mirzoev et al., 2020).

GCC countries recognize the risks of dependence on oil for private sector activity and its ability to create jobs. To this moment, the oil sector still generates half of the gross domestic product of the Gulf Cooperation Council countries, which automatically links economic growth rate of change to the size of oil revenues. In GCC countries, the need for economic diversification has become even more pressing. The coronavirus pandemic-caused worldwide economic downturn caused Brent crude prices to drop from $64 per barrel at the beginning of 2020 to a low of $23 in April of that same year (World Bank, 2023a). The GCC countries, which ran budget deficits during the pandemic recession, are under a great deal of pressure because of this.

In addition to these risks, the GCC countries are already anticipating a period of decline in global demand for oil in the long term, which will gradually reduce the returns on oil exports.

This chapter aims to identify the most important factors that go into determining the degree of economic diversification in the six Gulf Cooperation Council countries, relying on an experimental approach using cross-sectional series models to measure the impact of fixed capital formation, exchange rate, trade openness, and per capita GDP on economic diversification. Through a set of economic variables in the GCC countries during the period of 2000 to 2022, the pooled OLS method, the fixed effects method, and the random effects method were used. The results showed that there is an inverse relationship between fixed capital formation and the economic diversification index, which means that there is diversity in the formation of fixed capital, which the public and private sectors contribute to.

3.2 LITERATURE REVIEW

Depending on the use, there are several definitions of "diversification." Within the field of political economy, the study's conceptual framework states that diversification is typically associated with exports, particularly with policies that attempt to lessen reliance on a restricted number of export commodities that could be vulnerable to changes in both price and volume or long-term losses (Routledge Encyclopedia of International Political Economy, 2001: 360). The word "diverse," which literally means "different, unlike, distinct, or separate," is where the phrase "diversification" originates (Pitts & Hopkins, 1982).

Export diversification and economic (product) diversification are the two main categories of economic diversification. A common definition of economic diversification is the process by which the economy creates a wider range of commodities and services.

Export diversification pertains to intentional measures aimed at modifying the proportions of commodities in the current export blend, incorporating novel items into the export assortment, and/or venturing into uncharted geographic markets. Both kinds are seen to stimulate economic expansion, foster an atmosphere that encourages wise investment, and lessen macroeconomic volatility in the short term.

Economic diversification, as it relates to oil-producing nations like the GCC countries, entails lessening reliance on the oil industry as the primary source of funding for public budgets by developing non-oil industries, exporting non-oil products, and creating non-oil revenue streams. It also implicitly entails a smaller role for the public sector and a larger role for the private sector.

Economic diversification occurs at the national level when a nation's excessive reliance on a small economic base is lessened. Supporting manufacturing and other non-resource sectors as service sectors including tourism, cultural events, etc., is the first step in shifting the production base away from the extractive industry in resource-dependent nations.

El Beblawi (2011) offers a helpful distinction. He separates the manufacturing sector into two groups: sectors dependent on oil and industries that replace imports. The oil-based industries include refineries, the sizable petrochemical industry, and energy-intensive sectors like aluminum in addition to the extraction of oil and gas. He makes the point that oil-based companies are typically state-owned because they are large-scale, capital-intensive projects.

The most important reasons for economic diversification can be summarized by the following (The Ministry of Planning, 2006):

1. Economic diversification will be a wall of protection against the natural phenomenon known as the Dutch disease. This phenomenon occurs when the oil states exploit their natural wealth, including oil, which leads to high oil exports, resulting in a high value of the local currency compared to the foreign currency, which then affects negatively on the high prices of local commodities, and in return leads to a decrease in their ability to compete in global markets, and as a result imports rise and exports of non-oil products decrease.
2. The great dependence on oil resources leads to a reduction in productivity as the growing reliance on the oil industry hinders other sectors of the economy, particularly the industrial and agricultural ones, making economic diversification challenging. Decision makers respond by enacting protectionist policies to preserve economic activity, which erodes productivity and, consequently, reduces competitiveness and puts financial strain on the oil industry.
3. The oil sector, as a result of its dependence on large capital investments, is unable to absorb large numbers of employment, in addition to the fact that the quality of the employment required by this sector is the type that necessitates relatively high skill levels.
4. Economic diversification reduces the risk of economic exposure created by relying on a single export commodity instead of relying on a varied export base that would achieve greater stability in returns and lower instability in export earnings, expand export revenues and thus result in economic growth and development. With regard to imports, economic diversification will create a more balanced external trade sector.
5. Giving a greater role to the productive sectors such as industry, agriculture, and services will work to modify the structure of the national economy, and reduce the effects of shocks caused by low oil prices on the national economy.
6. It creates some planning difficulties for oil countries as a result of their great dependence on unstable oil revenues to cover their expenses in the public budget, including public investment.

From the foregoing, it is evident that the primary goal of economic diversification in oil-producing nations is to broaden the productive base in order to protect state revenues in particular and the national product in general from fluctuations and crises brought on by relying on a single commodity, like oil, as a major source of these revenues. In other words, economic diversification reduces the impact of shocks on the economy and fosters economic stability, which is a goal that every nation should strive for. To do this, the contribution of the remaining (non-oil) sectors to the gross domestic product must be increased in exchange for a decline in the contribution of the primary (oil) sector, but without lowering oil production or exports.

Oil and gas exporters, along with other commodity exporters, have prioritized economic diversification as a policy goal and an objective of their economic policies in order to mitigate these risks.

Economic diversity is essential for long-term economic growth and development because it creates more balanced economies. It would assist in lessening vulnerability to volatility and uncertainty in the world oil market and preventing the associated boom bust cycles for the GCC countries and other producers and exporters of fossil fuels. More diverse economies have reduced production volatility, which is linked to better chances for economic growth and decreased levels of general economic uncertainty for individuals, corporations, and governments (MBRSG, 2024: 81).

3.3 EFFORTS OF DIVERSIFICATION IN THE GCC COUNTRIES

Prior to 2007, the GCC countries had prosperity and economic progress due to the tendency of oil prices to rise; however, the era from 2008 to 2023 was characterized mostly by significant volatility in oil prices, which had a significant impact on the economies of the GCC countries. Brent crude oil prices peaked in early 2008 at $140 per barrel, but by 2009 they had dropped precipitously to $61.7 per barrel. However, prices then rose, reaching $111.3 per barrel in 2011 before dropping once more to $52.3 per barrel in 2015 (Figure 3.1). The COVID-19 pandemic in 2020 caused a severe reduction in oil prices; prices fell from 74.49 US dollars in December 2019 to 23.04 in April 2020, and all of the GCC countries saw sharp declines in their GDP.

The economy of the GCC countries in general is characterized by concentration, as the extractive industries sector contributed 41.9% of the gross domestic product in 2005, but the efforts made by these countries to diversify their economy achieved positive results that became clear in the decline in this percentage to 30.1% in 2021. However, this percentage varies between countries, as it reached the lowest percentage in Bahrain (18.3%), while the highest percentage in Kuwait was 39.2%, as Figure 3.2 shows.

The financial revenues of the Gulf Cooperation Council countries are affected by fluctuations in oil prices, as oil revenues represent the largest proportion of the total public revenues of those countries. Despite the efforts made by those countries to diversify their revenues, oil revenues still represent more than half of public revenues, and this is clear in the data in Figure 3.3.

The Economic Diversification Index (EDI) scores for the GCC countries paints an intriguing picture. Previous EDI editions revealed that Bahrain had led the way in diversification in 2000 before the UAE overtook it. This was

Source: https://www.macrotrends.net/1369/crude-oil-price-history-chart

Figure 3.1 *Brent crude oil price (1995–2023)*

due to the country's implementation of several reforms, such as the establishment of free zones that successfully drew in investments and produced jobs, as well as the active participation of the private sector and EDI. Among the GCC countries, Kuwait continues to lag behind, it ranked 105 among 112 countries include in the report. Over time, Saudi Arabia and Oman have made the most improvements. It's interesting to note that in 2022, EDI scores decreased in all GCC countries, with the output sub-index experiencing the largest loss (MBRSG, 2024: 69).

Previous results showed that the GCC countries have made significant progress in the field of economic diversification during the past two decades. The Global Economic Diversification Index was published in 2022. It measured and ranked countries on the extent of their economic diversification from a multi-dimensional angle, exploring diversification of economic activity, international trade, as well as diversification of government revenues (away from a dependence on natural resource or commodity revenue) for a total of 90 nations across the 2000–2019 period (MBRSG, 2023: 16). The index has proven this as all GCC countries achieved an increase during the period 2000–2022 (see Figure 3.4). The United Arab Emirates and Bahrain obtained higher scores

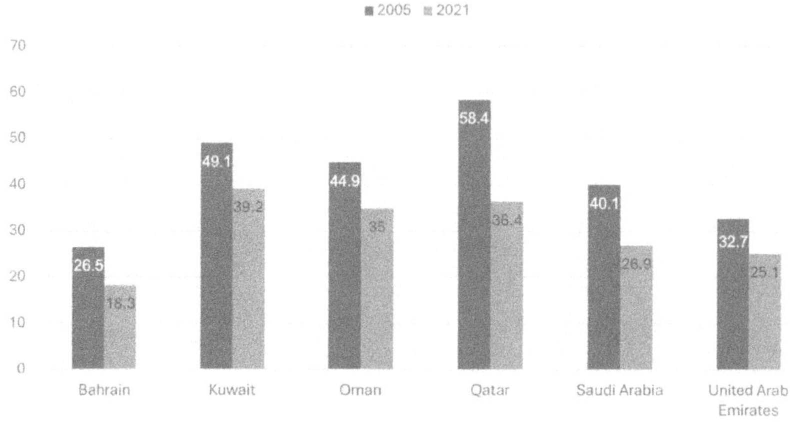

Source: Arab Monetary Fund, Unified Arab Economic Report, different issues, different years.

Figure 3.2 *The share of the extractive industries sector in the gross domestic product of the Gulf Cooperation Council countries during the period (2005–2021)*

compared to their counterparts, while the Kingdom of Saudi Arabia and the Sultanate of Oman improved their results significantly compared to the year 2000, whereas Kuwait remained in the bottom 20 in the world.

The GCC countries have long been driven to diversify their economies by creating profitable industries outside of oil and gas due to the anticipated decline in hydrocarbon reserves and earnings.

The GCC's private sector remains mostly dependent on government-funded initiatives and consumption, which are eventually financed by oil and gas earnings. The GCC's leaders need to move past the failures of past diversification initiatives and provide incentives for genuine economic growth that is not dependent on the oil and gas industry, either directly or indirectly. In order to diversify their sources of income, GCC nations should accumulate sovereign wealth funds and steer clear of initiatives that call for continuous government funding or subsidies. This group includes a large number of white elephants, or massive projects financed by the government. Lastly, GCC nations need to engage their people in wealth and economic diversification initiatives—this should include encouraging saving and investing at the individual level.

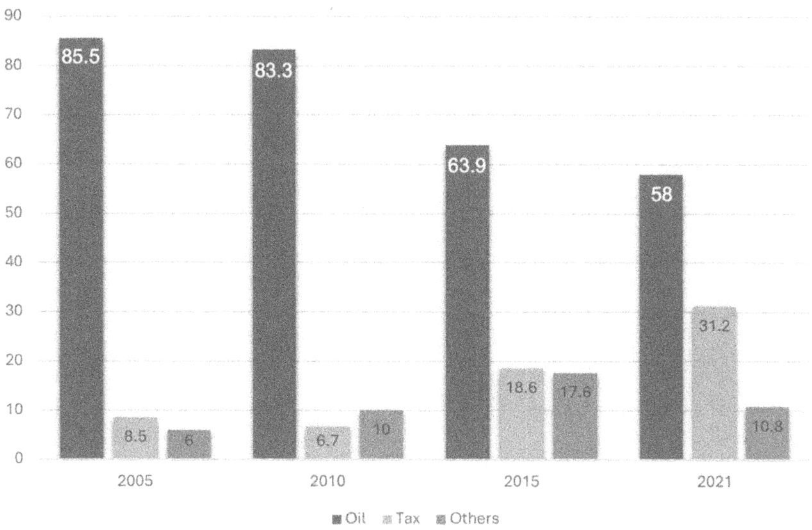

Source: Arab Monetary Fund, Unified Arab Economic Report, different issues, different years.

Figure 3.3 *Share of revenues from the total general revenue for the period (2005–2021)*

3.4 METHODOLOGY

The influence of fixed capital formation, fixed exchange rates, trade openness, and per capita GDP through a set of factors in the GCC countries between 2000 and 2022 will be assessed using the panel data methodology. The following is how these variables have been expressed:

The Herfindahl–Hirschman Index (HHI), a measure of economic diversification in the gross domestic product of the countries under study throughout the specified period, is the dependent variable.

The HHI index has a value between zero and one. If the index's value is one, it indicates that there is no economic diversification, and if it is zero, there is total economic diversification.

There were four independent variables used:

1. Fixed capital formation (FCF)
2. Exchange rate (ER)
3. Trade openness (TO)
4. Per capita GDP (PcGDP)

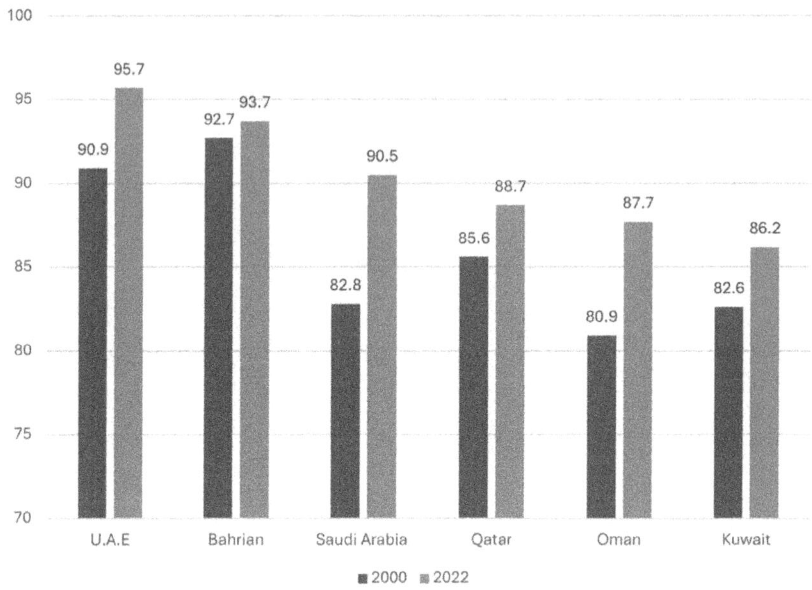

Source: Mohammed bin Rashid School of Government (MBRSG) (2024: 14).

Figure 3.4 *Economic Diversification Index for GCC countries (2000–2022)*

Additionally, the study of Levy-Yeyati & Sturzenegger (2007) demonstrated the inverse relationship between economic growth and the exchange rate, i.e., as the value of the local currency declines relative to foreign currencies, consumers favor local items.

The trade openness index and the economic diversification index, or the predominance of raw materials in GCC exports and the incapacity of non-oil exports to compete on a worldwide scale in international trade, were found to be positively correlated by the study.

Per capita did not determine economic diversification, according to a recent association between per capita, GDP, and the economic diversification index. This suggests that the GCC countries rely on other criteria to determine economic diversification.

So, the research chooses these variables for these reasons:

1. Gross capital formation is one factor that mediates the relationship between government spending and economic growth. Economic growth

is mostly influenced by gross capital formation, which takes the form of generated resources like structures, machinery, and equipment, in order for a country to diversify its economic basis from resource-based to non-resource-based industries.

2. Exchange rate policy is considered the most important tool of macroeconomic policies because it constitutes, alongside other policies, a mechanism effective to protect the local economy from internal and external shocks. A competitive and stable real exchange rate must be included in the assortment of tools intended to diversify exports and production while fostering macroeconomic growth and stability.
3. According to Van den Berg and Lewer (2007), the transfer of knowledge and technology is facilitated not just by international trade but also by related activities including international marketing, market research, product planning, and foreign travel. Therefore, under specific conditions, trade would be permitted by globalization to increase ideas and information, which would, in turn, promote economic progress. Because of their natural resource dependence, exporting countries suffer; importers of energy have benefited from the openness of their economies and have shown effectively the relationship between openness, growth, and diversification is positive.
4. The relationship between diversification and economic growth has been the main focus of research on export diversification; numerous studies have found a positive correlation between export diversification and per capita income (Al-Marhubi, 2000; Cavalcanti et al., 2014; Hausmann et al., 2007; Mau, 2016). Due to reverse causality, it is challenging to prove a causal relationship between the two variables; however, some research, like that done by Mau (2016), has shown that while there is some evidence that diversification level is influenced by per capita income, the relationship between diversification and GDP per capita is stronger. More economic integration is seen to promote growth through diversification as labor moves into capital-intensive industries (Mau, 2016).

The dependent variable: The variable of economic diversification (HHI) has been expressed, which is an indication of economic diversification in the gross domestic product of countries under study where the index was calculated according to the following equation:

$$\mathrm{HHI} = \frac{\sqrt{\sum_{i=1}^{N}\left(\frac{Xi}{X}\right)^{2}} - \sqrt{1/N}}{1-\sqrt{1/N}} \tag{3.1}$$

Where:

N = Number of sectors contributing to the GDP.
Xi = The value of the contribution of one sector to the GDP.
X = Total value of GDP.
The value of the HHI coefficient ranges between zero and one ($0 \leq \text{HHI} \leq 1$).
If (HHI = 0). This means that there is complete diversification in the economy.
If (HHI = 1). This means that the amount of diversity is non-existent.

Five independent variables have been relied upon in this research, which are as follows:

1. Forming fixed capital and expressed in relation to the percentage of the gross domestic product of the Gulf Cooperation Council countries during the study period.
2. The exchange rate: The price of the local currency is against the US dollar in each country under study.
3. Commercial openness: It is expressed by the total imports plus total exports divided into the gross domestic product within one year in each country under study.
4. The per capita GDP: It means the per capita GDP during one year in each country of the study.
5. Economic diversity is essential for long-term economic growth and development because it creates more balanced economies. It would lessen exposure to volatility and uncertainty in the world oil market and assist the GCC and other producers and exporters of fossil fuels to avoid the associated boom–bust cycles. Less production volatility is linked to better chances for economic growth and less overall economic uncertainty for individuals, companies, and governments in countries with greater diversity (Mohammed bin Rashed School Government, 2022: 23).

3.5 SPECIFICATION OF THE PANEL DATA MODEL

3.5.1 Fixed Effects Model (FEM)

The panel data model will be estimated by adopting the FEM static effect in order to determine the effect of each independent variable on economic diversification that represents the approved variable of the model (HHI) for each of the Gulf Cooperation Council countries separately, as the cross sectional data (CSD) is combined with time series data (TSD) according to the technology of inserting fake variables (dummy variables) as zeros in the process of organizing the total model data, which is as follows:

Cross section = GCC countries × number of variables = 6 × 4 = 24 independent variables.
Time series = period of study (2000–2022) × GCC countries = 23 × 6 = 138.
Total model of panel data (FEM) = 138 × 24 = 3312 observations of independent variables and dependent variables (HHI) = 6 × 23 = 138 giving 3450 total observations.
Where:

Xij: Independent variables, *i* indicates countries *i* = 1, 2, 3, 4, 5, 6.

1. Saudi Arabia
2. UAE
3. Qatar
4. Kuwait
5. Bahrain
6. Oman.

j: Independent variables = 4.

3.5.1.1 Results for panel data by Fixed Effects Model (FEM)

Regression Analysis: HHI versus X11: X64.

The regression equation is (Table 3.1):

$$HHI = 0.50 - 0.181\ X11 - 0.0219\ X12 + 0.00691\ X13 - 0.000026\ X14 + 0.031\ X21 + 0.10584\ X22 - 0.07928\ X23 + 0.0502\ X24 - 0.176\ X31 + 0.00246\ X32 + 0.00206\ X33 + 0.000002\ X34 - 1.93\ X41 - 0.00552\ X42 + 0.00660\ X43 - 0.000003\ X44 + 1.89\ X51 + 0.04175\ X52 + 0.00275\ X53 - 0.000059\ X54 - 1.22\ X61 + 0.00328\ X62 - 0.00016\ X63 + 0.000013\ X64$$

3.5.1.2 Fixed Effects Model analysis

On the econometrics and statistical indicators, the model and the estimated parameters were statistically acceptable and with a significant effect on tests (F, T), and the value of the selection coefficient was good (0.79), which represents the impact of independent variables on the approved variable (HHI), while the remaining percentage (0.21) was the effect of the random variable.

The FEM model did not suffer from mis-specification, this means errors and inaccuracies are absent in the model and assumptions adopted in the study. Also, the value of the variation enlargement factor (VIF) did not exceed the tenth level of value to confirm the absence of the problem of linear pluralism, as well as the value of D.W. = 1.89 demonstrated the lack of a problem of self-association, and because the value of correlation transactions was smaller than the two challenge laboratories, according to the clean test, this is evidence of the absence of a problem of non-homogeneity and that the data of the time chain is stable through cross sections.

Table 3.1 *Regression results*

Variable	Coefficient	Standard error of Coefficient	T	P	VIF
Constant	0.500	1.084	3.46	0.046	-
X11	−0.1812	0.2950	−7.61	0.000	9.236
X12	−0.021874	0.006004	−3.64	0.000	8.916
X13	0.006913	0.001295	5.34	0.000	3.024
X14	−0.00002648	0.000127	−2.08	0.040	3.675
X21	0.0314	0.3037	4.04	0.010	8.601
X22	0.105837	0.006113	3.95	0.042	7.743
X23	0.079276	0.005196	6.79	0.007	2.175
X24	0.050156	0.000244	8.64	0.000	9.022
X31	−0.1761	0.3044	−3.58	0.004	8.671
X32	0.002463	0.002344	2.05	0.006	4.036
X33	0.002056	0.001808	3.14	0.002	2.516
X34	0.00000160	0.0000234	5.68	0.000	7.117
X41	−1.931	0.436	−9.79	0.000	2.297
X42	−0.005524	0.003362	−6.64	0.003	9.661
X43	0.006602	0.003811	3.73	0.001	6.951
X44	−0.00000279	0.000471	−4.59	0.000	5.833

Variable	Coefficient	Standard error of Coefficient	T	P	VIF
X51	1.888	1.209	3.59	0.002	6.449
X52	0.041747	0.00302	5.53	0.000	3.135
X53	0.002745	0.001090	2.52	0.003	7.298
X54	−0.00005932	0.002182	−2.72	0.005	4.367
X61	−1.220	1.921	−1.973	0.067	5.730
X62	0.003277	0.002426	2.354	0.009	2.401
X63	−0.000159	0.001783	−0.09	0.059	9.884
X64	0.00001263	0.00001180	1.997	0.067	7.821

Note: S = 0.0653603, R-Sq = 79.0%, R-Sq(adj) = 76.1%, PRESS = 0.805589, R-Sq(pred) = 63.33%.
Source: Author.

Table 3.2 *Analysis of variance*

Source	DF	SS	MS	F	P
Regression	24	1.243313	0.051805	12.13	0.000
Residual error	113	0.482733	0.004272	-	-
Total	137	1.726045	-	-	-

Source: Author.

Table 3.3 *Unusual observations*

Obs.	X11	H.H	Fit	SE Fit	Residual	St Residual
1	3.75	0.28900	0.14209	0.02835	0.14691	2.49R
10	3.75	0.25600	0.39489	0.03774	−0.13889	−2.60R
16	3.75	0.72600	0.31118	0.03537	0.41482	7.55R

Note: Durbin-Watson (D.W.) statistic = 1.89181, Lack of fit test, Possible curvature in variable X12 (P-Value = 0.080), Possible curvature in variable X14 (P-Value = 0.005), Possible lack of fit at outer X-values (P-Value = 0.000), Overall lack of fit test is significant at P = 0.000.
Source: Author.

The economic analysis of the model examines the impact of the study variables across GCC countries, as presented below.

From the values and reference of the estimated parameters of the FEM standard listed in Table 3.4, it turns out that the arrangement of countries in terms of impact and economic performance in achieving important steps in the process of economic diversification was in the following order the state of the Emirates occupies the first level in terms of the size of the teachers and the positive impact of three parameters on economic diversification, then the Kingdom of Bahrain in the second level in terms of the size of the positive impact of the estimated teachers, then the State of Qatar, the third, the Kingdom of Saudi Arabia is fourth, the Sultanate of Oman is the fifth, and finally the State of Kuwait, whose weakest impact was in the field of diversification of the Kuwaiti economy, it was three parameters with a negative impact on the variable Certified (see Table 3.4).

Table 3.4 *Estimated parameters of the FEM standard*

Value of Coefficient	Variable	Country
−0.1812	X11 = ER	1. Saudi Arabia
−0.0219	X12 = FCF	1. Saudi Arabia
0.00691	X13 = CO	1. Saudi Arabia
−0.000026	X14 = Income	1. Saudi Arabia
0.031	X21 = ER	2. UAE
0.10584	X22 = FCF	2. UAE
−0.07928	X23 = CO	2. UAE
0.0502	X24 = Income	2. UAE
−0.176	X31 = ER	3. Qatar
0.00246	X32 = FCF	3. Qatar
0.00206	X33 = CO	3. Qatar
0.000002	X34 = Income	3. Qatar
−1.93	X41 = ER	4. Kuwait
−0.00552	X42 = FCF	4. Kuwait
0.00660	X43 = CO	4. Kuwait
−0.000003	X44 = Income	4. Kuwait
1.89	X51 = ER	5. Bahrain
0.04175	X52 = FCF	5. Bahrain
0.00275	X53 = CO	5. Bahrain
−0.000059	X54 = Income	5. Bahrain
−1.22	X61 = ER	6. Oman
0.00328	X62 = FCF	6. Oman
0.00016	X63 = CO	6. Oman
0.000013	X64 = Income	6. Oman

Source: Author's own construction.

3.5.2 Random Effects Model (REM)

The panel data model will be estimated by adopting the REM method in order to determine the moral effect of each independent variable on economic diversification that represents the approved variable of the model (HHI) in a comprehensive way for the Gulf Cooperation Council (GCC) states as the CSD data is combined and successive to the countries above during the study years and as follows:

Cross section = number of variables = four independent variables.
Time series = period of study (2000–2022) × GCC countries = 23 × 6 = 138.
Total model of panal data (REM) = 138 × 4 = 552 observations of independent variables.
HHI: dependent variables for GCC = 6 × 23 = 138.
Independent variables (138 × 4): Exchange rate (ER), Fixed capital formation (FCF) (% of GDP), Commercial openness (CO), GDP per capita income for GCC countries (Income).
1. Saudi Arabia, 2. UAE, 3. Qatar, 4. Kuwait, 5. Bahrain, 6. Oman.
Results for: Panel Data b Random Effects Model (REM).
Regression Analysis: HHI.

The regression equation (Table 3.5) is:

HHI = 0.296 – 0.0142 ER + 0.00284 FCF –0.000434 CO – 0.000002 Income

Table 3.5 Panel data by Fixed Affect Model

Predictor	Coefficient	SE Coefficient	T	P	VIF
Constant	0.29559	0.04321	6.84	0.000	-
ER	–0.014230	0.005982	–2.38	0.019	1.355
FCF	0.002838	0.001265	2.24	0.027	1.230
CO	–0.0004341	0.0002891	–2.20	0.036	1.099
Income	–0.00000198	0.00000064	–3.11	0.002	1.545

Notes: S = 0.100710, R-Sq = 71.8%, R-Sq(adj) = 69.5%, PRESS = 1.44026, R-Sq(pred) = 66.56%.
Source: Author.

Table 3.6 reports the results of the analysis of variance for the estimated regression model, indicating that the model is statistically significant at the 1% level. Table 3.7 presentes the sequential sum of sequare (Seq SS) for the expanatory variables included in the regression model.

First, for the econometrical and statistical indicators, the model and the estimated parameters were statistically acceptable and with a moral impact regarding (F, T) tests, and the value of the selection coefficient was good (0.71). The Random Effects Model (REM) did not suffer from the problems of economic measurement, and the value of the Variance Inflation Factor (VIF) did not exceed the tenth level of value to confirm the absence of the problem of linear pluralism. Similarly, the value of D.W. = 1.98 demonstrated the lack of a problem of self-association, and because the value of the correlation transactions was smaller than the two challenge laboratories, according to the clean

Table 3.6 *Analysis of variance*

Source	DF	SS	MS	F	P
Regression	4	0.37710	0.09428	9.30	0.000
Residual error	133	1.34894	0.01014	-	-
Total	137	1.72605	-	-	-

Note: There are no replicates. Minitab cannot do the lack of fit test based on pure error.
Source: Author.

Table 3.7 *Sequential sum of squares for explanatory variables*

Source	DF	Seq SS
ER	1	.20245
FCF	1	0.03220
CO	1	0.04411
Income	1	0.09834

Source: Author.

Table 3.8 *Unusual observations*

Obs	ER	H.H	Fit	SE Fit	Residual	St. Residual
16	3.75	0.72600	0.26045	0.02069	0.46555	4.72R
45	3.67	0.09400	0.12009	0.03805	−0.02609	−0.28 X
46	3.67	0.05300	0.11244	0.03899	−0.05944	−0.64 X
110	0.38	0.07600	0.29006	0.01341	−0.21406	−2.14R
111	0.38	0.08900	0.29032	0.01428	−0.20132	−2.02R
113	0.38	0.08300	0.29385	0.01378	−0.21085	−2.11R

Notes: R denotes an observation with a large standardized residual. X denotes an observation whose X value gives it large leverage. Durbin-Watson statistic = 1.989374.
Source: Author.

test, this is evidence of the absence of a problem of non-homogeneity and that the data of the time chain is stable through cross sections.

Second, for the economic analysis of the model, the statistically acceptable model of the estimated change shows the impact of independent variables on economic diversification in the Gulf Cooperation Council countries, and that most of the effects were negative and can be justified as follows:

1. The exchange rate variable was the sign of this variable negative to confirm the failure of economic policies in raising the competitiveness of the economies of the countries in order to stimulate the process of economic diversification, despite the low level of negative impact, but it means the GCC states need to review their economic policies on amending the system of exchange rate with the competitiveness of its economies against the foreign market, and then improve the level of economic diversification.
2. Fixed capital variable: This variable was the only one with a positive value to prove the positive impact of capital in stimulating the pace of the economic diversification process in the GCC countries. However, the value of this variable parameter was weak in effect, showing the weakness of the GCC countries' procedures in developing the productive bases in their economies.
3. The pure foreign trade variable: The negative parameter of this variable proves the ineffectiveness of the commercial policy of the GCC countries regarding the development and diversification of its economic structures, and this opens the way for the decision makers to review previous policies and correct foreign trade trends in a way that develops the national economy towards production, thus promoting the diversification of the national economy.
4. The average variable of per capita income: Despite the weak impact of this variable, the negative reference to it gives an indication that the high incomes in the GCC countries were towards encouraging imported products compared to local products, and therefore this variable has contributed to the harmful economic diversification policies in the GCC countries. It was not a variable aid to stimulating local demand towards locally produced goods, meaning it had a negative impact on economic diversification.

3.6 CONCLUSIONS

1. The differences in the level of economic diversification between the economies of the Gulf Cooperation Council states, as it became evident that

Kuwait has the lowest level of economic diversification and the United Arab Emirates the most.

2. As the standard model's results made evident, one of the components necessary for economic diversification is fixed capital.
3. The exchange rate factors, commercial openness, and the per capita component of the overall indicator of economic diversity in the GCC countries all have a negative effect.

BIBLIOGRAPHY

Al-Marhubi, F. (2000). Export diversification and growth: An empirical investigation. *Applied Economics Letters*, *7*(9), 559–562.

Arab Monetary Fund, Joint Arab Economic Report, different issues, different years. https://www.amf.org.ae/en/publications/reports/joint-arab-economic-reports

Cavalcanti, T., Mohaddes, K., and Raissi, M. (2014). Commodity price volatility and the sources of growth. *Journal of Applied Econometrics*, *30*(6), 857–873.

El Beblawi, H. (2011). Gulf industrialization in perspective. In J.-F. Seznec and M. Kirk (Eds.), *Industrialization in the Gulf: A Socioeconomic Revolution*. London: Center for Contemporary Arab Studies, Georgetown University/Routledge, pp. 185–197.

Hausmann, R., Hwang, J., and Rodrik, D. (2007). What you export matters. *Journal of Economic Growth*, *12*(1), 1–25.

Levy-Yeyati, E., and Sturzenegger, F. (2007). Fear of floating in reverse: Exchange rate policy in the 2000s. https://www.researchgate.net/publication/252583333_Fear_of_Floating_in_Reverse_Exchange_Rate_Policy_in_the_2000s_1

Mau, K. (2016). Export diversification and income differences reconsidered: The extensive product margin in theory and application. *Review of World Economics*, *152*(2), 351–381.

Ministry of Planning, Republic of Iraq (2006). *Iraq Country Economic Memorandum 2006: Pathways to Diversification*. Ministry of Planning, Baghdad.

Mirzoev, T. N., Zhu, L., Yang, Y., Zhang, T., Roos, E., Pescatori, A., and Matsumoto, A. (2020). *The Future of Oil and Fiscal Sustainability in the GCC Region*. IMF, Departmental Paper no. 20/01. https://www.imf.org/-/media/files/publications/dp/2020/english/fofsgccea.pdf

Mohammed bin Rashed School of Government (MBRSG) (2022). *Global Economic Diversification Index 2022*. Dubai, UAE.

Mohammed bin Rashid School of Government (MBRSG) (2023). *Global Economic Diversification Index 2023*. https://nassersaidi.com/wp-content/uploads/2023/02/Global-Economic-Diversification-Index-2023.pdf

Mohammed bin Rashid School of Government (MBRSG) (2024). *Global Economic Diversification Index 2024*. https://economicdiversification.com/app/uploads/2024/02/Global-Economic-Diversification-Index-2024_Full-report.pdf

Pitts, R. A., and Hopkins, H. D. (1982). Firm diversity: Conceptualization and measurement. *Academy of Management Review*, *7*(4), 620–629.

Routledge Encyclopedia of International Political Economy (1st ed.) (2001). "Diversification", volume edited by R. J. B. Jones. London: Routledge.

Van den Berg, H., and Lewer, J. J. (2007). *International Trade and Economic Growth* (1st edition). Abingdon, UK: Routledge.

World Bank (2023a). *Gulf Economic Update Structural Reforms and Shifting Social Norms to Increase Women's Labor Force Participation.* Middle East and North Africa Region, Fall 2023.

World Bank (2023b). *World Bank Commodity Price Data (The Pink Sheet), "Monthly Brent Prices in Nominal US Dollars, 1979 to Present".*

World Bank. (2024). *World Bank Data.* https://ycharts.com/indicators/kuwait_gross_fixed_capital_formation_percent

APPENDIX

The economic diversification index was estimated for some years for the Gulf Cooperation Council countries by adopting general trend equation models and simulation models for average values. These methods are the best ways to adopt values that are close to the real values provided that the economies are in a state of economic and political stability, which is what characterizes these countries during the years (see Tables 3A.1, 3A.2, 3A.3, 3A.4, and 3A.5).

Table 3A.1 HHI index for GCC countries (2000–2022)

Country	Saudi Arabia	UAE	Qatar	Kuwait	Bahrain	Oman
2000	0.289	0.175	0.198	0.223	0.243	0.268
2001	0.173	0.148	0.174	0.147	0.252	0.375
2002	0.172	0.132	0.157	0.123	0.261	0.329
2003	0.210	0.140	0.168	0.126	0.237	0.296
2004	0.264	0.175	0.183	0.184	0.239	0.472
2005	0.317	0.202	0.194	0.254	0.231	0.411
2006	0.343	0.220	0.263	0.280	0.297	0.354
2007	0.362	0.208	0.255	0.250	0.299	0.381
2008	0.428	0.202	0.231	0.304	0.318	0.474
2009	0.256	0.100	0.226	0.129	0.322	0.443
2010	0.295	0.140	0.227	0.259	0.284	0.403
2011	0.381	0.208	0.239	0.371	0.276	0.382
2012	0.283	0.209	0.215	0.361	0.295	0.375
2013	0.249	0.200	0.184	0.330	0.258	0.369
2014	0.200	0.162	0.195	0.294	0.235	0.394
2015	0.726	0.079	0.183	0.125	0.182	0.425
2016	0.057	0.034	0.192	0.112	0.105	0.337
2017	0.074	0.0410	0.221	0.133	0.076	0.378
2018	0.108	0.072	0.207	0.185	0.089	0.389
2019	0.086	0.066	0.176	0.198	0.097	0.414
2020	0.164	0.085	0.158	0.216	0.083	0.366
2021	0.097	0.094	0.197	0.233	0.086	0.405
2022	0.112	0.053	0.172	0.281	0.095	0.378

Source: Author.

Table 3A.2 *Exchange rate for GCC countries (2000–2022)*

Years	Saudi Arabia	UAE	Qatar	Kuwait	Bahrain	Oman
2000	3.75000	3.67250	3.64000	0.30675	0.38000	0.38000
2001	3.75000	3.67250	3.64000	0.30668	0.38000	0.38000
2002	3.75000	3.67250	3.64000	0.30391	0.38000	0.38000
2003	3.75000	3.67250	3.64000	0.29801	0.38000	0.38000
2004	3.75000	3.67250	3.64000	0.29470	0.38000	0.38000
2005	3.75000	3.67250	3.64000	0.29200	0.38000	0.38000
2006	3.75000	3.67250	3.64000	0.29017	0.38000	0.38000
2007	3.75000	3.67250	3.64000	0.28421	0.38000	0.38000
2008	3.75000	3.67250	3.64000	0.26882	0.38000	0.38000
2009	3.75000	3.67250	3.64000	0.28778	0.38000	0.38000
2010	3.75000	3.67250	3.64000	0.28660	0.38000	0.38000
2011	3.75000	3.67250	3.64000	0.27597	0.38000	0.38000
2012	3.75000	3.67250	3.64000	0.27993	0.38000	0.38000
2013	3.75000	3.67250	3.64000	0.28358	0.38000	0.38000
2014	3.75000	3.67250	3.64000	0.28456	0.38000	0.38000
2015	3.75000	3.67250	3.64000	0.30085	0.38000	0.38000

Years	Saudi Arabia	UAE	Qatar	Kuwait	Bahrain	Oman
2016	3.75000	3.67250	3.64000	0.30213	0.38000	0.38000
2017	3.75000	3.67250	3.64000	0.30334	0.38000	0.38000
2018	3.75000	3.67250	3.64000	0.30195	0.38000	0.38000
2019	3.75000	3.67250	3.64000	0.30361	0.38000	0.38000
2020	3.75000	3.67250	3.64000	0.31010	0.38000	0.38000
2021	3.75000	3.67250	3.64000	0.31010	0.38000	0.38000
2022	3.75000	3.67250	3.64000	0.31010	0.38000	0.38000

Source: IMF, International Financial Statistics(IFS) database.

Table 3A.3 *Fixed capital formation (FCF) for GCC countries (2000–2022) (%) GDP*

Years	Saudi Arabia	UAE	Qatar	Kuwait	Bahrain	Oman
2000	17.35	N.A	20.10	10.67	16.38	15.45
2001	18.26	20.97	29.07	14.31	16.97	17.05
2002	18.01	21.07	32.64	17.13	23.11	18.64
2003	18.29	20.79	34.84	16.63	23.57	21.91
2004	19.15	18.68	31.48	14.98	22.51	24.36
2005	19.31	18.37	34.29	14.63	25.68	22.01
2006	20.45	17.57	41.88	15.94	29.49	23.86
2007	23.65	23.57	46.01	20.46	33.55	28.66
2008	22.80	23.37	41.11	17.63	34.52	30.61
2009	25.75	28.91	42.95	17.98	25.25	33.30
2010	24.43	23.90	31.27	18.20	26.04	21.66
2011	22.41	20.83	28.7	14.12	21.06	28.55
2012	22.11	20.27	27.14	13.38	26.83	27.65
2013	23.46	17.75	27.82	14.50	24.76	29.94
2014	24.92	19.06	31.79	16.54	25.60	29.82
2015	29.35	22.61	45.84	25.22	24.07	34.01
2016	25.60	23.64	48.86	30.11	25.76	39.29
2017	23.94	18.73	42.60	25.33	28.34	33.32
2018	20.72	17.12	40.65	25.67	29.46	30.49
2019	22.38	18.36	43.73	25.21	27.79	28.95
2020	24.09	20.20	43.84	N.A	28.89	31.75
2021	24.29	20.23	36.79	N.A	24.61	25.61
2022	24.63	20.23	30.80	18.11	25.0	26.0

Sources: World Bank (2024). World bank data. https://ycharts.com/indicators/kuwait_gross_fixed_capital_formation_percent, https://www.indexmundi.com/facts/qatar/gross-capital-formation, https://data.worldbank.org/indicator/NY.GDP.MKTP.CD?end=2010&locations=QA&start=2000.

Table 3A.4 *Commercial openness*

Years	Saudi Arabia	UAE	Qatar	Kuwait	Bahrain	Oman
2000	56.893	80.267	83.592	70.504	119.463	73.932
2001	53.919	81.889	83.413	68.993	110.104	76.465
2002	55.244	85.201	77.618	63.902	112.643	75.730
2003	62.531	94.632	77.670	66.142	110.961	72.632
2004	67.006	108.896	77.793	69.367	115.155	70.978
2005	73.119	110.363	80.446	75.088	122.957	77.415
2006	74.583	109.165	82.932	72.134	122.750	71.764
2007	77.850	119.076	82.106	73.322	114.367	84.300
2008	82.454	135.913	82.594	76.195	125.611	87.180
2009	67.086	130.054	74.571	70.402	95.797	82.206
2010	67.777	126.253	78.486	80.277	105.903	87.044
2011	73.346	147.691	81.523	82.570	112.520	91.759
2012	73.329	170.787	87.644	83.983	99.707	92.409
2013	72.165	167.648	82.469	82.910	98.116	99.879
2014	67.344	154.680	78.574	82.045	96.879	86.323
2015	56.495	136.171	68.369	74.254	93.227	77.414
2016	48.610	156.721	58.899	70.469	75.582	70.760
2017	49.840	154.726	60.455	73.420	80.399	73.387
2018	50.962	162.003	63.748	78.003	87.072	73.799
2019	49.461	158.734	57.896	71.999	81.173	70.668
2020	42.470	139.299	53.554	64.044	77.260	81.658
2021	49.393	221.101	64.088	69.162	93.013	85.706
2022	54.240	225.418	69.355	76.772	103.037	91.252

Source: https://unctadstat.unctad.org/wds/ReportFolders/reportFolders.aspx

Table 3A.5 *GDP per capita income for GCC countries (2000–2022) (US$)*

Years	Saudi Arabia	UAE	Qatar	Kuwait	Bahrain	Oman
2000	17019	59062	53603	31662	21713	19355
2001	16403	56774	52994	30826	21681	19989
2002	15561	55284	54064	30893	21866	19592
2003	16917	57313	53428	35310	22349	18942
2004	17868	59967	61288	37986	22326	19028
2005	18295	58654	60386	40476	22027	19197
2006	18076	56297	63704	41161	21784	19737
2007	17700	48459	61932	41132	22014	20361
2008	18095	42517	62155	39860	21917	21804
2009	17072	35643	62413	35123	21157	22710
2010	17336	34541	69467	32569	21453	21783
2011	18803	36288	73493	33428	21907	20142
2012	19392	36568	72870	33009	22485	19889
2013	19526	38035	72013	31082	23013	19387
2014	19906	39242	69724	30282	23108	18694
2015	20442	41525	66985	29315	22795	18777
2016	20508	43458	64233	29134	22811	18800
2017	20028	43420	60551	27245	23019	18260
2018	20097	43644	60081	26665	23029	18257
2019	19806	43785	59621	25778	23414	18044
2020	18857	41276	58476	23930	22579	17662
2021	19622	42715	61023	24832	23407	18301
2022	21069	45698	63727	26914	24384	18857

Source: GDP Total (unctad.org).

4. Catalysts of change: the role of strategic sovereign wealth funds in the structural transformation of the GCC economies

Duncan Mayall

4.1 INTRODUCTION

Gulf Cooperation Council (GCC) governments have leveraged a number of tools to diversify their economies away from a reliance on hydrocarbon production, but one tool receiving particular attention from policymakers and external commentators are sovereign wealth funds (SWFs), specifically strategic SWFs.

According to the International Forum of Sovereign Wealth Funds (IFSWF), SWFs from the GCC manage in excess of $3 trillion (Global SWF, 2024). The first SWFs in the GCC were developed to save excess resource revenues and enhance intergenerational equity. However, in the last two decades, more SWFs, both in the Gulf and internationally, have been formed to foster domestic economic development.

Strategic SWFs are one of the four types of SWFs classified by the IFSWF. The types are:

- Savings funds: which the IFSWF notes 'are sometimes referred to as intergenerational savings funds because they have decades-long investment horizon' and 'are often set up by commodity-rich countries to save a portion of their resource wealth for the future'.
- Stabilisation funds: which the IFSWF describes as being 'designed as pools of capital which governments can draw on to smooth the budget'.
- Strategic funds: which the IFSWF notes 'acquire stakes in companies in strategic industries to nurture their development, promoting the growth of the wider economy and realising financial returns', 'may provide financing to early-stage companies in strategic industries, or buy long-term stakes to facilitate the development of more mature firms' and that 'some strategic funds will make direct investments in critical infrastructure projects,

occasionally using their local expertise to leverage co-investments from peer institutions'.

- Hybrid or multiple objective funds: where the IFSWF notes that 'many funds combine two or more of the functions listed above, mixing stabilisation, savings and development'.

Strategic SWFs accounted for 41% of the funds currently operational which were formed around the world from 2000 to 2020 and more than 30% of SWF assets, according to the IFSWF (2023). As specified by Global SWF (2024), strategic funds accounted for four of the five new SWFs created in 2023, and account for six of the ten SWFs in development as of January 2024.

This rise in prominence has been a comparatively recent shift. Strategic SWFs only accounted for 16% of those that were formed before 2000 (IFSWF, 2023). To the author's knowledge this growth has entirely come from the creation of new funds, rather than the repurposing of existing institutions. While the reasons behind the establishment of any SWF will largely be country-specific, there are two primary factors that have driven this shift.

First, strategic SWFs are commonly seeded with government-owned assets, such as equity stakes in state-owned companies, rather than being funded through resource revenues as is more common with stabilisation or savings funds. So, while SWFs are commonly associated with resource-rich countries with budget surpluses, strategic SWFs are increasingly being formed by countries with significant state-owned assets, but which run budget deficits. As SWFs are being deployed to serve different ends, more countries can establish them. One key element of this has been the emergence of Singapore's Temasek Holdings. Temasek's high-profile success, and Singapore's broader status as a development model, has been a key source of emulation as countries, explicitly or implicitly, look to the 'Temasek approach' for inspiration.

Second, many commentators have identified a resurgence of industrial policy and the willingness of governments to intervene in the domestic economy to achieve particular policy goals. For countries with significant sovereign wealth, whether in the form of resource revenues or state-owned assets, strategic SWFs may prove an effective tool in implementing industrial policy or competing against other markets for foreign direct investment (FDI).

Within the GCC countries, both factors apply to a certain extent. While there has been a degree of privatisation in previous decades, the state continues to exercise majority ownership of many of the largest industrial enterprises in the region. And while GCC economic development strategies highlight the importance of encouraging a greater role for the private sector, they continue to envisage an active role for the state.

Moreover, in the GCC there is the added attraction that increased investment in the domestic economy by SWFs has the potential to accelerate the region's economic diversification and structural transformation by crowding in capital to nascent, but strategically important sectors. In these industries, initial development may require investment at a larger scale or longer time frame for returns than many private sector investors would find attractive, while the region's financial sector may also lack the appropriate capability to divert private capital flows.

Furthermore, while the majority of investments made by strategic SWFs are made in their country of origin, there is also potential to link investments made in international markets to domestic economic development. For example, the investments by Saudi Arabia's Public Investment Fund (PIF) in the electric vehicle sector internationally, most notably its investment in Lucid Motors, can be partly seen as part of the country's broader ambitions to develop an electric vehicle manufacturing hub.

As a result, such investments are playing an increasingly central role within the GCC countries' economic development strategies. The most notable example is in Saudi Arabia, where the Public Investment Fund (PIF) is scheduled to invest an average of SAR150bn a year into the domestic economy from 2021 until 2025. To put this in context, this is a significant addition to the SAR189bn of capital expenditure outlined in the Kingdom's state budget for 2024 and equivalent to around 13% of the nation's Gross Fixed Capital Formation in 2023.

There has been limited analysis of the impact of domestic investment by strategic SWFs, however, recent research from the International Monetary Fund (IMF) has provided some initial data on the non-oil GDP multiplier of these investments. The IMF (2024) notes that 'ongoing analysis by staff (IMF, Korniyenko et al., forthcoming) suggests that domestic investments by GCC SWFs have a multiplier of around 0.4, in line with other domestic investments (of which 40 percent are estimated to be from SWFs in the GCC sample used).' This may suggest that although domestic investments conducted through SWFs in the GCC are intended to realise a financial return, they do so without reducing the multiplier effect compared to investment conducted through central government.

However, while increased investment creates opportunities, it also carries risks which policymakers will be keen to mitigate.

Investments not subject to rigorous standards of financial returns risk leading to a misallocation of resources which maximises neither commercial returns nor delivers significant broader economic returns. Furthermore, high levels of state investment which is not subject to market discipline also risks crowding out private sector investment.

To assess the impact of strategic SWFs and the function they are performing within the region's broader economic policymaking toolkit, it is important to establish the details of these SWFs' mandates. However, while the rise of strategic SWFs has been noted in the public commentary, less focus has been paid to the specific ambitions these funds are pursuing under the broader umbrella of domestic economic development.

This chapter aims to begin to address the current gap by looking at the strategic SWFs in the GCC and seeking to ascertain what these funds have set as their economic development objectives.

Furthermore, establishing what strategic SWFs are *attempting* to do is only one part of the challenge. To build a fuller picture of their role within the region's domestic economies, and the extent to which they have been successful, it will also be important to understand how they are seeking to *measure* that impact.

There are no universally agreed international standards for sovereign wealth funds when it comes to disclosing their activity, but the Generally Accepted Principles and Practices (GAPP), known as the Santiago Principles, set out in 2008, establish 24 principles of good governance, investment and risk management for SWFs and have been used by many funds to structure their disclosure practices. The Santiago Principles have also helped to provide a certain level of standardisation in how SWFs report their financial performance, with an increasing percentage of funds publishing data on their annual and longer-term financial returns (Maire et al., 2021). In some cases, these returns will be linked to benchmark targets, which can be of varying degrees of specificity. For example, Singapore's GIC states that it aims 'to preserve and enhance the international purchasing power of the funds placed in our care' while Australia's Future Fund is mandated to achieve 'at least the Consumer Price Index (CPI) +4.0 to +5.0 per cent per annum over the long term'.

However, it is important to note that the Santiago Principles focus strongly on financial returns and broader governance, reflecting the fact that when they were drafted, most SWFs were savings or stabilisation funds. They do not provide detailed guidance on measuring broader economic impact although they do not exclude the inclusion of this mandate.

Measuring broader economic impact is also challenging. As noted in Divakaran et al. (2022), 'adhering to a double bottom line mandate is complex', and that many funds 'particularly struggle to measure nonfinancial impact that is not quantifiable'. And while some impacts may be quantifiable at a certain level, for example, the number of jobs accounted for in the SWF's portfolio, they may not be amenable to a cost–benefit analysis or capture the full impact of a fund's investment.

Furthermore, the incentives for disclosing broader economic impact are less clear than for financial transparency. The SWF literature suggests that financial transparency is incentivised by the ability of funds to establish their legitimacy and maintain access to international capital and an ability to invest in key international markets. Governments or legislatures may benefit from data on economic impact when assessing the effectiveness of a SWF in meeting its objectives, however, the incentives for tracking and disclosing economic impact are potentially less immediate or urgent.

Combined, these factors mitigate against the likelihood of economic impact being measured and are likely to shape the form taken by any assessments of economic impact.

To assess how Gulf SWFs are addressing this challenge, this chapter will review what metrics, if any, strategic funds in the Gulf are using to measure the impact that they have on the broader economy. This also aims to shed light on the factors driving their decisions around the tracking and disclosure of their broader economic impact.

Finally, the GCC countries do not operate in a vacuum. Governments across the globe are establishing strategic investment funds and those from the GCC interact with those elsewhere. Consequently, this chapter will also explore strategic SWFs in other markets to establish a broader context.

4.2 LITERATURE REVIEW

Given their rapid emergence, there is little literature focused specifically on strategic SWFs as a grouping distinct from other SWFs. Indeed, even the establishment of 'sovereign wealth funds' as a category is a relatively recent development, with the term itself having been coined around twenty years ago in Andrew Rozanov's article 'Who Holds the Wealth of Nations?' (Rozanov, 2005).

Much of the early literature around SWFs reflected heightened concerns regarding foreign state ownership of sensitive assets and worries that, as Barbary et al. put it, 'sovereign wealth funds would make capital allocation decisions on non-commercial grounds and that this would distort financial markets' (Barbary et al., 2023).

Following these concerns, in the autumn of 2007, the International Monetary Fund convened the International Working Group of Sovereign Wealth Funds to draft the Santiago Principles.

This context helps to explain why the literature around SWFs is so frequently focused on their international investments and their financial returns rather than domestic investments and economic impact.

As Divakaran et al. (2022) highlight, 'Whereas the literature on SWFs provides a wealth of information related to investing abroad in foreign currency–denominated financial assets, limited guidance is available on the type of commercial, policy-driven domestic investment undertaken by [strategic investment funds].'

The consequence of this is that there is relatively little literature on the role these funds can play in domestic economic development, the specific goals of these institutions or how they are measuring their progress. However, literature in related fields can provide some guidance.

For example, Divakaran et al. (2022) provide analysis of sovereign investment funds (SIFs), institutions they define as 'special-purpose investment vehicles backed by governments or public institutions that seek a double bottom line of financial and economic returns', a categorisation which incorporates strategic SWFs, but also includes other entities which wouldn't fall under the umbrella of SWFs. Divakaran et al. (2022) also include within their list of strategic investment funds a number of funds which would not be classed as strategic SWFs, including development funds such as China's Silk Road Fund, industrialisation funds such as Saudi Arabia's Dussur and multinational funds such as Asia Climate Partners.

When it comes to the role these funds play in boosting economic development, much of the existing literature on sovereign investment funds focuses on the importance of additionality. Divakaran et al. (2022) argue that 'the primary argument for setting up a SIF [Strategic Investment Fund] is the extent to which a SIF's intervention can address market or government failures—that is, contribute additionality both to what exists in the market and to what is provided by the government'.

This is also a key consideration for GCC governments. The region's strategic SWFs are either explicitly tasked with helping to develop the domestic private sector or are envisaged as part of broader economic development strategies that aim to enhance diversification of the economy and the growth of the private sector.

When it comes to the precise aims of strategic SWFs or SIFs, the literature has focused on the importance of the broader economic impact being tied to the fund's mandate and the importance of a clear understanding of the relationship between financial and non-financial returns. Divakaran et al. (2022) argue that the broader economic mandate encompasses 'the expected impact on economic productivity and growth or on environmental and social variables' and that it 'should be clearly defined and publicly disclosed, and it should be directly based on the findings from detailed preliminary studies for the SIF'. As a reflection of the breadth of the aims adopted by these funds, they also note that the policy goal 'includes but is not limited to growing the economy, creating jobs, opening up economic opportunities for women and minorities, adapting to or mitigating climate change, boosting specific sectors or regions of the economy, and diversifying away from commodity reliance (in countries where that is the main industry)'.

However, while research such as Divakaran et al. (2022) and Melecky et al. (2023) include case studies of strategic SWFs and other state investors and works such as Halland et al. (2016) provide summary tables that outline the objectives and sectors of individual strategic investment funds, there does not appear to be any research which seeks to analyse which mandates are most common and how widely they are shared.

In part, this reflects the sector's relative newness and the limited literature to date. It also likely reflects the fact that mandates for strategic SWFs tend to reflect specific domestic requirements rather than being derived purely from a standard 'menu' of options.

In the GCC, strategic SWFs are designed to support specific national economic development strategies. Kotilaine (2024) notes that 'PIF plays a key role in pursuing the goals of Saudi Vision 2030 and the emergence or transformation of other funds in the region also tracks closely key development agendas: for example, the creation of Bahrain's Mumtalakat and the launch of the Kingdom's Economic Vision 2030'.

This approach is not unique to the GCC. For example, Divakaran et al. (2022) note that 'the board of FONSIS pre-screens investment projects for their compliance with Plan Sénégal Emergent, a government plan for the structural transformation and growth of the Senegalese economy, which FONSIS is mandated to support'.

When it comes to how strategic SWFs measure the impact on their domestic economy, there is little existing literature, although related literatures do provide some anecdotal evidence. Divakaran et al. (2022) examine the question of how to measure the 'double bottom line' from the perspective of sovereign investment funds and Melecky et al. (2023) examine it in detail from the perspective of a range of development finance institutions, including some strategic SWFs.

Halland et al. (2016) argue that 'in principle, the policy objectives of an investment should be expressed in terms of its [economic rate of return] estimated in accordance with one of several accepted methodologies', but concedes that 'none of the SIFs referred to in this paper use the [economic rate of return] to assess investment opportunities' and that 'in practice … most SIFs use simpler, albeit less comprehensive measures'.

Furthermore, while the economic rate of return stands as a theoretical best practice, it involves valuing discounted project benefits and costs using shadow prices. This necessarily introduces an element of subjectivity, meaning that even impact that is measured by economic rate of return will be imperfect and open to question. This chapter primarily focuses on how SWFs report on their performance so the focus is its use as an ex-post assessment of investment, but it is important to note that the development literature demonstrates that the economic rate of return is also used as an ex-ante measure to assess potential investments.

When it comes to the alternative measures adopted, Melecky et al. (2023), discussing development finance institutions, note that 'for small projects, the double bottom line can be expressed in terms of the IRR and of the social and environmental impact of the project using the IRIS+ impact measurement and management methodology developed by the Global Investment Impact Network' and that 'simpler practical alternatives for impact measurement could use benchmarking project indicators for beneficiaries (enterprises, households) against a control group (industry peers, nonbeneficiary households) using parallel trends in employment, value added, or GHG emissions (energy efficiency)' (Melecky et al., 2023).

Part of the reason that funds adopt this simpler approach, rather than a more comprehensive one based on the economic rate of return is, as Divakaran et al. (2022) highlight, the fact that 'nonfinancial impact is typically harder to measure than more easily quantifiable financial returns'. However, the broader SWF literature also sheds light on a further potential explanation of the limited focus paid to domestic economic impact. The impetus behind the writing of the Santiago Principles and an increased level of financial and operational transparency among SWFs is linked by many studies to the need to establish legitimacy (as argued, for example, in Monk, 2008) to maintain the ability to access markets in which they wish to invest and to continue to attract capital, whether debt or equity.

By contrast, the extent to which strategic SWFs increase the disclosure around the domestic economic impact of their investments is likely to have limited impact on these factors. Instead, pressure on strategic SWFs to demonstrate their broader economic impact is likely to come either from multilateral institutions, such as through the IMF's Article IV process, or, more pointedly, through domestic public opinion. Consequently, it is likely that the way in which these funds measure their impact is likely to be shaped by what is most likely to appeal to a public audience.

4.3 DATA

To assess how strategic SWFs are measuring and monitoring their goals, this chapter focuses on information published by SWFs themselves, while being informed by secondary analysis and commentary.

The primary focus of the analysis will be the strategic SWFs based in the GCC. This chapter uses the categorisation in IFSWF (2023) and focuses on strategic funds and 'hybrid' funds which include a strategic element. To provide a wider perspective, it also includes an analysis of a sample of strategic SWFs from outside of the GCC region. The sample has been chosen to include both advanced and emerging economies as well as examples frequently cited among international best practice.

The data analysed is the content published on the respective funds' English-language websites. The rationale for this is that it reflects the information about the fund that it wishes to put forward and should capture the most relevant material.

The key limitation of this approach is that it may miss some content. For example, many funds will not publish the legislation or executive orders that supported their creation on their websites and this material may include objectives that are not referred to elsewhere, particularly for funds which maintain only a minimal online presence. It also misses other sources of public communication by funds, such as media interviews or speeches and will miss any content that is published in local languages but not in English. Given the importance that most SWFs place on communicating with their domestic audiences, this may result in important information being missed.

Finally, it is important to note that of the seven GCC funds categorised as strategic funds by this approach, four are based in the United Arab Emirates. As a result, there is a risk that a simplistic analysis of the results could confuse characteristics of UAE funds for broader GCC trends.

4.4 METHODOLOGY

The primary approach in this chapter is a review of the content and documents published on the English-language websites of the strategic SWFs in the primary and secondary sample.

The first phase was an initial survey to establish some of the most common areas of focus.

Following this initial survey, five objectives relating to broader economic impact were identified. The contents and documents of each fund in the sample were then reviewed to establish whether the fund has identified each of these objectives.

The second phase was to repeat this process with the metrics these funds used to measure their broader economic impact. Following the initial survey, five broad categories of metrics were identified. The contents and documents of each fund in the sample were then reviewed to establish whether or not the fund discloses a metric under each of those broad categories.

The analysis uses the following definitions for each of these categories.

Objectives:

- Building national champions: Funds which state that they have as an objective, building the success of national companies on an international stage (in addition to the ambition to realise financial returns).
- Catalysing FDI: Funds which state that an objective is to catalyse or enable foreign direct investment into the local economy.

- Catalysing domestic private investment: Funds which state that an objective is to catalyse or enable higher levels of domestic private sector investment.
- Developing strategic sectors: Funds which identify economic sectors which they aim to enhance through their investment (directly or indirectly).
- Enhancing national reputation: Funds which state that they have as an objective enhancing the reputation of their home country through their activities.

Metrics:

- Job creation within portfolio: The fund provides a figure for the total number of jobs within their portfolio.
- FDI catalysed: The fund provides a figure for FDI that has been catalysed or induced by its investment projects or activities.
- Domestic private investment catalysed: The fund provides a figure for domestic private capital that has been catalysed or induced by its investment projects or activities.
- Climate impact: The fund discloses at least one metric around the environmental impact of its portfolio.
- Human capital development within portfolio: The fund discloses at least one metric regarding broader human capital development within its portfolio (for example, staff training, creation of jobs for nationals or specific forms of employment within its portfolio, such as female employment).
- GDP contribution: The fund publishes a figure for the contribution its portfolio makes to national GDP or provides a gross value added (GVA) calculation for projects.

The aim of this approach is to begin to quantify the areas of focus followed by strategic SWFs in the GCC, the broader economic impact metrics they report and the targets that they set in this regard (if any). It also aims to situate GCC strategic SWFs within the broader context of their international peers.

Clearly, this approach has limitations. The nature of the information it provides is, by its nature, high-level and imprecise. It also requires a degree of subjective judgement: while this chapter takes a relatively strict approach to defining whether any of a fund's objectives fits within the categories, there will inevitably be an element of subjectivity involved.

Furthermore, this approach only addresses explicit objectives and, therefore, may miss some implicit objectives. For example, many strategic SWFs, particularly within the GCC, include majority stakes in major national companies and aim to develop those businesses with regional and international expansion to enhance their financial returns. In practical terms, this may be indistinguishable from strategic SWFs that explicitly aim to promote national champions, but unless it is explicitly stated as an objective, this approach will not identify it.

Likewise, SWFs often have an important role to play in the development of local capital markets, something that is particularly the case within the GCC. This can come in the form of issuance of debt to support the development of a yield curve, providing liquidity as investors or by preparing companies for public listing and enhancing the breadth and quality of equities on the market. While this can play a significant role in enabling capital flows to support the development of non-oil sectors, it is not something explicitly stated as an objective by the strategic SWFs in this chapter.

Finally, by use of a binary yes/no measurement, this approach can disguise significant variation within those results. For example, one fund may only disclose relatively limited data on water use in its portfolio, while another discloses comprehensive scope 1, 2 and 3 emissions data. Under this methodology, both funds would be counted as disclosing a degree of climate impact.

4.5 RESULTS

The results of the assessments conducted are presented in tabular format below (Tables 4.1, 4.2, 4.3 and 4.4), where an 'X' marks that the relevant objective or metric is stated/applied by that fund and an 'X' in square brackets marks that the relevant objective or metric is stated/applied subject to clarification provided in the notes in the far-right column.

4.6 DISCUSSION AND ANALYSIS

GCC strategic SWFs have a strong stated emphasis on catalysing FDI and on developing strategic sectors. Six of the seven funds analysed state that developing strategic sectors is among their objectives, while four of the seven funds highlight catalysing FDI.

This finding would appear to fit with the broad analysis of the GCC economy as established in the introduction. Developing strategic non-oil sectors is a key plank in GCC countries' diversification efforts and strategic SWFs are being tasked with supporting these initiatives. Many of the priority sectors for these SWFs require significant capital expenditure, for example, tourism, renewable energy, advanced manufacturing, and the use of strategic SWFs both to deploy public capital in this area and catalyse private capital would seem in line with the region's broader economic objectives. Likewise, given that SWFs are, by definition, long-term investors, these significant projects are also well suited to their investment horizons.

Table 4.1 Objectives: GCC strategic SWFs

Fund	Building national champions	Catalysing FDI	Catalysing domestic private investment	Developing strategic sectors	Enhancing national reputation	Notes
Public Investment Fund	X	X	X	X	-	-
Mubadala Investment Company	X	X	-	X	-	-
Bahrain Mumtalakat Holding Company	-	-	-	X	-	-
Oman Investment Authority	-	X	-	X	-	-
ADQ	-	X	X	X	-	-
Emirates Investment Authority	-	-	-	-	-	-
Investment Corporation of Dubai	-	-	-	X	-	-

Source: Author's analysis.

Table 4.2 *Objectives: selected other strategic SWFs*

Fund	Building national champions	Catalysing FDI	Catalysing domestic private investment	Developing strategic sectors	Enhancing national reputation	Notes
Fundo Soberano de Angola	-	-	-	-	-	-
The Sovereign Fund of Egypt	X	X	X	X	-	-
Indonesia Investment Authority (INA)	X	X	X	X	X	-
Ireland Strategic Investment Fund (ISIF)	-	[X]	[X]	X	-	Aims to catalyse co-investment which captures both FDI and domestic private capital.
Khazanah Nasional BHD	X	X	X	X	-	-
Temasek Holdings	-	-	-	X	-	-
Türkiye Wealth Fund	X	X	X	X	X	-
COFIDES	X	X	X	X	-	-

Source: Author's analysis.

Table 4.3 *Metrics: GCC strategic SWFs*

Fund	Job creation with portfolio	FDI catalysed	Domestic private investment catalysed	Climate impact	Human capital development within portfolio	GDP contribution	Notes
Public Investment Fund	X	[X]	[X]	-	-	X	Reports a figure for total external investment catalysed, which includes both FDI and domestic private capital.
Mubadala Investment Company	-	-	-	-	-	-	-
Bahrain Mumtalakat Holding Company	X	-	-	-	X	X	Disclosed figures for the contribution of its portfolio to GDP in previous annual reports, although not in the latest.
Oman Investment Authority	X	X	-	-	X	-	-
ADQ	X	-	-	-	-	X	-
Emirates Investment Authority	-	-	-	-	-	-	-
Investment Corporation of Dubai	-	-	-	-	-	-	-

Source: Author's analysis.

Table 4.4 Metrics: selected other strategic SWFs

Fund	Job creation with portfolio	FDI catalysed	Domestic private investment catalysed	Climate impact	Human capital development within portfolio	GDP contribution	Notes
Fundo Soberano de Angola	-	-	-	-	-	-	-
The Sovereign Fund of Egypt	-	-	-	-	-	-	-
Indonesia Investment Authority (INA)	X	X	X	X	-	-	-
Ireland Strategic Investment Fund (ISIF)	X	[X]	[X]	X	X	X	Reports a figure for 'co-investment' which captures both FDI and domestic private capital.
Khazanah Nasional BHD	-	-	-	-	X	-	-
Temasek Holdings	-	-	-	X	-	-	-
Türkiye Wealth Fund	X	-	-	X	X	-	-
COFIDES	X	-	-	X	X	X	-

Source: Author's analysis.

The focus on catalysing FDI also seems to reflect the broad needs of the GCC economies. In part, FDI can play a role in helping to unlock additional capital for the development of non-oil sectors. But arguably, the related spillover effects and their impact on productivity growth are equally important to these investors. Outside of the energy sector, GCC economies have seen poor labour productivity performance in recent decades, with labour productivity declining 2% per year on average from 2000 to 2018 (Kotilaine, 2024) and growth supported by increased capital and labour inputs. Through localisation of technology and expertise and other spillover effects, FDI (particularly greenfield investment) has the potential to increase productivity and enhance the prospects for long-term diversification.

Strategic SWFs' ability to de-risk investment, for example, by acting as cornerstone investors in projects or providing significant capital in joint ventures, has the potential to play an important role in catalysing this FDI and these results suggest that GCC governments see them as playing a part in these efforts.

It is worth noting that while only two of the seven GCC funds reference building national champions among their objectives and none reference enhancing reputation, in many instances this may reflect a difference between explicit and implicit objectives more than a significant tangible difference with those who explicitly pursue those objectives. The majority of GCC strategic SWFs include within their portfolio majority stakes in key national companies such as Emirates Airlines (Investment Corporation of Dubai), ALBA (Mumtalakat) and Etisalat (Emirates Investment Authority), including those with a growing regional and international footprint. In practice, therefore, most GCC strategic SWFs are tasked with managing key state-owned enterprises and supporting their international expansion. Furthermore, certain strategic SWFs in the GCC have demonstrated a willingness to invest elsewhere in the region (for example, PIF has established investment companies in six countries across the Middle East: Reuters, 2022), suggesting that investing in local companies' regional and international expansion would not be a barrier.

Likewise, no Gulf SWF has an explicit objective to enhance the broader reputation of their home country in the way that the Indonesia Investment Authority (INA) and Türkiye Wealth Fund do. Türkiye Wealth Fund argues in its annual report that it 'strengthens our nation's economy thanks to its reputability in the international financial community' while Indonesia's INA cites 'favourable media attention and actively engaging in global conferences' as examples of its 'active role in enhancing Indonesia's standing to entice potential investors'.

However, in practice several SWFs in the GCC appear to fulfil a similar function. For example, PIF has emerged as one of the most prominent Saudi Arabian institutions on the international stage, while Mubadala has also consistently played a high-profile international role, albeit more restricted to the business and investment sphere.

So, in practical terms, their activity has a significant impact on how their home country is seen on the global stage, even if such an objective is not explicitly stated.

There are relatively limited examples of strategic SWFs, whether in the GCC or elsewhere, measuring their broader economic impact and those metrics adopted are 'simpler, albeit less comprehensive measures' than the economic rate of return (Halland et al., 2016).

Within the GCC, the most cited metric is job creation within the portfolio. This would seem aligned with two key theses outlined above. First, that strategic SWFs are likely to select metrics that are relatively easy to calculate. Second, strategic SWFs are more likely to select and emphasise metrics that will appeal to the public audience of their home market.

This may also partly explain the fact that three GCC SWFs publish figures for the GDP impact of their portfolio, despite it being relatively rare in an international context. These funds' portfolios often account for a significant proportion of the national economy (for example, government estimates have suggested that Mumtalakat accounts for 8% of Bahrain's GDP; Gulf Daily News, 2024) and such a disclosure may provide a means of demonstrating that they are delivering value.

There are relatively few examples of strategic SWFs publishing metrics for the FDI that they have catalysed. However, within the GCC, the Oman Investment Authority discloses both the value of the investment opportunities it has developed and the value of investment agreements, while PIF discloses a figure for the total amount of external investment it has catalysed, which includes both local investment and FDI. In both instances, catalysing investment was a prominent element of these funds' objectives and both funds are also explicitly closely tied to their respective national development strategies (Oman Vision 2040 and Vision 2030).

One area in which GCC funds appear to disclose less information relative to international peers is regarding climate impact. None of the GCC funds in the primary sample provides a measure of its impact on the climate while four of seven funds in the secondary sample do. One interpretation of this disparity is that, as major hydrocarbon producers, GCC states place a lower priority on climate change and that they see action against it as being counter to their national interests. However, it should also be noted that all GCC countries have established net zero targets as part of the Paris Agreement and that many have announced ambitious targets regarding renewable energy production, as well as other climate mitigation initiatives, many of which include a leading role for strategic SWFs.

An alternative interpretation would focus on local norms and the principal audience for the funds' communication. Among some of those international funds that disclose the environmental impact of their portfolio this disclosure is arguably a more deeply rooted norm within their home country: COFIDES in Spain would be an example of this. In other instances, the disclosure may reflect a desire to align with the norms of international institutional investors who are a primary audience. For example, the Indonesia Investment Authority is strongly focused on attracting international investment into projects in Indonesia. Closer alignment to the norms of those investors could be seen as a part of this effort. The GCC funds, by contrast, would seem to focus their disclosure on those areas which would have highest salience for a domestic public audience. In the event that the salience of climate change rises within the GCC, it may be the case that the focus on climate-related disclosures rises alongside this.

4.7 CONCLUSION

It is clear that strategic SWFs have been tasked with a significant role in the economic transformation of the GCC economies. And, with new strategic SWFs announced in Dubai and Kuwait in the second half of 2023, it seems likely that this trend will continue. This chapter has aimed to outline in greater detail what these institutions have been tasked with achieving, how they are measuring their impact and how they compare to their international peers.

The key role with which these funds appear to have been tasked is the development of strategic sectors of the economy. In the case of the GCC, these are non-oil sectors that are designed to support broader diversification agendas. The exact approaches to this objective will vary fund by fund, but there are some clear areas of commonality.

Each of these funds owns majority stakes in key national companies, so their shareholding in these companies plays an important role in their efforts to develop the broader sector around them. Indeed, Mubadala and PIF both speak specifically about helping national companies to compete on a regional or international level. This could be achieved through a range of approaches, including providing additional financing for investment, via engagement through the SWFs appointed board representatives or through leveraging the international networks that SWFs have developed.

In addition to managing and developing key companies within these sectors, several of these funds have set objectives to attract more private sector capital, whether local or international. In many cases, this has been through investment in new joint ventures with multinationals. As an example of this, in October 2023, PIF and Pirelli Tyre S.p.A. announced a joint venture agreement to build a tyre manufacturing facility in Saudi Arabia. It was announced that PIF would own 75% of the joint venture and that Pirelli would own the remaining 25% while acting as 'a strategic technology partner to support the development of the project by providing technical and commercial assistance' (Pirelli, 2023). This would suggest a model in which PIF is providing capital that de-risks the investment from the perspective of the foreign firm, while also benefitting from the technology and expertise of a global leader in the sector.

This investment is incorporated within a broader series of initiatives in the automotive sector, one of the 13 economic sectors that PIF identified as areas of focus within its 2021–2025 strategy. These initiatives include PIF's investment in the American electric vehicle manufacturer Lucid Motors, a joint venture agreement with Hyundai Motor Company, which aims to manufacture 50,000 vehicles per year within the Kingdom (Argaam, 2023), and the Electric Vehicle Infrastructure Company, a joint venture between PIF and Saudi Electricity Company (Public Investment Fund, 2024), among others.

While PIF is arguably an exceptional case among strategic SWFs, particularly regarding the scale of its domestic investments, the joint venture approach has been adopted by other SWFs in the region in developing key sectors and boosting FDI.

Other approaches used by strategic SWFs in the region in developing strategic sectors of the economy include the creation of wholly owned companies and acquisitions of stakes in international leaders in the field.

The first of these has the advantage of relative simplicity and these companies can gain access to international expertise through the hiring of experienced international executives. However, it has the downside of increasing the risk of crowding out private investment in the sector. To a certain degree, this can be mitigated through a commitment to reduce the SWF's shareholding in these companies once they reach a certain level of maturity, for example, through an IPO. Indeed, Saudi Arabia's Crown Prince Mohammed bin Salman, chairman of the Public Investment Fund, has indicated a desire to reduce the fund's ownership share in mature assets and a target of conducting a public listing for any new venture within five years of it reaching profitability (Al Arabiya English, 2021).

The second of these is a less direct route but can have the advantage of giving SWFs a deeper understanding of the sector and access to networks and expertise that can be used in developing the sector domestically. One downside is that in the case of a minority investment, the impact of this approach may be difficult to quantify. A second is that, particularly in the case of an investment in which the SWF takes on majority ownership of the company, this may open it to many of the concerns that are identified in the SWF literature: namely that the SWF is leveraging its ownership stake to cause the firm to make decisions in the national interest of its home country at the expense of the company's existing home market or its best commercial interests.

This chapter also examines how Gulf SWFs are measuring the broader economic impact of their activity and places this in a wider context of strategic SWFs and other analogous institutions globally.

First, GCC strategic SWFs are like other SWFs internationally in that they measure their domestic economic impact through relatively straightforward metrics. Whereas national and multinational development banks are more likely to assess the impact of projects through an estimate of the economic rate of return, strategic SWFs have adopted a range of simpler proxy measures from job creation to external capital catalysed, to GDP contribution. While the Ireland Strategic Investment Fund publishes a separate economic impact report, which aims to measure the impact of the investment catalysed by the fund, this report continues to utilise simpler measures and remains the exception rather than the rule.

Second, the metrics chosen by funds in the GCC and elsewhere appear to support the hypothesis that the choice of metrics is influenced by the priorities of their key audiences. In the case of GCC funds, this has translated into a relative focus on domestic job creation and human capital development and, to a lesser degree, on the attraction of FDI. By contrast, GCC funds appear to be less likely at this stage to measure the broader climate impact of their portfolio, although this may change as climate becomes a more salient issue in these countries.

This chapter marks an initial analysis of what strategic SWFs in the Gulf are looking to achieve and their role in the region's economic transformation, but it leaves considerable ground uncovered.

Further research could extend this analysis by looking at the activity conducted by SWFs, rather than simply their stated objectives, one of the key shortcomings of the approach adopted here. It could also examine the extent to which a fund's mandated reporting requirements, for example, whether it reports to parliament, a head of state or specific government ministry, influences how it measures its broader economic impact.

More research could also focus on the scale of local equity ownership and domestic investment being undertaken by these funds. Public data in these areas are generally limited but this may help to provide a clearer differentiation between the strategic SWFs in the region and their relative roles and influence within their countries' economies. While funds such as PIF are central to their home country's economic strategy, others in the region play a more marginal role. The relative scale of capital deployed domestically may help to clarify the picture. Likewise, it could examine the financial and economic returns achieved in these investments, to assess the extent to which funds have succeeded and to assess how investments by strategic SWFs compare with capital expenditure conducted by central government.

Given the broader global growth of these funds and the launch of new strategic SWFs, it is likely that this is a subject that will continue to grow in importance as Gulf states look to calibrate the right level and type of state support for their economic development and diversification. And as they attract more capital it is also likely that more focus will be paid to the progress of these institutions and the extent to which they have been successful in their aims (although it may be the case that the extent to which this translates into additional monitoring and disclosure of their broader economic impact by these funds will depend on the extent to which it is a salient issue for the domestic public).

DISCLOSURE

The author is the chief economist at a government advisory firm and, through this role, advises certain Gulf SWFs mentioned in this chapter. The views expressed in this chapter are the author's own and do not reflect those of his employer or those of any SWF he advises.

BIBLIOGRAPHY

Al Arabiya English (2021). "Saudi Crown Prince Mohammed bin Salman Interview on Vision 2030 [English subtitles]." YouTube, April 28, 2021. https://www.youtube.com/watch?v=Y1HfRhfHwUc

Al-Hassan, Abdullah, Michael Papaioannou, Martin Skancke, and Cheng Chih Sung (2013). "Sovereign Wealth Funds: Aspects of Governance Structures and Investment Management." IMF Working Paper, no. 13/231 (November 2013).

Ang, Andrew (2010). "The Four Benchmarks of Sovereign Wealth Funds." October 2010.

Argaam (2023). "PIF, Hyundai Motor Sign JV Agreement on Automotive Manufacturing Plant in Saudi Arabia." *Argaam*, October 22, 2023. https://www.argaam.com/en/article/articledetail/id/1678528

Bagnall, Allie, and Edwin Truman. (2013). "Progress on Sovereign Wealth Fund Transparency and Accountability: An Updated SWF Scoreboard." *Policy Brief*, no. 13–19. Washington, DC: Peterson Institute for International Economics.

Barbary, Victoria, Adam D. Dixon, and Patrick J. Schena (2023). "The Evolving Landscape of Sovereign Wealth Funds in a Changing World Economy: How Resilient Are the Santiago Principles?" In *Weaponising Investments* Volume I, edited by Jens Hillebrand Pohl, Joanna Warchol, Thomas Papadopoulos, and Janosch Wiesenthal, pp. 17–36. Springer Studies in Law & Geoeconomics. Cham: Springer.

Chhaochharia, Vidhi, and Luc A. Laeven (2009). "The Investment Allocation of Sovereign Wealth Funds" (July 8, 2009). Available at SSRN: https://ssrn.com/abstract=1262383.

Clark, Peter B., and Ashby H. B. Monk (2015). "Sovereign Development Funds: Designing High-Performance, Strategic Investment Institutions." SSRN, September 30, 2015.

Das, Udaibir S., Adnan Mazarei, and Han van der Hoorn (2010). "Economics of Sovereign Wealth Funds: Issues for Policymakers." Washington, DC: International Monetary Fund.

Divakaran, Shanthi, Håvard Halland, Gianni Lorenzato, Paul Rose, and Sebastian Sarmiento-Saher (2022). "Strategic Investment Funds: Establishment and Operations." Washington, DC: World Bank Group.

Dixon, Adam (2014). "Enhancing the Transparency Dialogue in the 'Santiago Principles' for Sovereign Wealth Funds." *Seattle University Law Review, 37*(2): 581–595.

Dixon, Adam, Patrick Schena, and Javier Capapé (2022). *Sovereign Wealth Funds: Between the State and Markets*. Newcastle-upon-Tyne: Agenda Publishing.

Gelb, Alan, Silvana Tordo, Håvard Halland, Noora Arfaa, and Gregory Smith (2016). "Sovereign Wealth Funds and Long-Term Development Finance Risks and Opportunities." Washington, DC: World Bank Group.

Global SWF (2024). *Annual Report: State-Owned Investors Powering Through Crises*. New York: Global SWF.

Gulf Daily News (2024). "Mumtalakat 'contributes 8pc to GDP'." Accessed May 15, 2024. https://www.gdnonline.com/Details/1300563/Mumtalakat-%E2%80%98contributes-8pc-to-GDP%E2%80%99#:~:text=Sovereign%20wealth%20fund%20Mumtalakat's%20contribution,Telecommunications%20Minister%20Mohammed%20Al%20Kaabi

Halland, Håvard, Michel Noël, Silvana Tordo, and Jacob J. Kloper-Owens (2016). "Strategic Investment Funds: Opportunities and Challenges." WB Policy Research Working Paper 7851.

IFSWF (2022). "A Year of More: IFSWF Annual Review 2021." London: IFSWF.

IFSWF (2023). "Investing in Uncertain Times: IFSWF Annual Review 2022." London: IFSWF.

IFSWF (2024a). "Powering Change: Building Resilience in a Transforming Climate." London: IFSWF.

IFSWF (2024b). "Santiago Principles." Accessed May 8, 2024. https://www.ifswf.org/sites/default/files/santiagoprinciples_0_0.pdf

International Monetary Fund (IMF) (2024). *Saudi Arabia: 2024 Article II Consultation: Press Release and Staff Report*. Washington, DC: IMF.

Kotilaine, Jarmo T. (2024). *Sustainable Prosperity in the Arab Gulf: From Miracle to Method*. Abingdon, UK: Routledge.

Maire, Julien, Adnan Mazarei, and Edwin Truman (2021). "Sovereign Wealth Funds are Growing More Slowly, and Governance Issues Remain." Policy Brief, no. 21–3. Washington, DC: Peterson Institute for International Economics.

Meggison, William, Diego Lopez, and Asif Malik (2021). "The Rise of State-Owned Investors: Sovereign Wealth Funds and Public Pension Funds." *Annual Review of Financial Economics, 13*: 247–270.

Melecky, Martin, Pasquale Di Benedetta, Ismael Ahmad Fontan, Ganbaatar Jambal, and Michel Noel (2023). *Braced for Impact: Reforming Kazakhstan's National Financial Holding for Development Effectiveness and Market Creation*. Washington, DC: World Bank.

Ministry of Finance, Saudi Arabia (2024). *Budget Statement: Fiscal Year 2024*. Riyadh: Ministry of Finance.

Monk, Ashby H. B. (2008). "Recasting the Sovereign Wealth Fund Debate: Trust, Legitimacy, and Governance." *New Political Economy, 14*(4): 451–468.

Pirelli (2023). "PIF and Pirelli Announce Joint Venture to Establish Leading Tire Manufacturing Facility in Saudi Arabia." Pirelli, press release, October 26, 2023. https://press.pirelli.com/pif-and-pirelli-announce-joint-venture-to-establish-leading-tire-manufacturing-facility-in-saudi-arabia/

Public Investment Fund. Electric Vehicle Infrastructure Company (EVIQ) (2024). "Public Investment Fund." Accessed May 8, 2024. https://www.pif.gov.sa/en/our-investments/our-portfolio/electric-vehicle-infrastructure-company-eviq/

Reuters (2022). "Saudi Arabia's Wealth Fund Sets Up Investment Firms in Five Mideast Countries." October 26, 2022, accessed June 17, 2024. https://www.reuters.com/world/middle-east/saudi-arabias-wealth-fund-sets-up-investment-firms-five-mideast-countries-2022-10-26/

Rozanov, Andrew (2005). "Who Holds the Wealth of Nations?" *Central Banking*, *15*(4) (May 2005): 52–57.

Schena, Patrick, and Richard Collins (2023). "Implementing the Santiago Principles: Lessons from Member Self-assessments." London: IFSWF.

Stone, Sarah, and Edwin Truman (2016). "Uneven Progress on Sovereign Wealth Fund Transparency and Accountability." Policy Brief no. 16–18. Washington, DC: Peterson Institute for International Economics.

Truman, Edwin M. (2009). "A Blueprint for Sovereign Wealth Fund Best Practices." *Revue d'économie financière*, *9*(1): 429–451.

5. Economic diversification and sustainability in GCC countries: the role of information technology

Umara Noreen, Attayah Shafique and Zaheer Ahmed

5.1 INTRODUCTION

Information technology plays an important role in the economic and structural development of the Gulf countries through digitalization. Economic diversification and sustainability are the two important issues highlighted in the sustainable development goals (SDGs). Nowadays, the economies are more focused and moving towards technological advancements in all sectors of the economy. Building capacity for digital development enhances the country's capabilities to promote innovation, create knowledge, and disseminate information. Digital networks increase communication as well as allow people, regions, and nations to collaborate and share information aimed at fostering growth and sustaining development. In fact, organizations cannot exist today and expect to stay competitive without adequate information technology systems. Artificial intelligence, cloud computing, home and business security blockchain, drones, and Internet of Things (IoT) are some of the developing trends today that are revolutionizing the multiple industries.

The increasing focus on digital transformations and data abundance is merging the real and virtual worlds, shaping the economic landscape. The ability to harness this big data will define the competitiveness of nations, including the Gulf Cooperation Council (GCC) countries, in global and regional markets. This leads to modern trends such as cost reduction in payments, enhanced accessibility of goods and services, and the exploration of new income sources. Each country within the group, Bahrain, Qatar, Kuwait, the United Arab Emirates, Oman, and Saudi Arabia is actively pursuing initiatives to digitize their economies (Aidrous et al., 2021).

For GCC countries, external knowledge enhances the economy's readiness to diversify output, create employment opportunities, and improve global competitiveness.

It has been observed that the Gulf Cooperation Council (GCC) countries are facing several structural economic challenges that hinder their ability to move towards economic diversification and sustainability. Mishrif (2018) argued that recent years have witnessed substantial infrastructure investments in GCC nations, notably in construction and real estate, yet this measured progress prompts critical questions. Why haven't the Gulf's aspirations for resource-driven industrialization materialized? Despite ample capital and cheap energy, why haven't GCC countries fostered an industrial framework conducive to global competitiveness, barring the heavily subsidized petrochemical sector? Moreover, the overwhelming reliance on imports, around 98%, increases the doubts about the sustainability of the Gulf development model. While no definitive answers exist, one feasible explanation for industrialization setbacks could be the GCC's focus on a service-based economy. Hence, diversification now involves directing resources to education, healthcare, finance, tourism, aviation, and real estate, with GCC nations viewing it as a long-term strategy amid continued reliance on oil revenues (Luciani, 2012). Therefore, this chapter aims to explore the different economic challenges and problems that the GCC countries (Saudi Arabia, Kuwait, the United Arab Emirates, Qatar, Bahrain, and Oman) face and highlights the role of information technology in dealing with these problems. Moreover, it also explains the relationship between economic diversification and sustainability in the GCC region.

This research has chosen GCC countries because they exhibit both geographical and economic convergence. For instance, they share similarities in economic structure, with a significant reliance on non-renewable energy sources and oil revenues. Additionally, they are all major petroleum exporters endowed with abundant natural resources, which has led to rapid economic expansion but has also resulted in significant environmental consequences. In contrast to the global average, Gulf countries tend to have a relatively limited range of exports but boast a comparatively high real GDP per capita (Satrovic & Adedoyin, 2022).

The current study attempts to answer the following questions:

1. What is the relationship between information technology and economic diversification in the GCC region?
2. What are the current economic challenges and the different strategies for economic diversification and sustainability faced by GCC countries?
3. What is the role of information technology in dealing with the problems of economic diversification and sustainability?

4. What is the relationship between economic diversification and sustainability in the GCC region?

To answer these questions, mixed research methods are used that are quantitative and qualitative. In this chapter, the data of different diversification factors are considered like gross domestic product, imports, exports, employment, fiscal budget, etc. of the GCC countries (Bahrain, Kuwait, Oman, Qatar, Saudi Arabia, and UAE). In addition to this, different sectors are also selected like energy, mining, manufacturing, etc. For measuring sustainability, the sustainability matrix or ESG (Environmental, Social, and Governance) is used. Different quantitative tools will be used to analyze data like correlation, regression, and descriptive statistics. The diversification of the economy coupled with information technology (digitalization) improves the overall performance of the firms/country. The findings of this chapter have important implications for the government and policymakers to be more focused on economic diversification when creating development agendas and to rigorously measure and monitor economic diversity in evaluating the success of their policies. This chapter recommends that long-term sustainable growth/sustainability is more important for any economy to become competitive. Moreover, this chapter recommends that, in the era of technology, it helps in the diversification at the micro as well as macro level of the country.

5.2 LITERATURE REVIEW

In the 1930s, oil discovery reshaped the Gulf region, fueling rapid growth in the GCC countries: Kuwait, Qatar, Bahrain, UAE, Oman, and Saudi Arabia. Nationalization of the oil industry empowered monarchies, relying on low-priced energy to consolidate power.

The area has emerged as one of the wealthiest globally, thanks to its vast hydrocarbon resources, boasting 30% of the world's proven oil reserves and 22% of its confirmed natural gas reserves, especially remarkable given the relatively small populations of the nations. Oil, natural gas, and petrochemical sectors continue to be pivotal contributors to both national income and government revenues across GCC countries (Ben Hassen, 2019). However, this reliance led to vulnerability to oil price fluctuations, undermining long-term development. With oil forming the backbone of their economies, shifts in prices directly impact these states, threatening their stability, notably during the 2015–2016 oil price decline. The GCC leadership has harbored concerns for numerous years regarding the enduring sustainability of its hydrocarbon revenue (Al Naimi, 2022; Al-Qahtani et al., 2022).

For nearly 50 years, the GCC region has heavily relied on revenue from hydrocarbon resources, which are essential to their economies. Changes in the prices of these resources directly affect the economies of these rentier states. This dependency was evident during the sharp decline in oil prices in 2015 and 2016 (Mishrif, 2018). Moreover, subsidies and low domestic oil prices increased local consumption, putting pressure on oil exports and posing a threat to the region's energy security. With the GCC region possessing significant portions of the world's crude oil and gas reserves, economic diversification is crucial to mitigate this risk and navigate dynamic changes across political, demographic, and economic realms (IRENA, 2023).

Hvidt (2013) describes the GCC countries as "allocation states," where the rulers of those countries distribute favors, public goods, and services as rents. However, there are problems with this approach. Even though it might seem like they are doing well, these Gulf rentier states are actually vulnerable to changes in global oil prices. This system does not help the GCC nations grow because the funds they rely on are unpredictable for their people and economies (Hvidt, 2013).

The COVID-19 pandemic had a profound impact on global health systems and also inflicted damage on socio-economic development and people's lives worldwide (United Nations, 2020). It led to a significant downturn in the global economy in 2020, resulting in increased unemployment and poverty on a global scale (Weiss et al., 2021). However, the extent of economic damage varied greatly, with some countries being heavily affected while others fared better during the crisis. The lack of economic diversification exacerbated the shock, particularly evident in industries overly reliant on tourism or oil extraction (Pitterle & Niermann, 2021). Indeed, the pandemic had a dual impact on GCC nations. While containment measures saved lives, they also triggered demand and supply shocks (Ollero et al., 2021). Oil demand plummeted in 2020 due to pandemic-induced lockdowns, causing prices to drop below zero for the first time in history, resulting from a significant decline in economic activity. Low oil prices weakened foreign balances, posing budgetary constraints for high-debt countries. Consequently, GCC countries implemented various measures to mitigate economic harm, including tax packages and financial injections. Spending on pandemic-related health and economic issues raised concerns about achieving long-term economic development goals (Ben Hassen & El Bilali, 2022; Oxford Business Group, 2024). Furthermore, the pandemic triggered an economic crisis, prompting regional governments to intensify their efforts towards economic diversification. It underscored the region's imperative to reduce its reliance on oil, enhance competitiveness in the private sector, and demonstrate the severe consequences of delaying reforms (Ollero et al., 2021). Since 2021, oil prices have been steadily increasing. Due to the Ukraine war, they surpassed USD 120 per barrel in the first quarter of 2022. Similarly, global natural gas prices have risen, elevating energy security as a top priority for major importers. This situation could potentially accelerate the global transition to green growth and emphasize the necessity for economic diversification in the GCC region (The World Bank, 2024).

Economic diversification involves shifting from dependence on a single income source, such as oil and gas revenues in the case of the GCC countries, to a more balanced economy where other sectors like industry, agriculture, and tourism play significant roles. Economic diversification also facilitates the attainment of the UN's Sustainable Development Goals (SDGs). These goals, consisting of 17 objectives established in 2015 by all UN member states under the "2030 Agenda for Sustainable Development," are aimed to be accomplished by 2030. The UN characterizes the SDGs as a comprehensive action plan striving to "end poverty, protect the planet, and ensure that by 2030 all people enjoy peace and prosperity" (UNDP, 2024).

Throughout 2020 to now, the GCC governments remained committed to implementing reforms aimed at diversifying their economies and fostering private sector growth. These structural reforms, including greater involvement of the private sector and increased flexibility in labor markets, played a pivotal role in sustaining the momentum of private sector development and laying the groundwork for a robust post-COVID economic recovery. Oman, for instance, undertook extensive reforms to restore fiscal stability and sustainability. Notable fiscal measures implemented during this period included the introduction of a 5% VAT rate starting in April 2021, targeted subsidy rationalization to support vulnerable social groups, prudent management of the public wage bill, and constraints on public sector employment. Similarly, Saudi Arabia revised its *Kafala* system to enhance job mobility for expatriate workers. In addition to reforms aimed at enhancing the business environment, GCC authorities prioritized investment in critical sectors such as telecommunications to facilitate economic diversification. The profound impact of the pandemic on the global oil sector served as a stark reminder of the importance of diversification efforts. Despite the opportunities presented for transitioning towards knowledge-based economies, challenges stemming from functional, structural, and cultural factors persist, underscoring the complexities associated with this transformation (Al Naimi, 2022) (see Figures 5.1, 5.2, and 5.3).

5.2.1 Current Economic Challenges, Economic Diversification, and Sustainability Issues in the GCC Region

Currently, the GCC countries are facing many economic challenges and adopting several strategies for economic diversification and sustainability. The foremost challenge to diversify the economy and revenues is to generate non-oil income and shift away from oil. However, the GCC countries have been

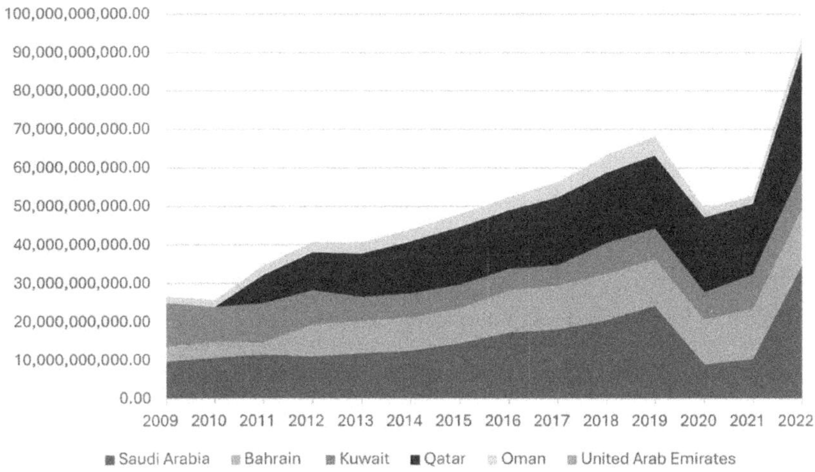

Source: Created by authors based on World Development Indicators, The World Bank (2024).

Figure 5.1 *Service export (US $) in GCC region from 2009 to 2022*

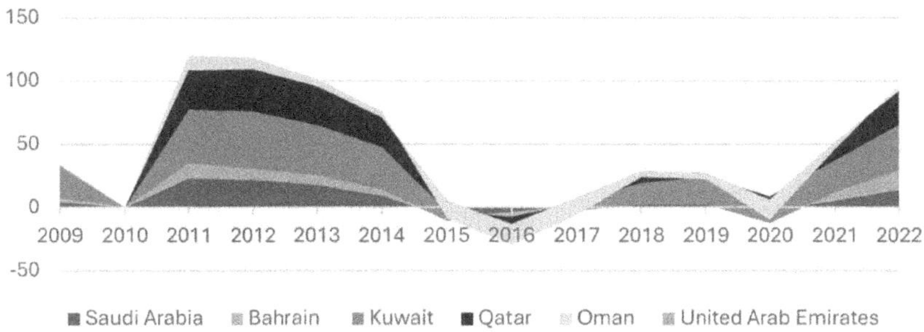

Source: Created by authors based on World Development Indicators, The World Bank (2024).

Figure 5.2 *Current account balance (% of GDP) in GCC region from 2009 to 2022*

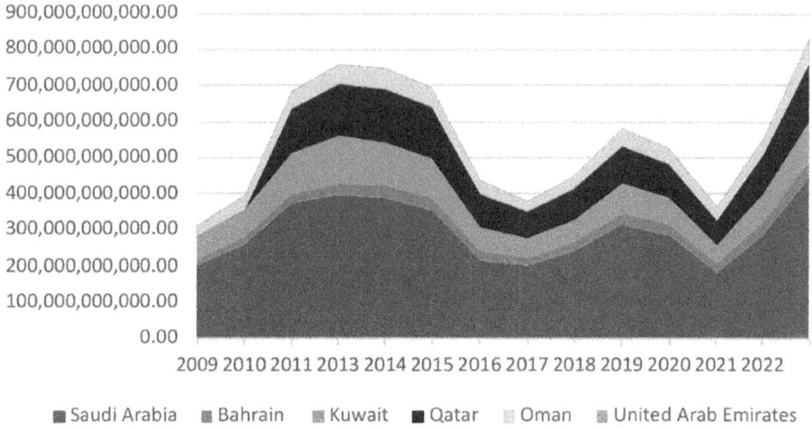

Source: Created by authors based on World Development Indicators, The World Bank (2024).

Figure 5.3 *Exports of goods and services (US $) in GCC region from 2009 to 2022*

planning to shift away from the dependence on oil for many years. In this regard, they have mentioned the strategy in national development plans since 1980. However, oil income still dominates the fiscal revenues of GCC countries (Aljawareen, 2017).

According to an International Monetary Fund (IMF) report in 2016, 77% of the revenues of Saudi Arabia, 64% of United Arab Emirates, 80% of Qatar, and 88% of Oman are generated through oil resources. Aljawareen (2017) also stated that the lack of highly skilled human resources is another major challenge faced by the GCC for economic sustainability. In addition, the lack of human resources and skilled workforce arises from lack of education, training, and scientific research. To meet this challenge, the institutions should produce highly skilled, well-educated human resources capable of carrying out the tasks which will lead to entrepreneurship, however, currently, they fail to do so.

For GCC countries, the aim of economic diversification is not only to minimize the negative impact of oil price fluctuations; it is also a necessity as a diversified economy tends to be more stable and has the capacity to create jobs while being less susceptible to the boom and bust cycle of oil and gas prices. Such necessity has put diversification at the very core of economic development strategies and planning since the mid-1990s (Fasano & Iqbal, 2003). This is clearly evident in the national visions, where each GCC country stresses the importance of promoting entrepreneurship and supporting and increasing the role of the private sector in the economic development process (Mishrif, 2018).

Evidence of diversification may be seen in the decline in the share of oil and gas in GDP from 41% in 2000 to 33% in 2013 and increased spending on industrial infrastructure across the region, with UAE's spending increasing by over 400%, particularly in aviation, aerospace, and defense, in the past three years (Davidson, 2011). In food security, the GCC countries have strengthened their agro-security by the acquisition of large areas of farmland outside their own national borders and investing heavily in major agricultural projects in Sudan, Ethiopia, Egypt, Turkey, Ukraine, Kazakhstan, the Philippines, and Brazil (Al-Obaid, 2010; Woertz, 2013).

Saudi Arabia's economy is also largely dependent on oil revenues and the non-oil revenues accounted for only 13% of the Saudi general budget in 2018. Saudi Arabia's budget deficit is 4.6% of its total 2018 GDP, with the possibility that it could reach 6.4% or worse in the 2020 general budget (Hussein, 2020). Now in 2023, the budget deficit of Saudi Arabia is 2% of the gross domestic product.

Wirba (2017) argued that if creating a knowledge-based economy is the cognitive bridge to creating a diversified economy, then educational reform and investment in R&D provide the infrastructure for building that knowledge-based economy, which would enable Saudi Arabia to transition away from an oil-based economy. He also stated that success in building a knowledge-based economy represents the basis for improved global competitiveness.

Al Naimi (2022) stated that a strategy of economic diversification can sustain economic growth and minimize the risks of over-reliance on one sector. Recently, the GCC countries have started to look beyond their dependence on oil revenues, with ambitious national visions reflecting their plans for economic diversification. Saudi Arabia's National Vision 2030 declared that the Saudi economy would be reformed through economic diversification (Al Naimi, 2022). To achieve this, several pillars were identified as the basis for transforming the Saudi economy in order to reduce the risks associated with reliance on oil revenues. One of these pillars is the establishment of a knowledge-based economy.

Al Naimi (2022) concluded that oil remains the main engine of the Saudi economy. Given the volatility of global oil prices, the growing deficit in the Saudi general budget, and domestic challenges such as increasing numbers of unemployed youth and an unreformed educational system, the process of economic diversification in Saudi Arabia is likely to suffer from setbacks along the way.

5.2.2 Role of Information Technology on Economic Diversification

The significant evolution driven by information communication technology (ICT) has connected individuals and communities, improved their quality of life and expanded global opportunities, modern amenities, and productivity trends during the final decades of the 21st century (Avom et al., 2020; Naseem et al., 2021).

In this millennium, information communication technology will shrink the geographical barriers and bring sociocultural values closer together globally (Latif et al., 2018; Mohsin et al., 2021; Nasir & Kalirajan, 2016).

Scholars and researchers assess the impact of ICT on various aspects including economic growth, GDP, organizational infrastructure, international trade, financial systems, employment opportunities, and the democratic processes within a nation's populace (Bon et al., 2016; Sarfraz et al., 2022).

Certainly, the ICT infrastructure has intensified competition in attracting foreign direct investment, thereby reshaping the global landscape of economic growth (Al Asbahi et al., 2019; Sun et al., 2020; Yang et al., 2021).

The export of high-technology goods from GCC countries is evident, as depicted in Figure 5.4. A notable surge occurred particularly after 2019, aligning with the period of economic recovery in 2021 from the effects of the COVID-19 pandemic on GCC economies. When countries engage in high-technology exports, it signifies a strong presence and capability in the realm of information technology within that country. Such exports typically rely heavily on an advanced technological infrastructure, a skilled workforce,

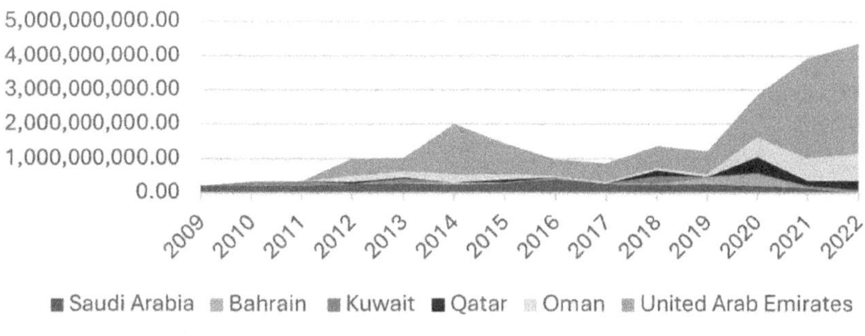

Source: Created by authors based on World Development Indicators, The World Bank (2024).

Figure 5.4 *High-technology export (US $) in GCC region from 2009 to 2022*

and innovative capabilities, all of which are nurtured and facilitated by robust information technology ecosystems.

Moreover, the capacity for high-technology exports reflects the country's innovation and research and development capabilities, which are closely intertwined with information technology. Advances in IT, such as artificial intelligence, big data analytics, and cloud computing, play a pivotal role in driving innovation across various sectors and are often integral to the development of high-tech products.

5.3 DATA AND METHODOLOGY

The purpose of this chapter is to explore the different economic challenges and problems that the GCC countries (Saudi Arabia, Kuwait, United Arab Emirates, Qatar, Bahrain, and Oman) face and highlights the role of information technology in dealing with these problems. Moreover, it also explains the relationship between information technology and sustainability with economic diversification in the GCC region.

Mixed research methods are used that are quantitative and qualitative. We used the qualitative method by exploring the literature to know about the current challenges related to the economic diversification and sustainability faced by GCC countries and role of information technology in dealing with the problems. Twenty-five research articles, reports, and economic reviews are studied

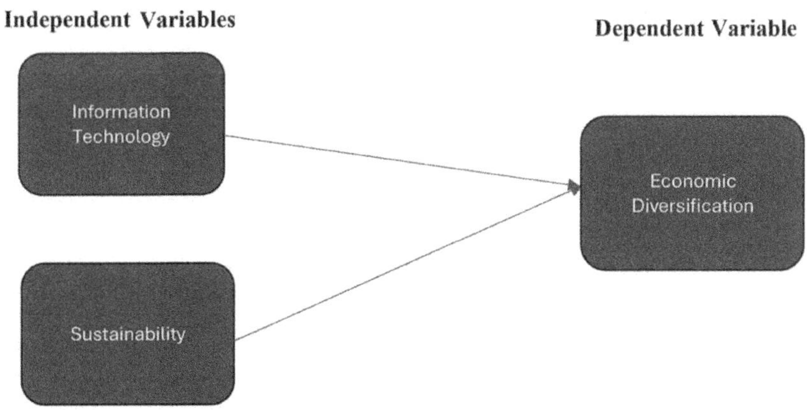

Source: Author.

Figure 5.5 *Theoretical framework*

and explored for this purpose. The quantitative method is used to explore the relationship of information technology and sustainability with the economic diversification by considering the GCC region.

The dataset used in this chapter was extracted from World Development Indicators published by the World Bank. The analysis was based on yearly data from a cross section of six GCC countries (Saudi Arabia, Kuwait, United Arab Emirates, Qatar, Bahrain, and Oman). The period considered for analysis is from 2005 to 2023. The framework and econometric model to present the relationship between the information technology and sustainability with the economic diversification are as shown in Figure 5.5.

The different proxies for the independent and dependent variables are used in the study. These proxies are used by different researchers in their studies like Al-shammari et al. (2022), Elmassah and Hassanien (2023), and Khuntia et al. (2018). The details are as shown in Tables 5.1 and 5.2.

Table 5.1 Proxies for different variables

Variables	Proxies
Information technology	The number of fixed telephone subscriptions per 100 inhabitants, the number of mobile cellular subscriptions per 100 inhabitants, the number of Internet users per 100 inhabitants, and fixed broadband subscriptions per 100 inhabitants
Sustainability	Environmental, social and governance factors
Economic diversification	Gross domestic product (US dollars), imports (% of GDP), exports (% of GDP), and employment (% of total labor force)

Source: Author.

Table 5.2 Abbreviations used for variables

Variables	Abbreviations
Information technology	IT
Sustainability	SUS
Gross domestic product	GDP
Imports	IMP
Exports	EXP
Employment	EMP

Source: Author.

5.3.1 Econometric Models

The panel multiple regression method is used for all six GCC countries. The equations are as follows:

$$\text{GDPit} = b0 + b1\,\text{ITit} + b3\,\text{SUSit} + \text{€it} \quad (5.1)$$

$$\text{IMPit} = b0 + b1\,\text{ITit} + b3\,\text{SUSit} + \text{€it} \quad (5.2)$$

$$\text{EXPit} = b0 + b1\,\text{ITit} + b3\,\text{SUSit} + \text{€it} \quad (5.3)$$

$$\text{EMPit} = b0 + b1\,\text{ITit} + b3\,\text{SUSit} + \text{€it} \quad (5.4)$$

Along with the panel multiple regression method, descriptive statistics and correlation are also applied.

5.4 RESULTS AND DISCUSSIONS

This section gives the results by performing correlation and panel multiple regression.

5.4.1 Correlation Analysis

Correlation is the statistical technique that is used to determine the relationship or association between two variables. The value of the coefficient of correlation ranges from +1 to −1. The direction of the relationship is indicated by the sign of the coefficient; a positive sign indicates a positive relationship, and a negative sign indicates a negative relationship. If the value of the coefficient of correlation is close to +1, this means that the variable is positively correlated; likewise, if the value of the coefficient of correlation is close to −1, the variables are said to be negatively correlated. Table 5.3 shows the correlation among the variables. Usually, we are interested in observing the relation between the independent and dependent variables. Table 5.3 represents the correlation matrix. In this study, the dependent variable GDP shows the strong relationship with IT and SUS. The other three dependent variables IMP, EXP, and EMP present a moderately positive relationship with IT and SUS.

Table 5.3 *Correlation matrix*

-	GDP	IMP	EXP	EMP	IT	SUS
GDP	1	-	-	-	-	-
IMP	0.18606	1	-	-	-	-
EXP	0.58875	0.04580	1	-	-	-
EMP	0.38543	0.22498	0.12965	1	-	-
IT	0.84874	0.34871	0.45213	0.23987	1	-
SUS	0.72563	0.39612	0.39765	0.44324	0.65329	1

Note: GDP = Gross Domestic Product, IMP = Imports, EXP = Exports, EMP = Employment, IT = Information Technology, SUS = Sustainability.
Source: Author.

5.4.2 Panel Multiple Regression

Panel multiple regression was adopted in this study because we are interested to see the effect of the two independent variables, that are information technology and sustainability, on gross domestic product, imports, exports, and employment one by one and across all six GCC countries. Table 5.4 shows the results related to the impact of information technology and sustainability on the gross domestic product of Saudi Arabia, Kuwait, United Arab Emirates, Qatar, Bahrain, and Oman.

Gross domestic product plays an important role in the evaluation of any economy. It represents the overall goods and services produced within the

Table 5.4 *Impact of information technology and sustainability on gross domestic product*

Variables	Coefficient Prob.	Std. Error	t-statistic	Prob.
IT	0.16224	0.03715	3.7005	0.0003***
SUS	0.44579	0.002458	9.5632	0.0000***
R-Squared	0.3895	-	-	-
Adjusted R-squared	0.3684	-	-	-
F-statistics	89.7189	-	-	-
Prob. (F-statistics)	0.00000	-	-	-

Note: ***$p < 0.01$, IT = Information Technology, SUS = Sustainability.
Source: Author.

boundaries of the country during a specific period. There are several factors that affect the production of goods and services within the country. Regression analysis shows that there is a positive and highly significant relationship of information technology and sustainability with gross domestic product with a $p < 0.01$.

Table 5.5 shows the relationship of information technology and sustainability with the imports of the countries (GCC). The results show that there is a negative and significant relationship between them at $p < 0.01$. As the awareness/improvement in the environmental, social, and governance issues increases, the imports are decreased. The other way, the organizations work properly and meet the criteria of achieving the sustainability in the economy. The better usage of information technology results in a decrease in imports.

Table 5.5 Impact of information technology and sustainability on imports

Variables	Coefficient Prob.	Std. Error	t-statistic	Prob.
IT	−0.044587	0.02698	−2.5932	0.0000***
SUS	−0.055677	0.03678	−2.60672	0.0002***
R-squared	0.31093	-	-	-
Adjusted R-squared	0.2954	-	-	-
F-statistics	79.3145	-	-	-
Prob. (F-statistics)	0.00000	-	-	-

Note: *** $p < 0.01$, IT = Information Technology, SUS = Sustainability.
Source: Author.

Table 5.6 of the study explores the positive and significant relationship between information technology and sustainability with exports at $p < 0.01$. This means that due to the introduction of information technology and improvement in the sustainability of the economy there is an increase in the exports coming from the different sectors of all the GCC countries.

Table 5.7 gives the relationship between information technology and sustainability with employment. The study found that a positive and significant relationship between them at $p < 0.1$. This means that the introduction of the information technology and improvement in the sustainability in the economy will lead to the creation of more employment opportunities in the important sectors of all the GCC countries.

Table 5.6 *Impact of information technology and sustainability on exports*

Variables	Coefficient Prob.	Std. Error	t-statistic	Prob.
IT	0.076541	0.02698	2.10765	0.02**
SUS	0.086443	0.05670	2.0768	0.03**
R-squared	0.37654	-	-	-
Adjusted R-squared	0.34123	-	-	-
F-statistics	73.3145	-	-	-
Prob. (F-statistics)	0.00000	-	-	-

Note: ** $p < 0.05$, IT = Information Technology, SUS = Sustainability.
Source: Author.

Table 5.7 *Impact of information technology and sustainability on employment*

Variables	Coefficient Prob.	Std. Error	t-statistic	Prob.
IT	0.08921	0.09854	2.00764	0.0785*
SUS	0.08654	0.0432	1.99873	0.0945*
R-squared	0.40543	-	-	-
Adjusted R-squares	0.38321	-	-	-
F-statistics	76.0987	-	-	-
Prob. (F-statistics)	0.00004	-	-	-

Note: * $p < 0.1$, IT = Information Technology, SUS = Sustainability.
Source: Author.

Tables 5.5 to 5.7 show the relationship of information technology and sustainability on different economic diversifications (GDP, imports, exports, and employment) in the GCC region. The diversification in different sectors, such as health, oil and gas, mining, manufacturing, transport, and logistics through the better usage of technology, as well as the introduction of new digital technology and trying to achieve sustainability in the economy, will enhance the gross domestic product, increase employment opportunities and exports, while imports start decreasing. Several studies show similar results.

5.5 CONCLUSION

The GCC countries (Saudi Arabia, Kuwait, United Arab Emirates, Qatar, Bahrain, and Oman) have an important position in the world as a result of their focus on information technology and sustainability to diversify into different sectors of the economy. This chapter particularly identifies the current challenges related to the economic diversification and sustainability faced by GCC countries and role of information technology in dealing with the problems. The quantitative method is used to explore the relationship of information technology and sustainability with economic diversification by considering the GCC region. Correlation and panel multiple regression have been performed to observe the relationships.

The results show the positive and significant relationship of information technology and sustainability with all the economic diversification proxies (GDP, exports, and employment) apart from with imports, which are negatively related. This means that when GCC countries are diversifying their economy by using information technology and sustainability, they are most likely increasing their gross domestic product, exports, and employment opportunities, while the imports of these countries will be decreasing. The GCC countries are among the world's top oil exporters, resulting in their economies being heavily dependent on the oil and gas sector. It is important for them to diversify and target other sectors of their economies. Diversification needs proper policies, finance, and coordination, which GCC countries are aiming to put in place to achieve their targets in the near future. There are significant challenges to achieving economic diversification. Most GCC countries suffer from weak institutions, lack of coordination between policymaking and policy implementation, small and ineffective private sectors, lack of innovation and limited investment in R&D, poorly skilled national workforces incapable of meeting the demands of the private sector, inefficient legal and regulatory systems, and lack of accountability and transparency. The literature also shows that severe implementation issues in the education, labor, and trade sectors, as well as fundamental weaknesses in the GCC economic structure, negatively affect economic diversification (Coury & Dave, 2010).

The diversification of the economy coupled with information technology (digitalization) improves the overall performance of the country. The findings of this chapter have important implications for the government and policymakers to be more focused on economic diversification when creating development agendas and rigorously measuring and monitoring economic diversity in evaluating the success of their policies. This chapter recommends that long-term sustainable growth/sustainability is more important for any economy to become competitive. Moreover, this chapter recommends that, in the era of technology, it helps in the diversification at the micro as well as macro level of the country.

ACKNOWLEDGMENT

The authors would like to thank Prince Sultan University, Riyadh, Saudi Arabia for their support.

REFERENCES

Aidrous, I. A., Asmyatullin, R. R., and Glavina, S. G. (2021). The development of the digital economy: GCC countries' experience. In A. V. Bogoviz and J. V. Ragulina (eds), *Industry Competitiveness: Digitalization, Management, and Integration* (vol. 1). Lecture Notes in Networks and Systems. Cham: Springer. https://www.semanticscholar.org/paper/The-Development-of-the-Digital-Economy%3A-GCC-Aidrous-Asmyatullin/9d12d6fb1c91ca2d4a6a6fe8751f3a0f3018928b

Al Asbahi, A. A. M. H., Gang, F. Z., Iqbal, W., Abass, Q., Mohsin, M., and Iram, R. (2019). Novel approach of principal component analysis method to assess the national energy performance via energy trilemma index. *Energy Reports*, *5*, 704–713. https://doi.org/10.1016/j.egyr.2019.06.009

Al Naimi, S. M. (2022). Economic diversification trends in the Gulf: The case of Saudi Arabia. *Circular Economy and Sustainability*, *2*, 221–230.

Aljawareen, A. F. (2017). Innovation in the GCC countries: An economic analysis. *Journal of Economics*, *5*(4), 51–62.

Al-Obaid, A. A. (2010). King Abdullah's Initiative for Saudi Agricultural Investment Abroad: A Way of Enhancing Saudi Food Security. Presentation by the Saudi Arabian Deputy Minister for Agricultural Research and Development to the Expert Group Meeting on Achieving Food Security in Member Countries in a Post-Crisis World, Islamic Development Bank, Jeddah, 2–3 May.

Al-Qahtani, M., Fekih Zguir, M., Al-Fagih, L., and Koç, M. (2022). Women entrepreneurship for sustainability: Investigations on status, challenges, drivers, and potentials in Qatar. *Sustainability*, *14*(7), 4091.

Al-shammari, A. S. A., Muneer, S., and Tripathi, A. (2022). Do information communication technology and economic development impact environmental degradation? Evidence from the GCC countries. *Frontiers in Environmental Science*, *10*, 875932.

Avom, D., Nkengfack, H., Fotio, H. K., and Totouom, A. (2020). ICT and environmental quality in Sub-saharan Africa: Effects and transmission channels. *Technological Forecasting and Social Change*, *155*(3), 120028. https://doi.org/10.1016/j.techfore.2020.120028

Ben Hassen, T. (2019). Entrepreneurship, ICT, and innovation: State of Qatar transformation to a knowledge-based economy. In Haitham M. Alkhateeb *Political, Economic and Social Issues* (pp. 193–208). Hauppauge, NY: Nova Publishers.

Ben Hassen, T., and El Bilali, H. (2022). Impacts of the COVID-19 pandemic on food security and food consumption: Preliminary insights from the Gulf Cooperation Council region. *Cogent Social Sciences*, *8*(1), 2064608.

Bon, A., Akkermans, H., and Gordijn, J. (2016). Developing ICT services in a low-resource development context. *Complex Systems Informatics and Modeling Quarterly*, *9*(12), 84–109. https://doi.org/10.7250/csimq.2016-9.05

Coury, T., and Dave, C. (2010). Oil, labor markets, and economic diversiaficatidn in the GCC: An empirical assessment. *Topics in Middle Eastern and North African Economics*, *12,* 1–45.

Davidson, C. M. (ed.) (2011). *Power and Politics in the Persian Gulf Monarchies.* London: Hurst Publishers.

Elmassah, S., and Hassanien, E. A. (2023). Economic development and environmental sustainability in the GCC countries: New insights based on the economic complexity. *Sustainability*, *15*(10), 7987.

Fasano, U., and Iqbal, Z. (2003). GCC countries: From oil dependence to diversification. IMF. inf.org/external/pubs/ft/med/2003/eng/fasano

Hussein, B. (2020). Energy sector diversification: Meeting demographic challenges in the MENA region. Atlantic Council, Washington.

Hvidt, M. (2013). Economic diversification in the GCC countries: Past record and future trends. Research paper no. 27: Kuwait Programme on Development, Governance and Globalisation in the Gulf States. The London School of Economics and Political Science, London.

IRENA (2023). Renewable energy statistics. Available online: https://www.irena.org/Publications/2023/Jul/Renewable-energy-statistics-2023 (accessed on 22 April 2024).

Khuntia, J., Saldanha, T. J., Mithas, S., & Sambamurthy, V. (2018). Information technology and sustainability: Evidence from an emerging economy. *Production and Operations Management*, *27*(4), 756–773.

Latif, Z., Yang, M., Danish, L., Latif, S., Ximei, L., Pathan, Z. H., Salam, S., and Jianqiu, Z. (2018). The dynamics of ICT, foreign direct investment, globalization and economic growth: Panel estimation robust to heterogeneity and cross-sectional dependence. *Telematics and Informatics*, *35*(2), 318–328. https://doi.org/10.1016/j.tele.2017.12.006

Luciani, G. (2012). Introduction: The resource curse and the Gulf development challenge. In G. Luciani (ed.), *Resources Blessed: Diversification and the Gulf Development Model* (pp. 1–28). Berlin: Gerlach Press.

Mishrif, A. (2018). Challenges of economic diversification in the GCC countries. In A. Mishrif and Y. Al Balushi (eds), *Economic Diversification in the Gulf Region, Volume II: Comparing Global Challenges* (pp. 1–19). Basingstoke: Palgrave Macmillan.

Mohsin, M., Naseem, S., Sarfraz, M., Ivascu, L., and Albasher, G. (2021). COVID-19 and greenhouse gas emission mitigation: Modelling the impact on environmental sustainability and policies. *Frontiers in Environmental Science*, *9*, 764294. https://doi.org/10.3389/fenvs.2021.764294

Naseem, S., Hui, W., Sarfraz, M., and Mohsin, M. (2021). Repercussions of sustainable agricultural productivity, foreign direct investment, renewable energy, and environmental decay: Recent evidence from Latin America and the Caribbean. *Frontiers in Environmental Science*, *9*, 784570. https://doi.org/10.3389/fenvs.2021.784570

Nasir, S., and Kalirajan, K. (2016). Information and communication technology-enabled modern services export performances of Asian economies. *Asian Development Review*, *33*(1), 1–27. https://doi.org/10.1162/ADEV_a_00059

Ollero, A. M., Alhmoud, K. B. R., and De Pinies Bianchi, J. R. (2021). *Gulf Economic Update: COVID-19 Pandemic and the Road to Diversification*. Available online: https://policycommons.net/artifacts/1805917/gulf-economic-update/2538669/ (accessed on 24 April 2024).

Oxford Business Group (2024). Spending or saving: How is the Gulf approaching 2022? Available online: https://oxfordbusinessgroup.com/articles-interviews/spending-or-saving-how-is-the-gulf-approaching-2022 (accessed on 24 April 2024).

Pitterle, I., and Niermann, L. (2021). The COVID-19 crisis: What explains cross-country differences in the pandemic's short-term economic impact? Available online: https://www.un.org/sites/un2.un.org/files/2021/08/wp174_2021.pdf (accessed on 24 April 2024).

Sarfraz, M., Mohsin, M., and Naseem, S. (2022). A blessing in disguise: New insights on the effect of COVID-19 on the carbon emission, climate change, and sustainable environment. *Environmental and Science Pollution Research*, *29*(20), 29651–29662. https://doi.org/10.1007/s11356-021-17507-1

Satrovic, E., and Adedoyin, F. F. (2022). An empirical assessment of electricity consumption and environmental degradation in the presence of economic complexities. *Environmental Science and Pollution Research*, *29*(52), 78330–78344.

Sun, H., Pofoura, A. K., Adjei Mensah, I., Li, L., and Mohsin, M. (2020). The role of environmental entrepreneurship for sustainable development: Evidence from 35 countries in Sub-saharan Africa. *The Science of the Total Environment*, *741*(6), 140132. https://doi.org/10.1016/j.scitotenv.2020.140132

The World Bank (2024). Economic diversification efforts paying off in GCC region but more reforms needed. Available online: https://www.worldbank.org/en/news/press-release/2023/11/22/economic-diversification-efforts-paying-off-in-gcc-region-but-more-reforms-needed (accessed on 24 April 2024).

UNDP (2024). Sustainable development goals. Available online: https://www.undp.org/sustainable-development-goals (accessed on 22 April 2024).

United Nations (2020). Shared responsibility, global solidarity: Responding to the socio-economic impacts of COVID-19. United Nations.

Weiss, M. A., Schwarzenberg, A. B., Nelson, R. M., Sutter, K. M., and Sutherland, M. D. (2021). *Global Economic Effects of COVID-19*. Washington, DC: Congressional Research Service.

Wirba, A. V. (2017). The role of research in knowledge economy within GCC countries. *European Journal of Business and Management*, *9*(3), 166–184.

Woertz, E. (2013). *Oil for Food: The Global Food Crisis and the Middle East*. Oxford: Oxford University Press.

Yang, Z., Abbas, Q., Hanif, I., Alharthi, M., Taghizadeh-Hesary, F., Aziz, B., and Muhammad, M. (2021). Short- and long-run influence of energy utilization and economic growth on carbon discharge in emerging SREB economies. *Renewable Energy*, *165*, 43–51. https://doi.org/10.1016/j.renene.2020.10.141

6. Encouraging the growth of innovative small and medium-sized enterprises (SMEs) as a pivotal strategy for diversifying resource-rich economies

Husam Arman, Ahmad Alawadhi and Shaikha Al-Fulaij

6.1 INTRODUCTION

The COVID-19 pandemic delivered a double whammy to economic activity. On the one hand, the pandemic reduced the labour supply (which led to a drop in output) due to restrictions on people's movements, plus the loss of labour due to COVID-19 deaths, quarantine, and hospital admissions of workers (Khamis et al., 2021). Containment measures such as total or partial lockdowns exacerbated the effective loss of labour supply. On the other hand, consumers were faced with a loss of income due to containment measures, workers' layoffs, fear of infection, and general uncertainty. Some sectors, such as tourism, restaurants, and transportation, were affected more than others. In general, SMEs were more vulnerable to the pandemic's economic effects due to the nature of the sectors in which they tend to operate, their lower financial resilience compared to large enterprises, and their limited resources. For example, the Federal Reserve Bank of New York (FDRNY) (2020) suggests that 50% of small enterprises in the US, which are defined by revenues (ranging from $1–40 million) and by employment (from 100–1,500 employees), work with less than 15 days of cash cover.

In 2020, global trade declined to its 2013 levels. Services linked to tourism and travel stagnated and had hardly recovered by 2022 (Yepez and Leimgruber, 2024). The COVID-19 pandemic was the worst for the world economy since the Great Depression in the 1930s. Measured in global real GDP, according to World Bank (2024) estimates, world GDP in real terms dropped from about $84.99 billion in 2019 to $82.5 billion in 2020 (2.7%) compared to the drop from $62.95 billion in 2008 to $62.1 billion in 2009 during the 2008–2009 financial crises (1.35%). Eventually world GDP in real terms recovered in 2021 to reach $87.66 billion (World Bank, 2024). According to Gagnon et al. (2023), structural characteristics of the economy influenced the extent of the pandemic's effect on the economy. For instance, it was smaller for economies that rely on manufacturing and exports in comparison to those dependent on services.

Countries have varied responses to the pandemic's economic consequences, with the United States in the lead, allocating an immediate $3 trillion to offset the damages inflicted on the US economy by COVID-19 (Lobosco, 2020). It was anticipated then that the lockdowns and other efforts to control the virus in Europe and the United States would likely lead to the largest quarterly decline in economic activity since 1933 (Smit et al., 2020), before bouncing back in the September 2020 quarter where the GDP movements moved from negative to positive for many developed countries (e.g. the UK from –19.8% to 15.5%, and the US from –9% to 7.4%).[1]

Due to the toll that COVID-19 has put on SMEs, countries have implemented measures to support SMEs in mitigating the economic effects of the COVID-19 pandemic. These measures vary across countries. Some countries focus on general measures that alleviate the economic effects on the economy as a whole, while other countries have put in place specific measures targeted towards SMEs (OECD, 2020).

In Kuwait, the government designed a rescue plan that eased access to liquidity, reduced interest rates, lowered provisions on loans and reserves requirements for banks, and encouraged the banking system to offer credit lines to affected companies. In tandem, specialized government agencies (and private philanthropic parties) provided cash support to families and individuals hit hard by the pandemic. Government rescue efforts focused on the private sector, which is composed of heterogeneous sets of size, paid-up capital, access to credit, value-added assets, and investments.

Among several measures, the government rescue plan included an additional KD500 million for ministries and government departments for the fiscal year 2020/2021 (KPMG, 2020), which represented 0.47% of the 2020 Kuwait GDP. Concurrently, the Central Bank reduced Kuwait's official discount rate to a historic low of 1.5%, and the capital adequacy ratio was lowered from 13% to 10.5%. To safeguard SMEs to the fullest extent possible, risk weight for such business firms was reduced from 75% to 25% (CBK, 2020). In addition, the limit of financing increased from 90% to 100%. Also, the loan to value (LTV) ratio was increased for properties, and Kuwait Banking Association announced a moratorium period of up to six months on bank loans, including a waiver of interest and charges (if any for postponement) for retail clients (citizens and ex-pats) and SMEs. In addition, the government allowed business owners in the private and oil sectors (not wholly owned by the state) to postpone social security contributions for six months (KPMG, 2020). According to

CBK (2020), the Kuwaiti government has doubled the wage subsidies allocated for Kuwaitis working in the private sector (including the self-employed) for a period of six months from April 2020 with a total cost of KD240 million.

SMEs were one of the most affected economic sectors since they lack resources and contingency plans, business continuity systems, and innovation capabilities (Rajapathirana and Hui, 2018). In addition to their contribution to the economy, SMEs are crucial in terms of job creation and contribution to society (Ayyagari et al., 2007; Koch, 2011; Schreyer, 2000; Yazdanfar and Öhman, 2015). For instance, SMEs have created around 85% of new jobs and provided two-thirds of the total private sector employment in the enlarged EU (European Commission, 2012). According to Wood (2023), employment fell in the European SME sector by 3% from 131.5 million in 2019 to 127.7 million post-pandemic.

Single-establishment firms, which are the case with most Kuwaiti SMEs, do not perform as well during the recession as multi-establishment SMEs (Davidsson et al., 1998). Particular emphasis should also be given to high-growth SMEs and those who work in high value-added sectors, often characterized by knowledge-intensive activities (Brinkley et al., 2012). These firms are high contributors to economic growth in employment and productivity (Autio et al., 2007). In the UK, 6% of businesses with the highest growth rates generated half of the new jobs (Bravo-Biosca and Westlake, 2009). This underscores the importance of designing policies that favour these types of enterprises (Shane, 2009).

Developed countries crafted various policy responses to support SMEs in surviving the severe impact of this crisis (OECD, 2020). For example, in the UK, a generous fund (£1 billion) has been allocated to support innovative firms hit by COVID-19, including a £500 million investment fund for high-growth companies impacted by the crisis, comprised of government and private sector funding. This is necessary for SMEs who have struggled financially, and it could affect their ability to sustain R&D and innovation (Roper and Turner, 2020).

In a study to investigate the pandemic impact on 100,000 businesses across 51 developing countries, the results showed that the shock of the pandemic had a severe and persistent negative impact on sales across various sectors (Apedo-Amah et al., 2020). The results indicate that although nearly 90% of businesses reopened ten weeks after the outbreak's peak, the negative impact on sales remained significant. Similar studies on SMEs demonstrated the negative impact on liquidity, business activity, and closure (Barrero et al., 2020; Bartik et al., 2020).

Some empirical studies in GCC demonstrated the impact of COVID-19 on SMEs (Al-Sanjary and Khalifa, 2021; Refass et al., 2023), the role of technology as a survival strategy (Mishrif and Khan, 2023), key enablers for SMEs' export performance and lessons learned from COVID-19 and other crises (Elsharnouby et al., 2024), and the future of SMEs beyond COVID-19 (Refass et al., 2023). Although COVID-19 severely affected SMEs in GCC countries, it has pushed them to accelerate technology adoption, improve the supply chain and logistics, and increase their agility. However, such a shift in work practices and processes has yet to be tested in terms of productivity and sustainability.

COVID-19 was an extreme wave of change that forced many SMEs to adjust their culture and strategies, and many survived due to their ability to adapt or the generous government support, especially in developed countries. In the modern world, it seems that change will be the norm, and many more waves of change are expected to affect all businesses, and SMEs in particular. The future is embracing Industry 4.0 with its related technologies, such as artificial intelligence (AI), the internet of things (IoT), blockchain, 3D printing, and others. Those are advancing very quickly, AI in particular, and can potentially disrupt many businesses. SMEs might be the most vulnerable due to a lack of complexity in their products and processes.

Besides the technology challenges and opportunities, the region has many uncertainties due to geopolitical risks. The ongoing war on Ukraine and the war on Gaza continue to destabilize the economic and business conditions, in addition to the preexisting global trade wars. Since the GCC region is the world energy hub, such disturbances can have a severe impact on businesses, including SMEs.

Hence, understanding the critical success factors of SMEs during crises can enable decision-makers to craft effective policies to support SMEs in tackling the aforementioned technological and political changes.

This chapter contributes to the recent studies about the impact of COVID-19 on SMEs, and investigates the SMEs' ability to survive severe crises such as COVID-19 and whether innovative firms are more resilient. This was reflected in two key research questions: "Were the innovative firms more resilient than their non-innovative counterparts?" and "Were the innovative firms more responsive than their non-innovative counterparts?" The chapter also recommends a list of practical strategies to enhance the role of SMEs in economic diversification.

6.2 BACKGROUND

6.2.1 Micro, Small, and Medium Enterprises (MSMEs) in Kuwait

In the case of GCC countries, and Kuwait in particular, micro, small, and medium enterprises' (MSMEs) role has been insignificant in contributing to socio-economic life. In Kuwait, micro firms are those that employ 1–10 people (including establishments with one employee), small with 11–49 employees, and medium-sized firms with 50–249 employees.

Kuwait's economy heavily depends on oil entirely owned by the state and crowds out the private sector, particularly MSMEs. According to the latest figures from Kuwait's Central Statistical Bureau (CSB), MSMEs' contribution to GDP in Kuwait, measured as the value-added generated by MSMEs, amounted to only 15% of non-oil GDP in 2019 following the above definition of MSMEs. In terms of employment, MSMEs employed 315,520 workers in 2019 (excluding the oil sector), which is around 37.7% of total employment. This is a meagre percentage compared to the large number of SMEs firms in the business sector (98.9%), which demonstrates the very low productivity of this sector and the need for policy intervention (Arman and Ramadhan, 2021).

Suppose we incorporate the analysis of micro firms in Kuwait, as outlined in a Kuwait Institute for Scientific Research (KISR) report (Arman et al., 2021). In that case, a noticeable trend emerges wherein MSMEs exert significant dominance in the business sector, especially within the micro category. The sheer number of MSMEs, particularly micro-enterprises, underscores their prevalence in the economic landscape. However, a closer examination reveals a concerning disparity in their contributions to total output, output growth, value-added, and Kuwaiti employment, indicating a minimal and declining impact from 2003 to 2016.

This scenario mirrors a common challenge observed in many emerging economies, known as the "missing middle" phenomenon. In Kuwait's context, this phenomenon manifests as a concentration of micro and small firms in the MSME sector, with a conspicuous absence of medium-sized enterprises. Astonishingly, only 410 medium-sized firms exist in Kuwait, constituting a mere 1% of the entire MSME landscape. This statistic raises alarm bells, pointing towards a low natural progression of businesses from small to medium size.

Furthermore, the stark contrast in the growth trajectories between MSMEs and large firms in Kuwait adds another layer of complexity. A dichotomy becomes apparent, particularly evident in the finance sector's performance. Although weakly interrelated, these two segments operate as distinct entities, emphasizing the need for a closer examination of the challenges and dynamics influencing MSMEs in Kuwait's economic landscape. In this chapter, we drop the micro firms and we only focus on SMEs, since they are more potent to innovation scalability, significance in economic contribution, and policy relevance in Kuwait where employment of nationals is a critical need.

6.2.2 The Role of Innovation in SMEs Performance

There is almost a consensus that innovation is a vital determinant of economic growth, development, and economic well-being. Economists, politicians, technologists, and industrialists are all contributing to the subject of innovation. This, in part, is driven by its growing dominant role in economic development at large and by improving and sustaining countries' competitiveness in particular (Rosenberg, 2004).

Innovation has been critical in stimulating and sustaining high economic growth while improving and maintaining countries' competitiveness. Moreover, innovation has been considered a crucial driver for competitive success in many industries. The role of innovation in a firm's success has been demonstrated in many studies that have considered different measures. For instance, there is strong evidence of positive links between innovation and productivity growth at the firm level (Hashi and Stojčić, 2013; Lööf and Heshmati, 2006; Parisi et al., 2006).

The relationship between innovation and performance largely depends on the context. The range of contexts can include the age of the firm, the type of innovation, and the cultural context (Rosenbusch et al., 2011). Large firms are usually better equipped to reap the benefit of innovation and are more innovative than SMEs in the manufacturing sector (Damanpour, 1992). The four different types of innovations positively affect firm performance (Gunday et al., 2011) but can vary. Process innovations seem to produce extra productivity growth for large and small firms (Wakasugi and Koyata, 1997).

This chapter contributes to the literature by highlighting the innovation not just as a lever for economic performance enhancement but also as a buffer that can enable SMEs to survive during a severe exogenous crisis such as the one caused by COVID-19. A recent study in the Kingdom of Saudi Arabia (KSA) showed that the innovative SMEs managed better in terms of performance and likelihood of business survival in the face of the repercussions of COVID-19 (Adam and Alarifi, 2021), and perhaps the most important type of innovation to cope with the crisis and recession periods is the business model innovation (Clauss et al., 2021; Ucaktürk et al., 2011).

6.3 METHODOLOGY

The main objective of this chapter was to assess the impact of COVID-19 on SMEs and demonstrate the potential role of SMEs in economic diversification and how it can be enhanced. To address these objectives of this practical study, a straightforward methodology was used, encompassing desk research and empirical work. The literature review was essential to analyse the previous studies on the pandemic impact on businesses and the role of innovation. To understand the current situation in Kuwait, a fieldwork survey was designed to solicit SMEs' opinions on how COVID-19 impacted their business and what types of measures they took. In addition, a focus group was conducted with the SMEs' key stakeholders to reflect the government's perspective on the survey results and the government's response to support SMEs. Key stakeholders included the Supreme Council for Planning and Development, The National Fund for Small and Medium Enterprise Development, Kuwait Industrial Bank, Kuwait Foundation for the Advancement of Sciences, Central Bank of Kuwait, Ministry of Finance, and Kuwait Chamber of Commerce and Industry.

To assess the role of innovation on SMEs' resilience and responsiveness, two key research questions were formulated as follows:

1. Were the innovative firms more resilient than their non-innovative counterparts?
2. Were the innovative firms more responsive than their non-innovative counterparts?

To address the first question, the impact of COVID-19 was measured in terms of operations shutdown and layoff. In contrast, the responsiveness was measured using the availability of a business continuity management system (a management system to ensure business continuity during a crisis) and the use of technology, particularly ICT.

6.3.1 The Dataset

To investigate the impact of COVID-19 on SMEs in Kuwait and how they responded to the COVID-19 crisis, the project team surveyed 50 SMEs covering the main sectors. The small firms are those with 11–49 employees, while medium firms are those with 50–249 employees. The study involved all the SMEs' key stakeholders through a focus group with government or quasi-government agencies in September 2020 to share the survey's initial findings and solicit their opinion on the SMEs' perspective. The survey was conducted in August 2020; hence it covers about six months' experience since the start of the first phase of lockdowns.

In the survey, the targeted population was 184 SMEs. The team had data from a previous survey that KISR conducted in 2017 to measure the rate of enterprise innovation in Kuwait (Salih et al., 2018). The questionnaire part of measuring the impact of COVID-19 was similar to the local study of Bensirri (2020), but shorter, and the expectations from the government and responses from the Business Development Bank of Canada (BDC, 2020).

The survey was emailed to all firms, but only six questionnaires were filled out online. Due to COVID-19, all firms refused to meet face-to-face, so other methods were offered as additional data-gathering mechanisms. The interviews (44) were conducted using a remote audio/video interview technique, which lasted for an average of 30 minutes. The majority of the interviewees were senior managers, and a total of 50 valid questionnaires were returned.

The restrictions on opening times for firms due to COVID-19 made it hard to get a high response rate, although the research team had been in touch with the firms. Several reminders were sent, and phone calls were made to encourage the firms to participate. This resulted in a response rate of about 27.2%.

6.3.2 The Specifications of Models

To address the research questions that aim to measure the impact of COVID-19 on innovative firms and their responsiveness in comparison to non-innovative firms, two hypotheses are identified:

Hypothesis 1: There is a positive relationship between the firm's innovativeness and its resilience against the impact of COVID-19.

H1: The innovative firms are more likely not to shut down their operations.

Hypothesis 2: There is a positive relationship between the firms' innovativeness and their responsiveness to COVID-19 consequences.

H2a: The innovative firms are more likely to have business continuity measures.

H2b: The innovative firms are more likely to utilize technology to overcome challenges caused by COVID-19.

A list of variables is defined (Tables 6.1a, 6.1b, and 6.1c) to test the hypotheses mentioned above. The first group of variables are the dependent variables, and they measure impact and responsiveness (impact and responsiveness indicators). The second group and third group represent the independent variables. One measures different dimensions of a firm's innovation (innovation performance indicators), and the other describes the basic firm's demography (firm and sectors indicators).

Since our dependent variables are strictly binary, with one outcome being better than the other (ordinal), a logistic regression model is used (Wooldridge, 2006). A logit model estimates the probability of the dependent variable to be = 1 conditional on the values of the independent variables.

Table 6.1a List of variables used in the model, dependent variables: impact and responsiveness indicators

Variable name	Description
Impactshut	Dichotomous variable equal to 1 for firms which have shut down their operation due to COVID-19, and 0 if not
responsys	Dichotomous variable equal to 1 for firms that have a business continuity management system that can mitigate COVID-19 impact, and 0 if not
using_tech	Dichotomous variable equal to 1 for firms that have used technology to overcome constraints due to COVID-19, and 0 if not

Source: Author.

Table 6.1b List of variables used in the model, independent variables: innovation performance indicators

Variable name	Description
innovgen	Dichotomous variable equal to 1 for firms that have introduced any type of innovation in 2013–2015
innovative_product	Dichotomous variable equal to 1 for firms that have introduced product innovation in 2013–2015
innovative_process	Dichotomous variable equal to 1 for firms that have introduced process innovation in 2013–2015
innovative_admin	Dichotomous variable equal to 1 for firms that have introduced organizational innovation in 2013–2015
innovative_market	Dichotomous variable equal to 1 for firms that have introduced market innovation in 2013–2015
innovative_product_process	Dichotomous variable equal to 1 for firms that have introduced product or process innovation in 2013–2015
est_cooperated	Dichotomous variable equal to 1 for firms that have cooperated in any institution for innovation purposes in 2013–2015

Source: Author.

Table 6.1c List of variables used in the model, independent variables: firm and sectors indicators

Variable name	Description
fsize	Categorical variable represents size of firm; equal 1 if micro, 2 if small, and 3 if medium
firmage	Continuous variable represents the age of the firm in years
sectortwo	Dichotomous variable equal to 1 for firms in industry and 0 if in the service sector

Source: Author.

Our suggested logit model is as follows:

$$\Pr(Y_i = 1 \mid X_j) = F\left(B_0 + B_1X_1 + \ldots + B_iX_j\right) \tag{6.1}$$

Where

Y_i: is the dependent variables representing impact and responsiveness indicators described in Table 6.1a.

X_j: is the independent variables representing indicators innovation, firm, and sectors (Tables 6.1b and 6.1c).

B_1 to B_j are coefficients to be estimated.

Several logistic models were derived to test the hypotheses mentioned above. Four key models were used to measure the impact (shutdown and layoff) and responsiveness (business continuity and technology usage). In each model, three modes of innovation were measured using innovation in general (at least one type of innovation), each type of innovation, and the technological innovation as a separate measure since it is the most significant measure of innovation.

6.4 ANALYSIS AND RESULTS

The survey covered the main economic sectors according to Kuwait's Central Statistical Bureau (CSB) Annual Economic Establishment Survey, which are manufacturing, construction, trade, finance, and non-finance.[2] More than half of the firms were from the trade and non-finance sectors, 32% and 28%, respectively. Most of the firms were established before the year 2000 (36 firms), and 20% were micro, 50% were small, 30% were medium, and 27 firms were innovative. Innovation is considered in its broadest sense, utilizing Oslo Manual categorization, which includes product innovation, process innovation, organizational innovation, and marketing innovation (Mortensen and

Bloch, 2005). Product and process innovation represent technological innovation, while organizational and marketing innovation denote non-technological innovation (Gallouj and Weinstein, 1997).

6.4.1 Measuring COVID-19 Impact on SMEs

The results of the survey, which was conducted in August 2020, showed that the impact of COVID-19 on the surveyed SMEs proved to be damaging since it had caused many firms to suspend or shut down their operation. The non-financial sector (for example, restaurants) was the most affected, followed by construction and manufacturing (Figure 6.1). In terms of firm size, micro and small firms were the most affected ones. More than 70% of these firms were forced to suspend or shut down their operation. This figure is higher than international figures, where between 25% and 36% of small businesses reported possible closure, according to several surveys in various countries (McKinsey, 2020).

COVID-19 forced almost half of the innovative firms (51.9%) to suspend or shut down their operations, while the effect was higher for non-innovative firms (78.3%). Hence, innovation capability reduced the impact of COVID-19 by about 26% (Figure 6.2). This indicative figure was further investigated using the econometric models, where the innovation aspect was disaggregated and represented by separate regression models.

Table 6.2 depicts the results of the logistics regression models. Model 1 shows that innovation, in general, was not statistically significant in predicting

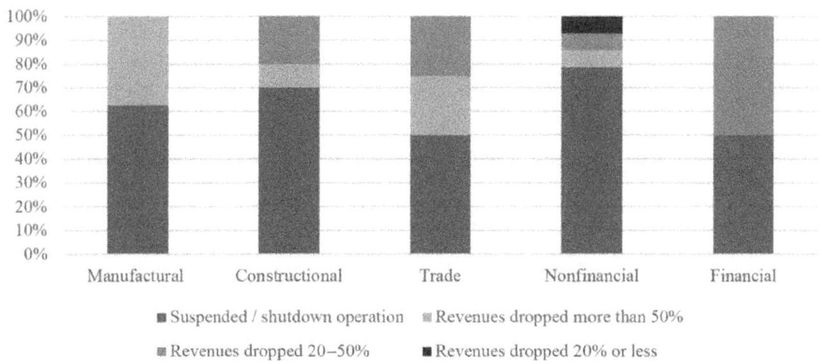

Source: Calculated from Kuwait's Central Statistical Bureau (CSB) Annual Economic Establishment Survey.

Figure 6.1 *COVID-19 impact on the last quarter revenues*

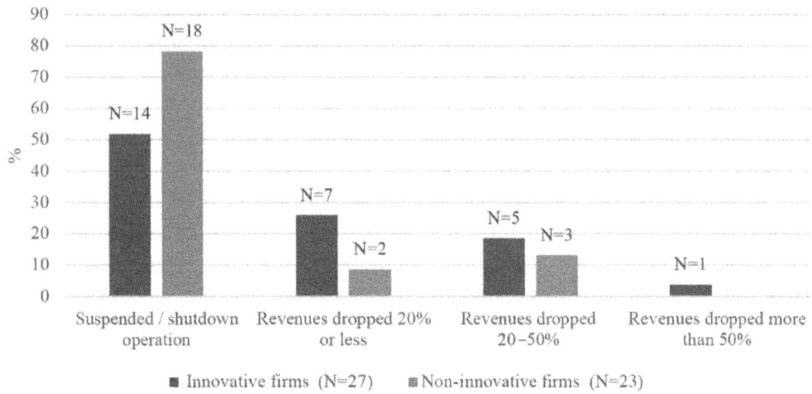

Source: Calculated from Kuwait's Central Statistical Bureau (CSB) Annual Economic Establishment Survey.

Figure 6.2 COVID-19 impact on innovative firms in terms of operation

shutdown. However, technological innovation (product or process innovation) was statistically significant ($p < .05$), and the sign of the coefficient confirms that the technological innovative firms are more resilient and less likely to shut down their operations (model 3). When innovation was disaggregated into its four types (model 2), product innovation was statistically significant ($p < .05$). It showed that it is the main differentiator (we dropped process innovation in this model due to the high correlation with product innovation 0.83, and when replaced by product innovation, it was not statistically significant). According to McKinsey's study, which surveyed about 300 senior executives in Europe, business model innovation was the most important strategic lever in addressing the crisis (McKinsey, 2021).

Another interesting observation is that the firms that have cooperated with science, technology, and innovation (STI) institutions were less resilient to the impact of COVID-19. Model 1 shows that the firm's size predicts the possibility of shutdown ($p < .1$), while Model 2 shows that it is the firm's age. Larger and older firms are more resilient in difficult times, such as the COVID-19 crisis.

Table 6.2 Logistic regression to measure COVID-19 impact in terms of shutdown

Variable name	(1) impactshut	(2) impactshut	(3) impactshut
firmage	−0.0484 (0.0304)	−0.0692* (0.0363)	−0.0400 (0.0313)
fsize	−1.099* (0.668)	−1.238 (0.789)	−1.063 (0.674)
sectortwo	−0.416 (0.734)	−1.053 (0.925)	−0.446 (0.743)
innovative_product	-	−1.796** (0.801)	-
innovative_process	-	-	-
innovative_admin	-	−0.412 (1.090)	-
innovative_market	-	−1.329 (1.197)	-
innovgen	−1.469 (0.894)	-	-
est_cooperated	0.671 (0.755)	1.543** (0.771)	1.162 (0.835)
innovative_product_process	-	-	−2.002** (0.835)
Constant	5.373** (2.343)	7.019*** (2.651)	4.993** (1.941)
AIC	67.13122	62.9689	64.48213
BIC	78.60335	78.26509	75.95427
Pseudo R-squared	0.1563	0.2812	0.1968
Prob. > chi2	0.334	0.1054	0.1018
Observations	50	50	50

Note: ***, **, and * represent 0.01, 0.05, and 0.1 significance levels respectively (p-value), robust standard errors in parentheses.
Source: Author.

6.5 MEASURING RESPONSIVENESS TO COVID-19

6.5.1 Business Continuity

Well-established firms usually have a system in place for securing business continuity during a crisis. This system enables firms to manage and mitigate the risks which could disrupt their essential processes and associated services (Gibb and Buchanan, 2006). To highlight the importance of this concept in the COVID-19 crisis, the International Labour Organization (ILO) issued practical guidance to implement a business continuity plan for SMEs (ILO, 2020).

The majority of firms in the survey (72%) did not have any business continuity systems to ensure the business was not disrupted entirely and continued to work and serve customers. Because all surveyed firms are SMEs, it was reasonable to see that only 16% had such a system, especially in emerging economies like Kuwait (Kato and Charoenrat, 2018). Although the situation seems similar when innovative firms are compared to the non-innovative regarding the availability of a business continuity management system (Figure 6.3), the regression analysis (Model 5) showed that organizational innovation was highly statistically significant ($p < 0.01$) (Table 6.3).

Interestingly, all the regression models in Table 6.3 showed that cooperation with STI institutions reduced the likelihood that the firm has a business continuity system (in Model 5, it was highly statistically significant at $p < .01$). Cooperation with STI institutions usually affects SMEs innovation performance positively (Zeng et al., 2010), but in our case such cooperation had a

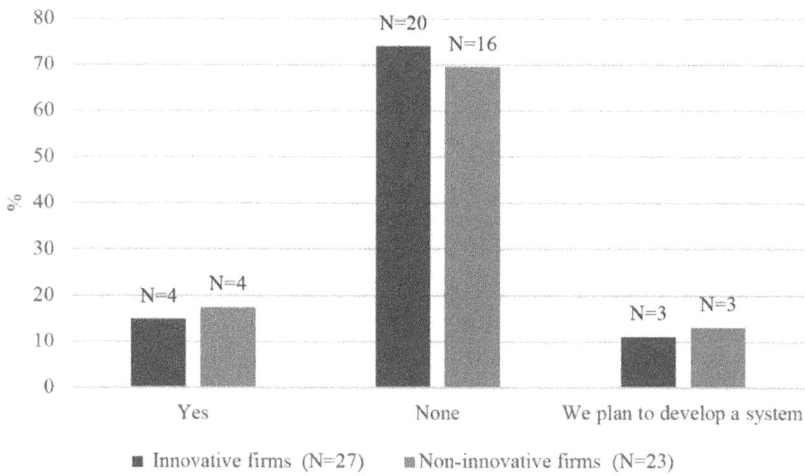

Source: Calculated from Kuwait's Central Statistical Bureau (CSB) Annual Economic Establishment Survey.

Figure 6.3 *The availability of a business continuity management system*

Table 6.3 Logistic regression to measure responsiveness to COVID-19 in terms of business continuity

Variable name	(4) responsys	(5) responsys	(6) responsys
firmage	0.0378 (0.0292)	0.0658 (0.0447)	0.0208 (0.0258)
fsize	0.216 (0.710)	0.670 (1.072)	0.157 (0.673)
sectortwo	−0.324 (0.912)	0.285 (1.358)	−0.480 (0.892)
innovative_product	-	−0.641 (1.021)	-
innovative_process	-	-	-
innovative_admin	-	3.559*** (1.299)	-
innovative_market	-	0.578 (1.432)	-
innovgen	1.481 (1.111)	-	-
est_cooperated	−2.530** (1.177)	−3.799*** (1.171)	−2.165* (1.180)
innovative_product_process	-	-	0.699 (0.899)
Constant	−3.553* (1.920)	−6.150* (3.704)	−2.285 (1.653)
AIC	50.09062	44.21287	51.78136
BIC	61.56276	59.50905	63.2535
Pseudo R-squared	0.2021	0.3583	0.0952
Prob. > chi2	0.1337	0.0116	0.2342
Observations	50	50	50

Note: ***, **, and * represent 0.01, 0.05, and 0.1 significance levels respectively (p-value), robust standard errors in parentheses.
Source: Author.

negative impact which requires further investigation considering the research context and the vulnerability issue.

New concepts such as business agility will be of great interest to SMEs to capitalize on the opportunity for digitization and rapidly develop capabilities that can help them survive the changes that the environment imposes upon them (Seetharaman, 2020). Hence, the government should consider introducing such strategies to SMEs in their planned capacity-building programs.

6.5.2 Technology Usage

Like many firms, SMEs were also forced to work remotely utilizing the available technology to continue their operation and serve customers during the partial and full lockdown, but it was not consistent among sectors. For instance, 50% of firms in the financial sector have used technology to work remotely, compared to only 13% of firms operating in manufacturing (Figure 6.4). These results are consistent with the recent IMF global study on tele-workability, although construction was worse than manufacturing in their tele-workability by sector analysis (Brussevich et al., 2020). The SMEs that managed to take advantage of digital resources were more responsive and performed better considering their limited resources (Caballero-Morales, 2021).

The innovative firms the team interviewed were better equipped to work remotely (Figure 6.5). About 63% of firms that had used technology to facilitate working remotely were innovative (37% of innovative firms used technology to work remotely, while 26.1% of non-innovative firms used it).

Although this descriptive analysis of the question about technology usage showed a difference between innovative and non-innovative firms, this was not reflected in the inferential analysis. Apart from market innovation (which was statistically significant at $p < .1$), the innovation didn't differentiate firms in

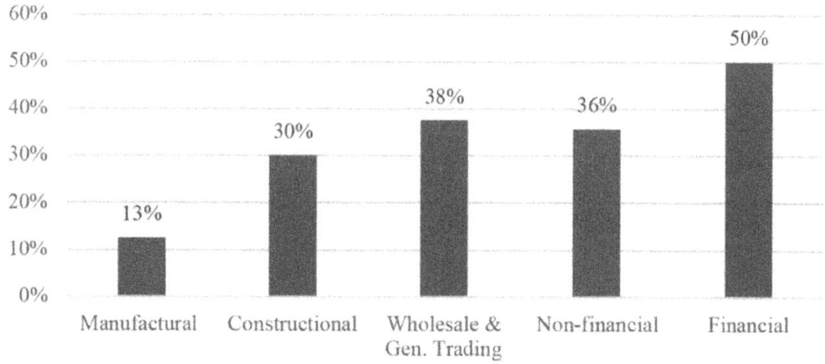

Source: Calculated from Kuwait's Central Statistical Bureau (CSB) Annual Economic Establishment Survey.

Figure 6.4 *Using technology to facilitate working remotely according to sector*

using technology during the COVID-19 crisis. However, the coefficient of all variables representing innovation in the models (including marketing innovation) had a positive sign (Table 6.4), which means that innovation and using technology are in the same direction.

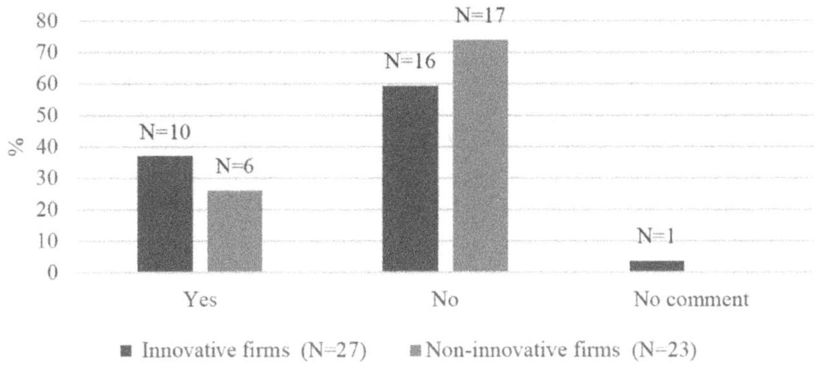

Source: Calculated from Kuwait's Central Statistical Bureau (CSB) Annual Economic Establishment Survey.

Figure 6.5 *Innovative firms using technology to facilitate working remotely*

6.6 ENHANCING THE ROLE OF SMEs IN ECONOMIC DIVERSIFICATION IN KUWAIT

GCC countries need to expand the private sector to increase their economic contribution to growth, diversify the economy, and, most importantly, create job opportunities. Miniaoui and Schilirò (2016) argue that innovation and entrepreneurship constitute the main drivers for diversifying and developing the GCC countries. However, there is a need to build the conditions for an environment conducive to innovation and to stimulate entrepreneurship with a particular focus on small and medium enterprises.

The sustained and healthy SMEs sector growth is critical to transitional economies (McIntyre, 2001). SMEs and innovation, when combined, can have a high socio-economic impact and public value for any country, and in the long run SMEs will need to innovate to survive (Vermeulen et al., 2003). However, SMEs are different, and they should be treated differently by policymakers. Innovation-driven SMEs (IDEs), as described by Aulet and Murray

Table 6.4 *Logistic regression to measure responsiveness to COVID-19 in terms of using technology*

Variable name	(7) using_tech	(8) using_tech	(9) using_tech
firmage	0.0629**	0.0859**	0.0534*
	(0.0321)	(0.0365)	(0.0305)
fsize	0.545	0.548	0.480
	(0.605)	(0.639)	(0.606)
sectortwo	−0.433	−0.247	−0.491
	(0.727)	(0.785)	(0.712)
innovative_product	-	1.195	-
		(0.765)	
innovative_process	-	-	-
innovative_admin	-	−0.850	-
		(0.820)	
innovative_market	-	1.956*	-
		(1.020)	
innovgen	1.435	-	-
	(0.971)		
est_cooperated	−1.111	−1.433	−1.153
	(0.823)	(0.894)	(0.863)
innovative_product_process	-	-	1.214
			(0.867)
Constant	−4.227***	−5.184***	−3.440**
	(1.592)	(1.813)	(1.338)
AIC	66.33011	66.26539	67.00854
BIC	77.80225	81.56157	78.48068
Pseudo R-squared	0.1525	0.2159	0.1419
Prob. > chi2	0.1014	0.1888	0.0748
Observations	50	50	50

Note: ***, **, and * represent 0.01, 0.05, and 0.1 significance levels respectively (p-value), robust standard errors in parentheses.
Source: Author.

(2013), require individually tailored policies to support them. These promising types of SMEs create innovations that have a clear competitive advantage and high-growth potential and pursue global opportunities in the long term. On the other hand, traditional SMEs are comfortable with slow growth, modest intention for economic impact, and serving local markets with conventional and limited competitive advantage.

The argument is prominent in technology-based enterprises where technological innovation is key in establishing such enterprises. These enterprises proved to be higher contributors to economic growth, both directly by their growth and indirectly through spillover, as demonstrated in Sweden's case (Lindholm Dahlstrand, 2007). The heart of these policies should be promoting innovation, which is key to SMEs' growth. The COVID-19 crisis showed that innovation is resourceful for survival during this event and key to business recovery and growth after the pandemic (Caballero-Morales, 2021).

Support for SMEs from the government should use a spray gun approach, instead, a defined criterion should be adopted. Considering the output of the above analysis from the literature, survey, and focus groups, any government support model should be designed to favour high-growth innovative SMEs that have a superior position in their contribution to the national economy and Kuwait Vision 2035 and their ability to employ Kuwaitis.

Kuwait has invested in SME development by establishing a large fund called The National Fund for SME Development with a total capital of two billion Kuwaiti dinar (about 6.5 billion US dollars). However, the challenge is to create high-value SMEs for economic diversification and employment. As discussed in the background section, much empirical evidence shows that innovation is the most important source of growth. Below is a list of practical strategies derived from recent relevant studies in Kuwait, among them are studies led by the main author of this chapter (Arman and Ramadhan, 2021; Arman et al., 2021; Salih et al., 2018):

1. Implement an effective SME innovation policy to foster value-added growth, leveraging the current surge in start-up and SME training initiatives.
2. Channel efforts towards supporting SMEs in high value-added sectors to enrich local economic activities and connect firms to the global supply chain.
3. Utilize the high-skilled national labour force and consider complementing it with skilled individuals from abroad to fuel entrepreneurship.
4. Devise government incentives to guide public and private efforts towards adopting and promoting high-value growth strategies.
5. Focus support programs on high-potential start-ups and SMEs, acknowledging the difficulty in predicting which ventures will grow rapidly.
6. Address obstacles faced by SMEs in the high value-added sector to increase their number and enhance their overall contribution to the national economy.

7. Celebrate SME successes at the national level to inspire and encourage potential entrepreneurs, showcasing the possibility of success despite the challenging business environment.
8. Foster economic diversification by enhancing existing business activities, expanding into adjacent sectors, and promoting the development of new ones.

The aforementioned recommendations are diverse and hence require different mechanisms and government organizations to orchestrate their implementation. For instance, the Kuwait SME Fund can play an important role in mobilizing the necessary resources while ministries such as the Ministry of Trade and Industry can facilitate the processes such as amending the regulatory framework for SMEs to ease the burdens related to SMEs' development. Moreover, new institutional developments, such as establishing a national STI Council, can help with implementing such initiatives.

6.7 DISCUSSION AND CONCLUSIONS

The SMEs sector has been promoted as a key driver in Kuwait's diversification agenda, one of the seven pillars of Kuwait Vision 2035. Kuwait's SMEs have been struggling for different reasons, including the lack of a conducive business environment, and their current contribution to GDP and employment is very limited compared to other countries. The COVID-19 crisis has deepened the problem. Therefore, supporting SMEs in Kuwait in this challenging time is crucial, especially for those who proved to be resilient and innovative.

The SMEs survey and other similar surveys in Kuwait showed that COVID-19 has severely impacted Kuwait SMEs and forced many firms to suspend or shut down their operation, particularly in non-financial sectors (Al-Rowaih et al., 2020; Bensirri, 2020). Most surveyed SMEs in Kuwait, including those in the current survey, demonstrated that they are not resilient and agile enough to cope with such a colossal crisis. This is due to the lack of resources and the inability to manage risk and ensure business continuity.

An in-depth analysis was performed, including descriptive analysis, to measure whether innovation capability has enabled SMEs in Kuwait to be more resilient to the crisis. This aspect was measured mainly by analysing the firms that were forced to shut down their operations. The econometric analysis showed that innovative firms and technological innovation are more resilient than their non-innovative counterparts. Moreover, the firms that have relationships with STI institutions are also more resilient. This confirms the importance of innovation and innovation cooperation for SMEs both during ordinary times and in difficult times such as the COVID-19 crisis. Another crucial factor was the firm's size and age, which proved significant in facing such difficult times. This can be attributed to the advantage of the more extensive experience and available resources used as a buffer.

Firms' responsiveness to the COVID-19 crisis was measured in terms of the availability of a business continuity management system and if the firm could use technology to continue its operation during the crisis. The analysis showed that there is a strong relationship between organizational innovation and the availability of a business continuity management system in firms. This reflects the importance of the dynamic organizational culture of innovative firms to adopt new ideas and anticipate challenges and hence respond better than others. Moreover, cooperation with STI institutions emerged again in this part of the analysis and showed that firms that cooperate in STI are more responsive than those that do not cooperate.

The use of technology exploded during the crisis, and many firms globally invested in the required IT infrastructure. Our analysis showed that 63% of firms that used technology to facilitate working remotely were generally innovative. However, innovative firms in marketing were the only high statistically significant in readiness to work remotely utilizing technology. The other types of innovations didn't show any statistically significant relationship.

The above results, in general, show the importance of innovation for SMEs. Hence, Kuwait's government should continue upgrading the regulatory framework to alleviate the factors that can hamper SMEs from innovating. It should also provide capacity-building programs to help SMEs innovate and grow.

Promoting high-growth and innovative SMEs can play an important role in advancing the speed of government diversification plans in the GCC, including Kuwait. The SMEs' development strategies in Kuwait, including the SMEs' fund, should be steered towards promoting technology-based firms and provide the support to conduct practical R&D activities and successful innovations.

ACKNOWLEDGEMENT

This chapter is part of a study financed by Kuwait Foundation for the Advancement of Science (KFAS), Grant PN20-17IC-04-CORONAL 58, and is an outcome of GRM 2024 Workshop No 4 GRC.

NOTES

1. https://www.stats.govt.nz/news/quarterly-gdp-bounces-back-but-covid-still-a-drag-on-annual-growth/
2. Non-finance includes education, health, hotels and restaurants, and other business services.

REFERENCES

Adam, N.A., and Alarifi, G. (2021). Innovation practices for survival of small and medium enterprises (SMEs) in the COVID-19 times: The role of external support. *Journal of Innovation and Entrepreneurship* 10(1): 15–16. Epub 2021 May 27.

Al-Rowaih, A., Al-Fozan, B., Al-Joan, A., and Alloghani, A. (2020). Special Study on COVID-19 impact on SMEs in Kuwait. Kuwait. https://www.alanba.com.kw/959019

Al-Sanjary, O.I., and Khalifa, M. (2021). Impact of COVID-19 pandemic on small and medium-sized businesses (SMEs) in the GCC. *International Journal of Green Management and Business Studies* 1(1): 29–49.

Apedo-Amah, M.C., Avdiu, B., Cirera, X., Cruz, M., Davies, E., Grover, A., et al. (2020). Unmasking the impact of COVID-19 on businesses. Policy Research Working Paper 9434. World Bank Group.

Arman, H., and Ramadhan, M. (2021). Critical success factors for small and medium-sized enterprises in resource-rich country context. *International Journal of Globalisation and Small Business* 12(3): 299–316.

Arman, H., Ramadhan, M., AlAwadhi, A., Al-Fulaij, S., and AlAli, A.M. (2021). Selecting alternative policies to support SMEs in the struggle due to COVID-19. Kuwait: KISR.

Aulet, W., and Murray, F. (2013). A tale of two entrepreneurs: Understanding differences in the types of entrepreneurship in the economy. Kauffman Institute Paper.

Autio, E., Kronlund, M., and Kovalainen, A. (2007). High-growth SME support initiatives in nine countries: Analysis, categorization, and recommendations: Report prepared for the Finnish Ministry of Trade and Industry. Helsinki: Ministry of Trade and Industry.

Ayyagari, M., Beck, T., and Demirguc-Kunt, A. (2007). Small and medium enterprises across the globe. *Small Business Economics* 29(4): 415–434.

Barrero, J.M., Bloom, N., and Davis, S.J. (2020). Covid-19 is also a reallocation shock. National Bureau of Economic Research (Working Paper 27137).

Bartik, A.W., Bertrand, M., Cullen, Z.B., Glaeser, E.L., Luca, M., and Stanton, C.T. (2020). How are small businesses adjusting to Covid-19? National Bureau of Economic Research (Working Paper 26989).

BDC (2020). Survey on the impact of COVID-19 on Canadian SMEs. Canada: BDC.

Bensirri (2020). COVID-19 Kuwait Business Impact Survey. Kuwait.

Bravo-Biosca, A., and Westlake, S. (2009). The vital 6 per cent: How high-growth innovative businesses generate prosperity and jobs. NESTA, London.

Brinkley, I., Hutton, W., Schneider, P., and Coates Ulrichsen, K. (2012). *Kuwait and the Knowledge Economy*. London: LSE.

Brussevich, M., Dabla-Norris, E., and Khalid, S. (2020). Who will bear the brunt of lockdown policies? Evidence from tele-workability measures across countries. IMF Working Paper.

Caballero-Morales, S. (2021). Innovation as recovery strategy for SMEs in emerging economies during the COVID-19 pandemic. *Research in International Business and Finance* 57: 101396.

CBK (2020). CBK offers regulatory stimulus package for local banks to face coronavirus fallout [02.04.20, PRESS RELEASE].

Clauss, T., Breier, M., Kraus, S., Durst, S., and Mahto, R.V. (2021). Temporary business model innovation: SMEs' innovation response to the Covid-19 crisis. *R&D Management* 52(2): 294–312.
Damanpour, F. (1992). Organizational size and innovation. *Organization Studies* 13(3): 375–402.
Davidsson, P., Lindmark, L., and Olofsson, C. (1998). Small firms and job creation during a recession and recovery. In Z.J. Acs, B. Carlsson, and C. Karlsson (eds), *Entrepreneurship, Small and Medium-Sized Enterprises and the Macroeconomy*. Cambridge: Cambridge University Press, pp. 286–309.
Elsharnouby, T.H., Elbanna, S., Farha, A.A., and Mauji, N. (2024). Exploring critical internal enablers to SMEs export performance: Evidence from Qatar. *Humanities and Social Sciences Communications* 11(1): 1–12.
European Commission (2012). Small companies create 85% of new jobs. Available at: https://ec.europas.eu/commission/presscorner/detai/en/ip_12_20.
FDRNY (2020). Can small firms weather the economic effects of COVID-19? Federal Reserve Bank of New York.
Gagnon, J.E., Kamin, S.B., and Kearns, J. (2023). The impact of the COVID-19 pandemic on global GDP growth. *Journal of the Japanese and International Economies* 68: 101258.
Gallouj, F., and Weinstein, O. (1997). Innovation in services. *Research Policy* 26(4): 537–556.
Gibb, F., and Buchanan, S. (2006). A framework for business continuity management. *International Journal of Information Management* 26(2): 128–141.
Gunday, G., Ulusoy, G., Kilic, K., and Alpkan, L. (2011). Effects of innovation types on firm performance. *International Journal of Production Economics* 133(2): 662–676.
Hashi, I., and Stojčić, N. (2013). The impact of innovation activities on firm performance using a multi-stage model: Evidence from the Community Innovation Survey 4. *Research Policy* 42(2): 353–366.
ILO (2020). *The Six-Step COVID-19 Business Continuity Plan for SMEs*. International Labour Organization.
Kato, M., and Charoenrat, T. (2018). Business continuity management of small and medium-sized enterprises: Evidence from Thailand. *International Journal of Disaster Risk Reduction* 27: 577–587.
Khamis, M., Prinz, D., Newhouse, D., Palacios-Lopez, A., Pape, U., and Weber, M. (2021). The early labor market impacts of COVID-19 in developing countries. Policy Research Working Paper, 9510.
Koch, E. (2011). *Challenges to SME Development in Kuwait*. Kuwait: UNDP.
KPMG (2020). *Kuwait: COVID-19 Government Relief Measures*.
Lindholm Dahlstrand, Å. (2007). Technology-based entrepreneurship and regional development: The case of Sweden. *European Business Review* 19(5): 373–386.
Lobosco, K. (2020). Congress has already approved more than $3trillion in coronavirus relief. Here's what happened to it. *WRAL News*. Available at https://www.wral./com /story/congress-has-already-approved-more-than-3 trillion-in-coronavirus-relief -heres-whats-happened-to-it/19129381/.
Lööf, H., and Heshmati, A. (2006). On the relationship between innovation and performance: A sensitivity analysis. *Economics of Innovation and New Technology* 15(4–5): 317–344.

McIntyre, R.J. (2001). *The Role of Small and Medium Enterprises in Transition: Growth and Entrepreneurship.* Basingstoke: UNU World Institute for Development Economics Research (UNU/WIDER).
McKinsey (2020). Which small businesses are most vulnerable to COVID-19 – and when. Available at: https://www.mckinsey.com/featured-insights/americas/which-small-businesses-are-most-vulnerable-to-covid-19-and-when
McKinsey (2021). Strategic resilience during the COVID-19 crisis. Available at: https://www.mckinsey.com/business-functions/strategy-and-corporate-finance/our-insights/strategic-resilience-during-the-covid-19-crisis#.
Miniaoui, H., and Schilirò, D. (2016). Innovation and entrepreneurship for the growth and diversification of the GCC economies. Munich Personal RePEc Archive.
Mishrif, A., and Khan, A. (2023). Technology adoption as survival strategy for small and medium enterprises during COVID-19. *Journal of Innovation and Entrepreneurship* 12(1): 53.
Mortensen, P.S., and Bloch, C.W. (2005). *Oslo Manual: Guidelines for Collecting and Interpreting Innovation Data.* Paris: Organisation for Economic Co-operation and Development (OECD).
OECD (2020). *Coronavirus (COVID-19): SME Policy Responses.* Paris: OECD.
Parisi, M.L., Schiantarelli, F., and Sembenelli, A. (2006). Productivity, innovation and R&D: Micro evidence for Italy. *European Economic Review* 50(8): 2037–2061.
Rajapathirana, R.J., and Hui, Y. (2018). Relationship between innovation capability, innovation type, and firm performance. *Journal of Innovation & Knowledge* 3(1): 44–55.
Refass, S., Lillywhite, J., Salem, F., Akrout, Z., Shaer, S., and Shibl, E. (2023). The future of SMEs in the UAE. Digital Economy Series.
Roper, S., and Turner, J. (2020). R&D and innovation after COVID-19: What can we expect? A review of prior research and data trends after the great financial crisis. *International Small Business Journal* 38(6): 504–514.
Rosenberg, N. (2004). *Innovation and Economic Growth.* Paris: OECD.
Rosenbusch, N., Brinckmann, J., and Bausch, A. (2011). Is innovation always beneficial? A meta-analysis of the relationship between innovation and performance in SMEs. *Journal of Business Venturing* 26(4): 441–457.
Salih, S., Arman, H., and Al-Qudsi, S. (2018). *An Action Plan for Improving Kuwait's Global Competitiveness Path: An Engine for Transformation into Knowledge Innovation Economy.* Kuwait: Kuwait Institute for Scientific Research.
Schreyer, P. (2000). Small and Medium-Sized Enterprises (SMEs); Employment creation and industrial policy. In W. Elsner and J. Groenewegen (eds), *Industrial Policies After 2000.* Dordrecht: Springer Netherlands, pp. 285–319.
Seetharaman, P. (2020). Business models shifts: Impact of Covid-19. *International Journal of Information Management* 54: 102173.
Shane, S. (2009). Why encouraging more people to become entrepreneurs is bad public policy. *Small Business Economics* 33(2): 141–149.
Smit, S., Hirt, M., Buehler, K., Lund, S., Greenberg, E., and Govindarajan, A. (2020). *Safeguarding our Lives and our Livelihoods: The Imperative of Our Time.* McKinsey & Company.
Ucaktürk, A., Bekmezci, M., and Ucaktürk, T. (2011). Prevailing during the periods of economical crisis and recession through business model innovation. *Procedia – Social and Behavioral Sciences* 24: 89–100.

Vermeulen, P.A., de Jong, J., and O'Schaughnessy, K.C. (2003). *Innovation in SMEs: An Empirical Investigation of the Input-Throughput-Output-Performance Model.* Zoetermeer: EIM.

Wakasugi, R., and Koyata, F. (1997). R&D, firm size and innovation outputs: Are Japanese firms efficient in product development? *Journal of Product Innovation Management* 14(5): 383–392.

Wood, J. (2023, 3 January). Europe's small businesses proved resilient to COVID-19 pandemic disruption. Here's what that means for SMEs. The World Economic Forum.

Wooldridge, J.M. (2006). *Introductory Econometrics: A Modern Approach.* New York: Thomson.

World Bank (2024). *World Development Indicators (WDI).* https://databank.worldbank.org/source/world-development-indicators/preview/on

Yazdanfar, D., and Öhman, P. (2015). Firm-level determinants of job creation by SMEs: Swedish empirical evidence. *Journal of Small Business and Enterprise Development* 22(4): 666–679.

Yepez, C., and Leimgruber, W. (2024). The evolving landscape of tourism, travel, and global trade since the Covid-19 pandemic. *Research in Globalization* 8(10): 100207.

Zeng, S.X., Xie, X.M., and Tam, C.M. (2010). Relationship between cooperation networks and innovation performance of SMEs. *Technovation* 30(3): 181–194.

7. Green credit lines in the Gulf Cooperation Council: evaluating opportunities, overcoming challenges, and assessing the impact on energy transition in Qatar

Islam Mohamed Mahmoud and Quosay Awad Ahmed

7.1 INTRODUCTION[1]

The financial sector's mandate is to manage risk, allocate capital, mobilize savings, and – as a financial intermediary – manage risk and maturity transformation and convenience denomination, all at the lowest possible transaction costs. It can have either an enabling role in the transition to a sustainable world or a hampering role depending on its actions (Battiston et al., 2021).

The public sector does and will still play the leading role in commissioning green infrastructure projects and to guide and "jump start" investment when needed. But transformational change will ultimately require large-scale private sector engagement (Corfee-Morlot et al., 2012). The transition requires a structural change in the financing patterns in terms of finance tenor and the result orientation to enable the private sector, including small and medium enterprises (SMEs) and large enterprises (LEs) to have a viable business case for green and renewable energy (RE) projects. However, a clear distinction between "green" and "brown" investments is essential to ensuring transparency and effectiveness in green finance.

Green credit lines (GCLs) are specifically designed to finance environmentally sustainable projects, such as renewable energy, energy efficiency, and pollution control, while conventional or "brown" investments typically fund projects associated with high carbon emissions, like fossil fuel extraction or traditional infrastructure developments. The key difference lies in the purpose and criteria: GCLs prioritize environmental benefits, offering favorable terms (e.g., lower interest rates, longer repayment periods) to encourage green projects, whereas brown investments focus on profitability without necessarily considering environmental impacts. Additionally, GCLs often adhere to strict sustainability standards and frameworks, ensuring alignment with global climate goals, while brown investments may contribute to environmental degradation through activities that increase carbon emissions and harm natural ecosystems.

Table 7.1 compares the conventional credit line and the GCL.

The Gulf Cooperation Council (GCC) economies have been heavily reliant on oil and gas export revenues, with a narrow export profile dominated by oil and gas. World Bank data ranks Qatar, Kuwait, the UAE, and Bahrain in positions one to four for the highest per capita emissions, with Saudi Arabia 10th, and Oman 12th (World Bank, 2020). While Qatar's per capita emissions are

Table 7.1 Difference between the conventional credit line and the green credit line

Feature	Credit line	Green credit line
Definition	A pre-approved loan amount that a borrower can access as needed, up to a specified limit	A specific type of credit line designed to finance environmentally friendly projects and initiatives
Purpose	Can be used for various purposes, such as working capital, debt consolidation, or emergency expenses	Exclusively used for projects that promote environmental sustainability, like renewable energy, energy efficiency, or pollution control
Eligibility	Based on creditworthiness, income, and other financial factors	Requires meeting specific criteria related to the project's environmental benefits and adherence to sustainability standards
Terms and Conditions	Interest rates, fees, and repayment terms can vary depending on the borrower's credit profile and the lender's policies	Often comes with more favorable terms than traditional credit lines, such as lower interest rates, longer repayment periods, or reduced fees, to incentivize green investments
Examples	Personal credit lines, business credit lines, home equity lines of credit	Green credit lines for renewable energy projects, energy-efficient building upgrades, or sustainable agriculture practices

Source: Authors' illustration.

the highest in the world, its small population means that total emissions are lower than those of Saudi Arabia and the UAE (Engineering Net Zero, 2022).

The GCC countries have progressively joined global forces to address climate change. They signed and ratified the Paris Climate Agreement and have submitted nationally determined contributions (NDCs) to the United Nations Framework Convention on Climate Change (UNFCCC), outlining their goals for mitigating and adapting to climate change. Notably, all GCC countries have pledged to achieve a net-zero target by the middle of the century. As of 2021, comprehensive national climate strategies, including adaptation ambitions, have been publicly declared by only three GCC states: the UAE, Oman, and Saudi Arabia (Al-Sarihi, 2021). Among them, Qatar's NDCs were submitted to the UNFCCC in November 2021, showing that the country is committed to reducing its greenhouse gase (GHG) emissions by 25% compared to a baseline scenario by 2030.[2] However, this is a complex challenge given Qatar's heavy dependence on oil and gas hydrocarbons' production, transformation, and consumption, which contribute significantly to the nation's gross domestic product and overall wealth (Al-Noaimi et al., 2023).

Large-scale projects require significant capital to develop and implement innovative technologies that can reduce emissions on a national scale. Simultaneously, SMEs play a vital role in the energy transition by fostering innovation and adopting sustainable practices at a smaller scale (IEA, 2021). Therefore, ensuring adequate funding for both large and small energy projects is essential. This financial support will enable the deployment of cutting-edge technologies and sustainable practices necessary for reducing emissions, allowing Qatar and other GCC countries to effectively achieve the energy transition and contribute to global climate goals (World Bank, 2021).

Green finance instruments, such as green bonds, green loans, grants, and carbon markets, are designed to fund projects that promote environmental sustainability and address climate change. Among these, GCLs stand out as impactful tools, providing pre-approved financing with favorable terms for green projects like renewable energy and energy efficiency. By offering lower interest rates, longer repayment periods, and technical assistance, GCLs help overcome funding barriers, particularly for SMEs, enabling faster adoption of sustainable practices.

The chapter adopts a comprehensive approach that includes a literature review and a conceptual framework to define and explain the opportunities and challenges of establishing GCLs by the financial institutions (FIs). It also presents a methodology for assessing the impact of GCL mechanisms on Qatar's energy transition goals. By examining publicly available and historical data, the chapter aims to evaluate the progress of establishing GCLs in the GCC, with a particular focus on Qatar.

To measure the potential and impact of the establishment of GCLs by the FIs, the chapter introduces two metrics: (1) an index to assess the potential of the country to successfully implement green credit programs based on its existing financial and regulatory infrastructure, and (2) an indicator which measures the expected influence of implementing GCL by the FIs within the country on advancing energy transition goal. These metrics will explore various aspects, including the performance of the FIs, governmental framework, internal capacities, and the energy transition target which are assessed qualitatively to judge the potentiality and impact of establishing GCLs.

The chapter enriches its findings by comparing Qatar, the United Arab Emirates (UAE), and Saudi Arabia (KSA). This comparative analysis aims to draw lessons from the sustainable finance experiences of these three countries. This provides a comprehensive perspective on the factors that may hinder or facilitate the success of GCLs in the GCC region.

7.2 LITERATURE REVIEW

7.2.1 Energy Transition Challenges in Qatar and the GCC

Founded in 1981, the GCC countries, Bahrain, Kuwait, Oman, Qatar, Saudi Arabia, and United Arab Emirates, together, cover a total area of 2410 km^2, have a total population of about 47 million and a GDP of $1.6 trillion or about $33,300 per capita (Almulla & Howells, 2014). The GCC countries rank among the highest countries in term of energy consumption per capita. Qatar ranks first, followed by Kuwait, United Arab Emirates, Bahrain, Oman, and Saudi Arabia. In comparison, the per capita energy consumption in Qatar is four times that in the United Kingdom and 20 times the average Indian's per capita energy consumption. This can be attributed to the harsh climate in the GCC region leading to high demand for air conditioning and cooling throughout the year. For instance, Qatar's per capita electricity consumption reaches approximately 17,500 kWh annually, with a significant portion dedicated to cooling, especially during peak summer months (World Bank, 2020). In contrast, colder countries like Germany exhibit lower per capita energy consumption for heating, averaging around 130–150 kWh/m^2 per year, thanks to better insulation, energy-efficient building designs, and a more diverse energy mix that includes renewables (European Commission, 2020). For example, the Passivhaus standard in Germany reduces heating energy needs to as low as 15 kWh/m^2 annually. This difference in energy demand highlights the efficiency and sustainability challenges faced by the GCC, where the reliance on electricity for cooling contrasts sharply with the more varied and efficient energy strategies in colder regions (IEA & LBNL, 2021). Also, low fuel prices over the past decades led to higher energy demand and less efficient energy use in the GCC countries (Sakhrieh, 2016).

The energy consumption across the GCC region showed an average annual growth rate (AAGR) of 6% to 7%, largely driven by the residential sector (which accounts for about 44% of the region's total consumption) (Wogan et al., 2017). Although GCC countries are not the world's largest emitters in terms of total GHG emissions and total GHG emissions per GDP, several Gulf countries fall in the top ten emitters in terms of GHG emissions per capita. Despite the fact that GCC countries collectively contribute about 2.7% of global greenhouse gas (GHG) emissions due to their oil and gas production (General Electric, 2021), they have embarked in wide-ranging reforms to achieve socio-economic transformation, as shown in Qatar National Vision 2030, Vision 2030 of Saudi Arabia, "We the UAE 2031", and Oman Vision 2040. The main progress areas are social and business-friendly reforms, efforts to enhance sustainability and resilience, investments in strategic industries and digital and green infrastructure (IMF, 2023). All the GCC countries are progressing with the SDGs' agenda implementation and four of the countries have already exceeded two-thirds of the overall SDG score, Qatar being one of them (IMF, 2023). The Gulf Arab states have already taken steps and developed institutional architecture conducive to mitigating the effects of climate change. Before the announcement of net-zero commitments, each GCC state launched initiatives, regulations, and programs intended to mitigate different aspects of climate change impacts (Al-Sarihi, 2021).

Qatar is taking a range of actions to reduce its greenhouse gas emissions; Qatar ratified the Kyoto Protocol in 2005 and submitted an initial National Communication to the UNFCCC in 2011. In 2012, Qatar demonstrated its leadership role and support for global action on climate change action by hosting the 18th Conference of Parties (COP18) to the UNFCCC and submitted their updated first NDC in 2021. In terms of the impact of climate change, Qatar's ND-GAIN Country Index[3] rank is 38. It is the 139th most vulnerable country and the 44th most ready country. The low vulnerability score and high readiness score of Qatar places it in the lower-bottom quadrant of the ND-GAIN Matrix, which means that adaptation challenges still exist, but Qatar is well positioned to adjust (University of Notre Dame, 2023). Table 7.2 presents an overview of Qatar's strategic initiatives aimed at sustainable development and climate action.

In their recent National Renewable Energy Strategy (QNRES), Qatar focuses on three main objectives: (1) reduce GHG emissions through sustainable policies and trends targeting 10% reduction in the annual GHG emissions; (2) increase RE penetration while maintaining network reliability targeting to increase RE share in the power mix from its current 5% to 18% by 2030; and

Table 7.2 Qatar's strategic plans for sustainable development and climate action

Category	Action/Plan	Description	Lead institution(s)
National Strategy	Qatar National Vision 2030	Outlines a long-term vision for economic diversification, environmental sustainability, and human development. Emphasizes a balanced approach to economic growth and environmental protection	Qatar General Secretariat for Development Planning (QGSDP)
Climate Change Strategy	Qatar National Environment and Climate Change Strategy (QNECCS)	Establishes a national framework for mitigating climate change impacts and adapting to a changing climate. Sets national climate targets, including those outlined in Qatar's NDC, and outlines various measures across different sectors	Ministry of Municipality and Environment (MME)
Nationally Determined Contribution (NDC)	Qatar's First NDC	Sets a national target to reduce greenhouse gas emissions by 25% by 2030 compared to a business-as-usual (BAU) scenario	Ministry of Municipality and Environment (MME)
Energy Sector	QatarEnergy Sustainability Strategy	Aims to reduce greenhouse gas emissions throughout the natural gas value chain. Focuses on improving energy efficiency, reducing methane emissions, and exploring carbon capture and storage (CCS) technologies	QatarEnergy
Renewable Energy (RE) Strategy	Qatar National Renewable Energy (RE) Strategy	Aims to increase the share of RE in the country's energy mix	Ministry of Municipality and Environment (MME)

Category	Action/Plan	Description	Lead institution(s)
Carbon Capture and Storage (CCS)	QatarEnergy CCS Research and Development	Explores the potential of CCS technologies to capture and store carbon emissions from the natural gas industry	QatarEnergy
Aero Emissions Reduction	The Qatar Airways' Fuel Optimization	Aims to reduce fuel consumption and carbon emissions from aircraft operations	Qatar Airways
Zero Emission Targets	N/A	N/A	N/A

Source: Prepared by the authors based on published data.

(3) maximize the socio-economic contribution from its RE targeting reduction in the average cost of electricity generation by 15% by 2030.

In conclusion, the literature review highlights the pressing energy challenges facing Qatar and the broader GCC region, characterized by high energy consumption per capita, significant greenhouse gas emissions, and a growing imperative for sustainable development. Moreover, there exists a pronounced ambition towards RE targets, signifying a pivotal shift towards a more sustainable and resilient energy future.

7.2.2 The Role of the Financial Sector and GCLs

Several empirical studies have shown that the financial sector can play an important role in reducing GHG emissions. Financial firms' ability to secure and allocate funds, and manage financial risks, are recognized as essential in response to climate change risks (UNEP Finance Initiative, 2015). Financial firms are adapting their traditional financial purpose, function, and philosophy, to change financial decision activities and products to reflect climate change risks and sustainability aims (GFANZ, 2021). However, several barriers currently inhibit green lending in developing countries. GCLs are considered useful in addressing some of these barriers to green lending, for example, an unfavorable investment environment can hinder the competitiveness of green investments compared to traditional alternatives. This lack of competitiveness stems from several factors. One major issue is the high upfront capital required for green projects, such as renewable energy plants, which often exceeds the initial costs of conventional fossil fuel investments. These projects also tend to have longer payback periods, making them less attractive to investors looking for quicker returns (IEA, 2021).

Additionally, the fossil fuel industry in many developing countries benefits from significant subsidies, creating market distortions that make it difficult for green projects to compete on a level playing field (IEA, 2023). Another challenge is the lack of financial instruments, such as risk guarantees, which increases the perceived financial risk of green investments, further reducing their appeal to potential investors (GEF, 2017).

Challenges also include a lack of viable projects, insufficient demand for financing, and limited financial knowledge and products (Shishlov et al., 2017). While the availability of finance through GCLs is crucial, it is not a standalone solution. If viable projects are lacking, the effectiveness of available financing is limited. However, GCLs can stimulate project development by offering technical assistance aimed at helping project developers to structure bankable green projects. GCLs serve a dual purpose as a financial tool. First, they aim to facilitate lending to projects with environmental benefits. Second, they seek to enhance the capacity of local FIs to expand the local green lending market[4] (Shishlov et al., 2017). Under a GCL arrangement, funds are typically provided by a public financial institution, whether it is national or international, to participating local FIs, who then lend them to developers of eligible green projects (SMEs and LEs). The eligibility of green projects is generally determined by either the public financial institution providing the funds or by adhering to internationally recognized frameworks such as the Green Bond Principles or standards set by the Climate Bonds Initiative. These frameworks ensure that projects align with global environmental goals, such as reducing carbon emissions or promoting renewable energy. This support helps build a pipeline of viable projects, thereby bridging the gap between available finance and project readiness (OECD, 2020). GCLs play a pivotal role in overcoming supply-side barriers by providing dedicated financing for green projects and leveraging the intermediation function of FIs (Shishlov et al., 2017; Smith et al., 2020). Additionally, GCLs may encompass technical assistance funded by the participating FIs, aimed at enhancing the capacity of local banks to finance green investment projects and/or assisting end-borrowers in structuring investment proposals.

Recent developments in the taxonomy of the Green Loan Principles (GLP) provide clear guidelines for distinguishing between green and brown projects. The GLP taxonomy, established by the Loan Market Association, outlines specific criteria that projects must meet to be considered environmentally sustainable. These criteria include improvements in energy efficiency, significant reductions in greenhouse gas emissions, and the promotion and development of renewable energy sources (LMA, 2021). For instance, projects aimed at enhancing energy efficiency might involve upgrading to energy-efficient appliances or retrofitting buildings to reduce energy consumption. Renewable energy projects could include the development of solar farms, wind energy installations, or hydroelectric power stations (LMA, 2021). The Climate Bonds Standard and Certification Scheme also offers sector-specific criteria to ensure that projects deliver genuine environmental benefits, particularly in high-impact areas like energy and transport (Climate Bonds Initiative, 2020). Similarly, the EU Taxonomy for Sustainable Activities provides a comprehensive framework for classifying environmentally sustainable economic activities. It includes detailed criteria across six environmental objectives, ensuring a broad and rigorous approach to sustainability (European Commission, 2020).

Conversely, brown projects are characterized by activities that significantly contribute to carbon emissions and environmental degradation. Examples of brown projects include fossil fuel extraction, coal mining, and the development of new oil and gas infrastructure. These activities are not aligned with the sustainability goals outlined by the GLP and other taxonomies and are typically excluded from green financing. The differentiation between green and brown projects is critical to avoid "greenwashing," where projects are misleadingly marketed as environmentally friendly without meeting the necessary sustainability criteria. Greenwashing can undermine the integrity of green finance and erode investor and public trust. By adhering to established taxonomies such as the GLP, EU Taxonomy, and Climate Bonds Standard, financial institutions can ensure that only genuinely sustainable projects receive green financing, thereby maintaining the integrity of green credit lines. This adherence involves rigorous assessment and verification processes to confirm that projects meet the relevant criteria and deliver the intended environmental benefits (Climate Bonds Initiative, 2020; European Commission, 2020).

Figure 7.1 illustrates the mechanism of GCL establishment by FIs.

7.2.3 Impact Assessment

GCLs play a pivotal role in promoting green investments by addressing financial and non-financial barriers throughout the lending process both from the supply and demand sides. Financial incentives embedded in GCLs – typically provided by national or international public financial institutions, such as development banks, government agencies, or international climate funds – such as concessionally and favorable terms, help alleviate supply-side challenges like high costs and perceived risks. Lower interest rates, longer tenure, and grace periods align loan terms with the lifecycle of green projects, thereby enhancing their financial feasibility. Moreover, incentives like performance payments and credit enhancements encourage the adoption of green lending practices among financial intermediaries (Aravamuthan et al., 2015).

Public FIs (such as international banks, development banks, central banks, climate funds and facilities, foundations or charitable organizations) facilitate GCLs by leveraging their access to stable financing and blending commercial

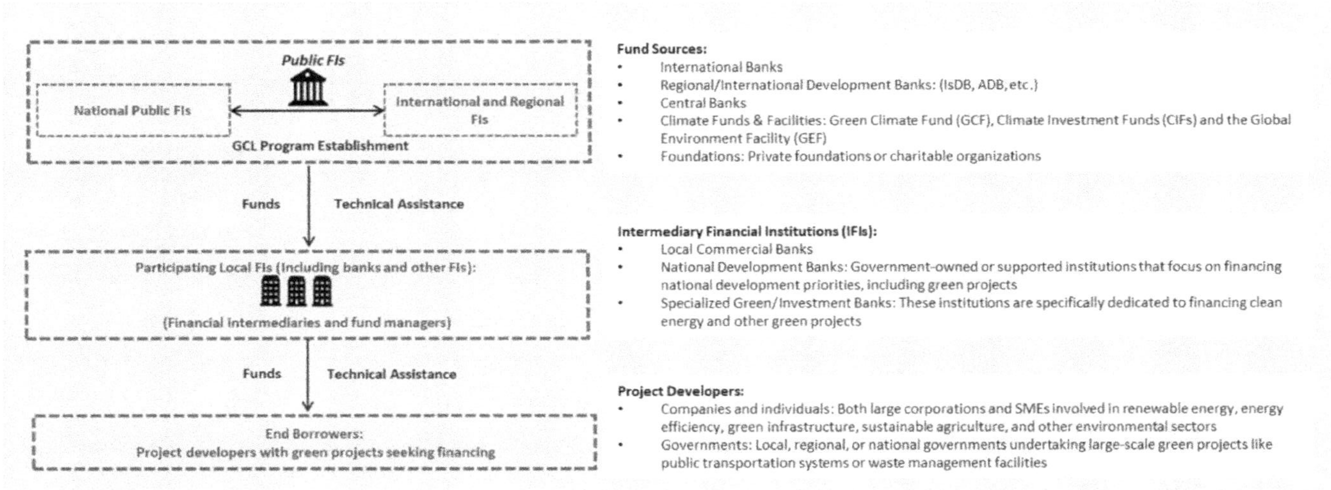

Source: Authors' illustration.

Figure 7.1 GCL mechanism

finance with concessional contributions, making green lending more appealing. These institutions can mobilize external public finance and private co-financing, thereby expanding the pool of available funds for green projects. However, empirical evidence on the extent to which financial benefits are passed on to end-borrowers remains limited (OECD, 2016). Non-financial benefits of GCLs are equally significant, with technical assistance programs addressing capacity gaps among financial intermediaries and end-borrowers (Enclude Limited, 2016).

The Qatari banking sector is increasingly recognizing the importance of environmental sustainability and is actively participating in the green finance movement. This shift aligns with Qatar's National Vision 2030. As a result, several Qatari banks have implemented green finance initiatives to promote environmentally friendly practices among businesses and consumers. According to secondary data published as of May 2024, GCLs are not yet established within the Qatari financial sector.

Table 7.3 provides a snapshot of key green finance initiatives offered by leading Qatari banks. It highlights the diverse range of products and services available, serving various segments of the market.

7.3 RESEARCH METHODOLOGY

7.3.1 Research Framework

The chapter proposes a conceptual framework to qualitatively assess the potential for GCL establishment by the FIs and its impact on energy transition in Qatar. The framework highlights two metrics:

Green Credit Line Implementation Potential Index (GCLIPI): this index assesses the potentiality of the GCL establishment by the FIs and considers three main factors: (1) Financial Institution Performance (based on common aspects specified by frameworks employed by many donors and development banks, such as those used by the World Bank), OECD Development Assistance Committee (DAC), International Finance Corporation (IFC), Green Climate Fund (GCF), and Asian Development Bank (ADB); (2) Governmental Frameworks (based on World Bank, 2023; ADB, 2023), and (3) FIs' Internal Capacities (derived from a review of various established GCL programs).[5] While these factors reflect the financial sector's readiness to integrate GCLs into their operations, they represent a preliminary assessment towards a more comprehensive evaluation.

The Green Credit Potential Impact Indicator (GCLPII): this indicator aims to provide a preliminary assessment of the potential impact of GCL establishment by the FIs on energy transition.

Table 7.3 Key green finance initiatives offered by leading Qatari banks

Bank	Green initiatives
Qatar National Bank (QNB)	Issued USD 600 million in green bonds
Doha Bank	Green car loans, green mortgage program, green credit cards, green accounts
Qatar Development Bank (QDB)	Green Financing Program: Provides preferential financing for eco-friendly projects and products
Qatar Central Bank (QCB)	Regulatory and Strategic Efforts: (1) Facilitates green bond issuance; (2) Collaborates with QDB for green financing initiatives; (3) Encourages environmental and social considerations in bank governance
Dukhan Bank	(1) ESG Strategy: Implements a comprehensive strategy with a focus on sustainable finance; (2) Green Products: Offers eco-friendly vehicle financing and partners with GORD for sustainable building practices
International Bank of Qatar (IBQ)	N/A
Qatar Islamic Bank (QIB)	(1) Sustainable Deposit: Sharia-compliant product allocating funds to environmentally and socially responsible projects. (2) Sustainability Strategy: Aims to be a leader in Sharia-compliant products; (3) Sustainable Finance: Aligns with UN SDGs and Qatar National Vision 2030; (4) Equator Principles: Adopted framework to manage environmental and social risks in financed projects
Masraf Al Rayan	(1) Sustainable Finance Framework: Promotes environmental and social objectives through financing activities; (2) Green Deposit: Qatar's first Sharia-compliant green deposit product; (3) Green Vehicle Finance Campaign: Offers competitive financing for electric and hybrid vehicles
Ahli Bank	N/A
Qatar International Islamic Bank (QIIB)	(1) Sustainable Finance Framework: Promotes environmental and social benefits through financing activities aligned with Green Bond Principles (GBP), Social Bond Principles (SBP), Green Loan Principles (GLP), and Social Loan Principles (SLP); (2) Green Financing Products: Offers financing for various green projects like RE, clean transportation, energy efficiency, and sustainable water management

Source: Compiled by the authors from multiple publicly accessible sources, including annual reports, official bank websites, and sustainability publications.

Figure 7.2 shows that the impact of GCL establishment for a country will be examined by three factors: the *performance of financial institutions* (FIs) as intermediaries, the overall *governmental frameworks*, and the *internal capacities* of the bank regarding the GCL-specific program. To further enrich the assessment, the framework proposes developing a GCL Implementation Potential Index (GCLIPI) for Qatar. This index will aggregate scores based on the three identified factors. Additionally, the GCLIPI score for Qatar will be compared with scores calculated for two other GCC countries namely, the UAE and Saudi Arabia (KSA). This comparative analysis will offer valuable insights into the relative strengths and challenges of each country's GCL potential within the regional context. In addition, to assess the Potential

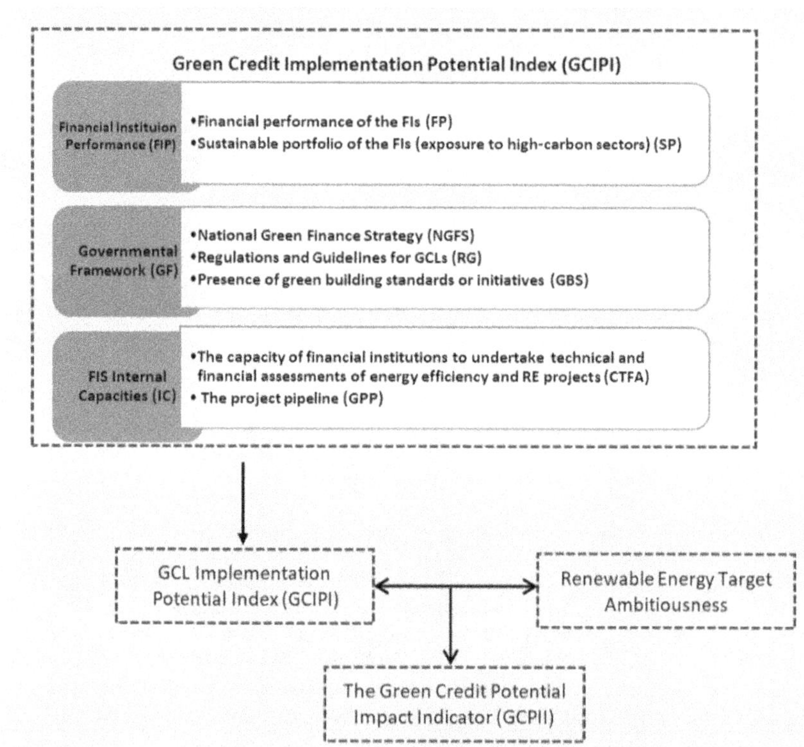

Source: Authors' own analysis.

Figure 7.2 *Conceptual framework for evaluating the GCL potential in GCC and impact on energy transition*

Impact of GCL, the framework incorporates an additional concept: *"RE Target Ambitiousness"*. This factor, independent of the GCL Potential index, represents a country's level of ambition for increasing its contribution from RE sources. A more ambitious target suggests a stronger commitment to RE, potentially leading to a higher GCL Potential Impact Indicator (GCLPII) score.

7.3.1.1 GCL Implementation Potential Index (GCLIPI)

The GCIPI assesses the potential of a country to successfully implement green credit programs based on its existing financial and regulatory infrastructure.

To assess the potential of GCLs in Qatar, the UAE, and the KSA, a comparative analysis using the GCL Implementation Potential Index (GCLIPI) is proposed. This index utilizes the publicly available information. Table 7.4 illustrates the GCLIPI factors, sub-indices, measurements, and data sources.

The index will be a composite score (0–100) derived from the weight of the three factors (Box 7.1):

1. Financial Institution Performance (30%)
2. Governmental Frameworks (40%)
3. Internal Capacities (30%).

BOX 7.1 CONCEPTUAL STRUCTURE OF THE GCL IMPLEMENTATION POTENTIAL INDEX (GCLIPI)

1. *The performance of the FIs (30%)*: Assesses the degree to which FIs are prepared to meet the Credit Line criteria. This factor is weighted at 30% and includes the following sub-indices:
   - *Financial Performance of the FIs – 50%*: this is measured by the "credit rating" of the FIs. Credit rating indicates the institution's ability to meet its financial obligations and reflects the overall financial health and stability of the institution. It is a critical factor in ensuring the trustworthiness and reliability of financial operations.
   - *Sustainability Portfolio – 50%*: refers to the efforts made to reduce exposure to high-carbon sectors. This involves assessing how banks contribute to or mitigate climate change, particularly through their financing decisions. One key metric for this is the ratio of loans to carbon-intensive sectors relative to total loans.
2. *Governmental Frameworks (40%)*: this component evaluates the broader policy and regulatory context that supports green finance. This factor is weighted at 40% and includes the following sub-indices:

- *National Green Finance Strategy – 33%*: measured by the presence of relevant information in published materials.
- *Regulations for GCLs – Reporting – 33%*: similar to the national strategy, this is assessed by evaluating the presence of relevant information in published materials.
- *Presence of Green Building Standards or Initiatives – 33%*: the assessment is based on the presence of relevant information in published materials.

3. *Internal Capacities (30%)*: this component focuses on the specific capabilities and activities related to specific GCL programs. This factor is weighted at 30% and includes the following sub-indices:
   - *Capacity of FIs to Undertake Technical and Financial Assessments of Energy Efficiency and RE Projects – 50%*: measured by examining the conduction of sustainable finance training programs.
   - *Green Projects Pipeline – 50%*: assessed by evaluating the presence of relevant information in published materials.

Source: Prepared by the authors.

The rationale for assigning these weights is grounded in the recognition of the fundamental importance of the governmental frameworks in ensuring the success and sustainability of the GCLs.[6] Even if the performance and the internal capacities of the FIs fully met, the absence of supportive governmental frameworks would significantly hinder the effectiveness of the GCLs. Given these insights, the governmental frameworks are prioritized with a 40% weight to reflect their critical role in supporting the GCLs' success. The comprehensive assessment of the *national green finance strategy, GCL regulatory and guidelines*, and *green building standards* ensures that the foundational conditions necessary for the GCL are in place. The FIs' performance is essential for defining the specific eligibility criteria for the FIs, focusing on the *financial performance* of the FIs and the commitment to the *sustainability (exposure to high-carbon sectors)*. Internal capacities focus on the specific design and implementation aspects of the GCL. This includes the *green finance expertise*, the availability of the *green projects pipeline*, among others. The sub-indices for each factor are illustrated in with relative importance percentage (out of 100%). A pre-defined scoring system (e.g., 0 for no evidence, 1 for limited evidence, 2 for moderate evidence, 3 for strong evidence) will be applied to each sub-index. Scores for each factor will be calculated and multiplied by their respective weights. The final GCLIPI score for each country will be the sum of the weighted factors' scores. The GCLIPI scores will serve as a starting point for assessing the potential impact on the energy transition. Figures, 7.3, 7.4, and 7.5 show the scale definitions, the model equations, and the benchmark matrix respectively.

Table 7.4 Scale definition for GCL Implementation Potential Index (GCLIPI): criteria and sub-indicators

Factors	Sub-indices	Abbreviation	Scale definition-No	Scale definition-Low	Scale definition-Moderate	Scla definition-High
Financial Institution Performance	Financial performance of the FIs	FP	D and SD (in default)	Low: ranging from CCC+, CCC, CCC–, CC, C	Med: ranging from BBB+, BBB, BBB–, BB+, BB, BB–, B+, B, B–	High: ranging from AAA, AA+, AA, AA–, A+, A, A–
Financial Institution Performance	Sustainable portfolio of the FIs (exposure to high-carbon sectors)	SP	No significant efforts to reduce exposure to high-carbon sectors	Some initial efforts towards sustainability, and minor reductions in high-carbon investments	Substantial commitment to sustainability, and moderate reductions in exposure to high-carbon sectors	Leader in sustainability, with aggressive targets and substantial reductions in high-carbon sector exposure
Governmental Frameworks	National Green Finance Strategy	NGFS	No evidence of a National Green Finance Strategy in publicly available data or reports	Indirect mention of a National Green Finance Strategy in publicly available data or reports, but no comprehensive details or dedicated strategy documents	Some documentation or references to a National Green Finance Strategy, possibly including high-level goals or intentions, but lacks detailed implementation plans or strategies	Clear evidence of a National Green Finance Strategy with documented goals, strategies, and initial implementation plans available in publicly published reports

Factors	Sub-indices	Abbreviation	Scale definition-No	Scale definition-Low	Scale definition-Moderate	Scla definition-High
Governmental Frameworks	Regulations and Guidelines for GCLs –Reporting	RG	No evidence of specific regulations or guidelines for Green Credit Lines (GCL) in publicly available data or reports	Direct mention of regulations or guidelines for Green Credit Lines (GCL), but no comprehensive details or dedicated regulatory framework	Some documentation or references to regulations or guidelines for Green Credit Lines (GCL), possibly including broad principles or intentions, but lacks detailed implementation guidelines or regulatory frameworks	Clear evidence of specific regulations or guidelines for Green Credit Lines (GCL), with documented criteria, eligibility requirements, and implementation guidelines available in publicly published reports
Governmental Frameworks	Presence of green building standards or initiatives	GBS	No evidence or acknowledgment of specific green building standards or initiatives in publicly available data or reports	Minimal or indirect mention of green building standards or initiatives, but no comprehensive details or dedicated framework	Some documentation or references to green building standards or initiatives, possibly including initial guidelines or principles, but lacks widespread adoption or comprehensive implementation	Clear evidence of specific green building standards or initiatives with documented criteria, certification processes, and adoption by stakeholders available in publicly published reports

Factors	Sub-indices	Abbreviation	Scale definition-No	Scale definition-Low	Scale definition-Moderate	Scla definition-High
Internal Capacities	The capacity of financial institutions to undertake technical and financial assessments of energy efficiency and RE project	CTFA	No evidence or acknowledgment of specific Sustainable Finance training programs or capacity building initiatives related to energy efficiency or renewable energy projects in publicly available data or reports	Indirect mention of Sustainable Finance training programs, but no comprehensive details or dedicated framework for energy efficiency or renewable energy projects	Some documentation or references to Sustainable Finance training programs, possibly including basic training or awareness sessions, but lacks comprehensive coverage of technical and financial assessments	Clear evidence of specific Sustainable Finance training programs with documented curriculum, training modules on technical and financial assessments for energy efficiency and renewable energy projects
Internal Capacities	The green project pipeline	GPP	No evidence or acknowledgment of a specific green project pipeline or renewable energy targets in publicly available data or reports	Indirect mention of green project pipeline or renewable energy targets, but no comprehensive details or dedicated framework for identifying and developing green project	Some documentation or references to green project pipeline or renewable energy targets, possibly including preliminary listings or intentions, but lacks a structured and detailed pipeline management system	Clear evidence of a specific green project pipeline with documented projects aligned with renewable energy targets, stages of development, and potential financing needs available in publicly published reports

Source: Prepared by the authors.

	1		**2**		**3**	
Factors	**Financial Institution Performance (30%)**	**Measurement**	**Governmental Frameworks (40%)**	**Measurement**	**Internal Capacities (30%)**	**Measurement**
Weighted sub-indices	Financial performance of the FIs (50%)	Measured by the credit rating	National Green Finance Strategy (33%)	Assessed by evaluating the presence of relevant information in published materials	The capacity of FIs to undertake technical and financial assessments of energy efficiency and RE project 50%)	Measured by examining the conduction of the Sustainable finance training program
	Sustainable portfolio of the FIs (exposure to high-carbon sectors) (50%)	Measured by the efforts to reduce exposure to high-carbon sectors (loans to carbon intensive sectors/ total loans)	Regulations for GCLs (33%)	Assessed by evaluating the presence of relevant information in published materials	The green projects pipeline (50%)	Assessed by evaluating the presence of relevant information in published materials
			Presence of green building standards or initiatives (33%)	Assessed by evaluating the presence of relevant information in published materials		
Date Sources	FIs websites, annual reports industry reports, central bank reports		Regulatory body websites, government policy documents		Government policy documents, national plans and related publications	
References	World Bank's Financial Intermediary Funds (FIFs) Framework, https://www.worldbank.org/en/programs/financial-intermediary-funds		WB, 2023, ADB, 2023, WB, Financing Energy Efficiency, Part 2: Credit Lines, 2018		Derived from a review of various established GCL programs	

Source: Prepared by the authors.

Figure 7.3 GCL Potential Index, factors, sub-indices, measurements and data sources

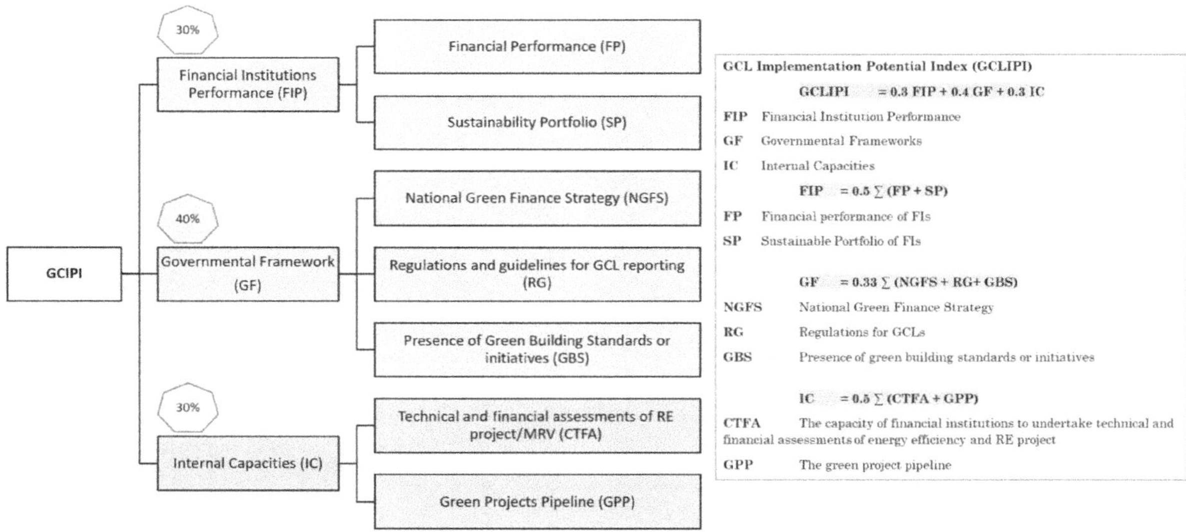

Source: Prepared by the authors.

Figure 7.4 Breakdown of the factors that compose the Green Credit Implementation Potential Index (GCLIPI)

Green Credit Potential Impact (GCPII)		Green Credit Implementation Potential Index (GCIPI)			
		0	1	2	3
Renewable Energy Target Ambitiousness (RETA)	1	0.5	1	1.5	2
	2	1	1.5	2	2.5
	3	1.5	2	2.5	3

GCPII Score	Category	Expected Impact of Green Credit Lines	Description
	No Impact	No expected positive impact on renewable energy adoption or transition	The country has low GCIPI and unambitious renewable energy targets, making green credit lines unlikely to significantly accelerate the energy transition
	Limited Impact	Potential for marginal improvements in renewable energy adoption, but significant barriers remain	The country has moderate GCIPI and/or limited renewable energy targets, suggesting that green credit lines might have a positive but constrained impact due to regulatory, financial, or technological limitations
	Moderate Impact	Green credit lines are likely to contribute to a noticeable acceleration of renewable energy adoption and a gradual energy transition	The country has good GCIPI and ambitious renewable energy targets, indicating a favorable environment for green credit lines to effectively support the transition to cleaner energy sources
	High Impact	Green credit lines are expected to play a crucial role in rapid renewable energy adoption and a transformative energy transition	The country has excellent GCIPI and highly ambitious renewable energy targets, creating a strong foundation for green credit lines to significantly catalyze the development and deployment of renewable energy technologies

Source: Prepared by the authors.

Figure 7.5 Benchmark matrix for the Green Credit Line Potential Impact Indicator (GCLPII)

GCLPII measures the expected influence of implementing green credit lines (GCL) by financial institutions (FIs) within a country on advancing energy transition goals.

As mentioned above, this indicator utilizes two factors namely; (1) the GCLIPI, and (2) the RE target ambitiousness which measures the level of ambition of a country's RE targets (see explanatory note 2). Data sources include government RE plans and international reports tracking RE targets. The RE target ambitiousness is scored based on a pre-defined scale (e.g., highly ambitious, moderate, ambitious with challenges; see Box 7.2) reflecting the target's level of ambition compared to current energy production. The indicator is calculated as a simple average of the GCLIPI score and the RE target ambitiousness score (after converting it to a numerical value) (see Figure 7.5).

BOX 7.2 SCALE DEFINITION FOR GCL POTENTIAL IMPACT INDICATOR (GCPII)

Highly Ambitious (3 Points)

The country has a target for RE exceeding a certain percentage of total energy generation by a specific year (e.g., 50% RE by 2040). This target should also be considered ambitious compared to the region's average or the country's current energy production level with suitable timeframe.

Moderate (2 Points)

The country has a RE target but it might be less ambitious than the "High" category (e.g., 30% RE by 2050). Targets with long timelines or unclear definitions might also fall into this category.

Ambitious with Challenges (1 Point)

The country has an ambitious target for high RE use, but significant efforts are required and challenges need to be addressed.

Source: Prepared by the authors.

7.4 ANALYSIS AND DISCUSSION

7.4.1 GCL Implementation Potential Index (GCLIPI)

This chapter has aimed to assess the GCL potential of Qatar compared to the UAE and the KSA by developing a GCL Implementation Potential Index. According to the first national survey on contributions of the FIs to the Green Economy,[7] the UAE appears to be the only country among the three with existing GCL within their green finance offerings. This suggests a potential head start for the UAE in terms of GCL implementation. Regarding the degree to which the financial system within the three countries is prepared to establish the GCL, which is measured by the financial performance, and the sustainable portfolio of FIs, Qatar and the UAE scored highest in this sub-indicator, indicating both the health of the FIs and higher commitment by the FIs to sustainability and energy transition. Regarding the governmental frameworks in the three countries, the analysis revealed that while each country has implemented supportive policies and taken steps towards green finance, the KSA demonstrated a more developed and comprehensive green financing framework. Qatar and the UAE could benefit from exploring similar initiatives to enhance their GCL potential. For the internal capacities (measured by the green finance expertise, green projects pipeline), while all three countries showed similar results regarding the green projects pipeline, the UAE demonstrates a documented effort regarding the sustainable finance training. Based on the factors analyzed, the UAE appears to be the most prepared for GCL establishment by the FIs and deployment. The KSA shows promise with a focus on building enabling governmental frameworks. While Qatar is possessing a strong financial sector, limitations in the enabling environment criteria hinder its immediate GCL readiness.

7.4.2 GCL Potential Impact Indicator (GCPII)

The RE target ambitiousness is assessed through reviewing the RE target for the three countries within the specified timeframe (Table 7.5). Qatar's RE target stands out as highly ambitious, aiming for a significant increase in the share of RE in the power mix by 2030 (from 5% to 18%) as documented in Qatar National RE strategy (Qatar National Renewable Energy Strategy, 2024). By facilitating access to financing for green projects, GCLs can play a crucial role in enabling Qatar to achieve its ambitious RE targets. Many studies demonstrate how GCLs can accelerate clean energy development by providing tailored financing solutions for RE projects (Brown & Jacobs, 2011).

Table 7.5 *RE target ambitiousness*

Country	RE target ambitiousness	Note	References
Qatar	National RE Strategy aiming to increase the RE contribution from 5% to 18% by 2030	A significant increase in RE contribution within a defined timeframe (2030) indicates a highly ambitious target	Qatar National RE Strategy, May 2024; REN21 Renewables Global Status Report 2023
UAE	The 50% target by 2050 represents a long-term vision but is still ambitious compared to the region's average	The 50% target by 2050 represents a long-term vision but is still ambitious compared to the region's average	UAE Net Zero by 2050 Strategic Initiative; IEA World Energy Outlook 2023
KSA	Saudi Arabia's Vision 2030 targets 50% of its electricity generation from RE sources by 2030	The 50% target by 2050 represents a long-term vision but is still ambitious compared to the region's average	Saudi Arabia Vision 2030; IEA Executive Director statement

Source: Authors' own analysis based on published documents and national plans.

For the KSA, the RE target is ambitious within the specified timeframe, however, there are many challenges that the KSA might encounter and thus the transition requires more effort. The result reveals that the KSA may witness high impact from establishing the GCL by the FIs given its GCL potential and RE target. Hence, the GCL potential impact indicator is the highest for the KSA given the challenging target of RE, the GCL might act as a catalyzer for enabling such transition. While the UAE demonstrates strong green finance initiatives, the relatively longer timeframe for RE targets reduces the potential impact of GCLs in accelerating the transition.

To sum up, the chapter compared the GCL potential of Qatar, the UAE, and the KSA. While the UAE has currently limited GCL products, the KSA possesses the strongest readiness of the financial sector. All three countries share similar green projects pipelines and ambitious RE targets, with Qatar having a particularly recenntly set high target. Analyzing GCL potential alongside RE target ambition, the chapter suggests the KSA has the highest GCL potential impact on energy transition. Qatar also shows promise due to its RE target, while the UAE's more moderate RE target leads to a relatively lower impact of GCLs. Overall, GCLs hold promise for the GCC, but each country needs to address its limitations to unlock the full potential of GCLs (see Figures 7.6a, 7.6b, 7.6c and Table 7.6).

Qatar	Sub-index weight	Score	Weighted scores	References
Financial Institutions Performance - country scale (FIP)	30%			(1, 2)
Financial Performance of the FIs	0.5	3	1.5	(1) Credit rating, S&P Global Ratings 2022
Sustainable Portfolio of FIs	0.5	2	1	(2) Loans to carbon intensive sectors/total loans, banks — Gulf Cooperation Council: 2022 Outlook
Sub-index score			**2.5**	
Weighted sub-index score			**0.75**	
Governmental Frameworks (GF)	40%			(3, 4,)
National Green Finance Strategy	0.33	1	0.33	(3) Qatar Central Bank's Plan (2017–2022) with intention to implement strategic actions on green finance
Regulations for GCL	0.33	0	0	No regulations found yet
Presence of green building standards or initiatives	0.33	3	0.99	(5) Qatar has 1,406 sustainability certified buildings, according to the Ministry of Environment and Climate Change
Sub-index score			**1.32**	
Weighted sub-index score			**0.528**	
Internal Capacities (IC)	30%			(5, 6, 7)
The capacity of financial institutions to undertake technical and financial assessments of energy efficiency and RE project	0.5	0	0	(5) Opportunities for the GCC to strengthen the sustainable finance ecosystem, PwC research adapted from the Atlantic Council, 2022 Official public resources, 2023 https://www.strategyand.pwc.com/m1/en/strategic-foresight/sector-strategies/financial-services/middle-east-green-finance/middle-east-green-finance.pdf
The Project Pipeline	0.5	2	1	(6) Qatar National Vision 2030 - Renewable Energy Goals
Sub-index score			**1**	
Weighted sub-index score			**0.3**	
Total GCL Implementation Potential Index	**1.578**			

Source: Authors' own analysis.

Figure 7.6a The results of scoring the sub-indices of the GCLIPI and references: Qatar

UAE	Sub-index weight	Score	Weighted scores	References
Financial Institutions Performance - country scale (FIP)	30%			(1, 2)
Financial Performance of the FIs	0.5	3	1.5	(1) Liquid assets/assets (%), S&P Global Ratings, 2022
Sustainable Portfolio of FIs	0.5	2	1	(2) Loans to carbon intensive sectors/total loans, banks — Gulf Cooperation Council: 2022 Outlook
Sub-index score			2.5	
Weighted sub-index score			0.75	
Governmental Frameworks (GF)	40%			(8, 9)
National Green Finance Strategy	0.33	2	0.66	(8) UAE Sustainable Finance Framework 2021–2031
Regulations for GCLs -Reporting	0.33	0	0	No regulation found yet
Presence of green building standards or initiatives	0.33	3	0.99	(9) Estidama Green Building Rating System (UAE)
Sub-index score			1.65	
Weighted sub-index score			0.66	
Internal Capacities (IC)	30%			(5, 10, 11)
The capacity of financial institutions to undertake technical and financial assessments of energy efficiency and RE project	0.5	1	0.5	(5) Opportunities for the GCC to strengthen the sustainable finance ecosystem, PwC research adapted from the Atlantic Council, 2022 Official public resources, 2023 https://www.strategyand.pwc.com/m1/en/strategic-foresight/sector-strategies/financial-services/middle-east-green-finance/middle-east-green-finance.pdf
The Project Pipeline	0.5	2	1	(10) Emirates NBD Green Financing Initiatives, UAE Energy Strategy 2050, Dubai Green Fund
Sub-index score			**1.5**	
Weighted sub-index score			**0.45**	
Total GCL Potential Index	**1.86**			

Source: Authors' own analysis.

Figure 7.6b The results of scoring the sub-indices of the GCLIPI and references: UAE

KSA	Sub-index weight	Score	Weighted scores	References
Financial Institutions Performance - country scale (FIP)	30%			(1, 2)
Financial Performance of the FIs (efficiency)	0.5	3	1.5	(1) Liquid assets/assets (%), S&P Global Ratings
Sustainable Portfolio of FIs	0.5	1	0.5	(2) Loans to carbon intensive sectors/total loans, banks — Gulf Cooperation Council: 2022 Outlook
Sub-index score			**2**	
Weighted sub-index score			**0.6**	
Governmental Frameworks (GF)	40%			(12, 13)
National Green Finance Strategy	0.33	3	0.99	(12) Green Financing Framework March 2024, https://ndmc.gov.sa/investorsrelations/Documents/Green-Financing-Framework-KSA-28March2024.pdf
Regulations for GCL	0.33	0	0	No regulation found yet
Presence of green building standards or initiatives	0.33	3	0.99	(13) MOSTADAM Certificate
Sub-index score			**1.98**	
Weighted sub-index score			**0.792**	
Internal Capacities (IC)	30%			(5, 14, 15)
The capacity of financial institutions to undertake technical and financial assessments of energy efficiency and RE project	0.5	0	0	Opportunities for the GCC to strengthen the sustainable finance ecosystem, PwC research adapted from the Atlantic Council, 2022. Official public resources, 2023 https://www.strategyand.pwc.com/m1/en/strategic-foresight/sector-strategies/financial-services/middle-east-green-finance/middle-east-green-finance.pdf
The Project Pipeline	0.5	2	1	(14) Green Financing Framework March 2024 and Giga projects
Sub-index score			**1**	
Weighted sub-index score			**0.3**	
Total GCL Implementation Potential Index	**1.692**			

Source: Authors' own analysis.

Figure 7.6c The results of scoring the sub-indices of the GCLIPI and references: KSA

As shown in Table 7.6, the three countries have good GCIPI and ambitious renewable energy targets, indicating a favorable environment for green credit lines to effectively support the transition to cleaner energy sources.

Table 7.6 The results of scoring the factors of the GCL Potential Impact Indicator

RE target ambitiousness	Score
National RE Strategy aiming to increase the RE contribution from 5% to 18% by 2030	3 – High
GCLIPI	1.58
GCL Potential Impact Indicator	2.29
The 50% target by 2050 represents a long-term vision but is still ambitious compared to the region's average	2.5 – Medium
GCLIPI	1.86
GCL Potential Impact Indicator	2.18
Saudi Arabia's Vision 2030 targets 50% of its electricity generation from RE sources by 2030	3 – High
GCLIPI	1.69
GCL Potential Impact Indicator	2.35

Source: Authors' own analysis.

7.5 CONCLUDING COMMENTS

This chapter adopted a qualitative conceptual framework to assess GCLs' potential in Qatar and the wider GCC region. It begins with a literature review that defined and explored the enablers, opportunities, and challenges associated with the potential and impact of GCLs. Building upon this foundation, the chapter presented a methodology to assess both the GCL establishment potential and the impact on achieving Qatar's energy transition goals compared with two GCC countries, namely, the UAE and the KSA. This methodology involved examining publicly published and historical data to evaluate the progress of GCL establishment and sustainable finance frameworks.

To comprehensively measure GCL potential and impact, the chapter utilizes two metrics: the GCL Implementation Potential Index and the GCL Potential Impact Indicator. The chapter identified the GCL potential across all three Gulf nations. While Qatar possesses a strong financial sector, limitations in its governmental frameworks hinder its immediate GCL readiness. However, Qatar's highly ambitious RE target, aiming for a significant increase in the share of RE in the power mix, necessitates innovative financing solutions like GCLs. The UAE emerged as the country with the strongest overall GCL potential based on the GCL Implementation Potential Index. This suggests a head start for the UAE in terms of practical GCL experience. This is attributed to its robust financial sector and the existence of current GCL products. The KSA demonstrated a more developed and comprehensive green financing framework. All three countries share ambitious RE targets and similar green project pipelines, highlighting a strong commitment to clean energy development.

7.5.1 Policy Recommendations

This chapter emphasizes the need for Qatar to prioritize the development of a comprehensive green financing and investment framework. Such a framework can address the limitations identified by the GCL Implementation Potential Index within the country's enabling environment. A well-designed framework should aim to enhance the competitiveness of green investments compared to traditional brown alternatives. The main objective is to reduce perceived high risks associated with the energy transition projects from the investor point of view. This will increase the investor base for this type of project which, in turn, will have a positive effect on the green projects pipelines. Furthermore, sufficient financial regulations will address the uncertainty and risk aversion among potential investors.

In addition to the overall finance and investment framework, Qatar can introduce policies that incentivize or require potential borrowers to participate in training programs on green project development and financing. These programs, potentially co-developed with the Qatari Central Bank and FIs, should equip borrowers with the necessary skills to develop technically sound and bankable green projects. This also will accelerate the increase in the investor base and green projects pipeline.

7.5.2 Financial Sector Recommendations

Qatar and the GCC region in general need to focus on capacity building within the banking sector; the FIs should prioritize building capacity within thorough targeted training programs. These programs should focus on equipping the finance-oriented team (bank staff) with the necessary expertise to assess green projects. Training should cover the technical, economic and financial, and socio-environmental attributes of the green loan and the underlying project. Bank staff must be proficient in technical terminologies such as energy efficiency measures, greenhouse gas emissions, CO_2 savings, efficiency factors, and baseline energy sources. A deep understanding of these concepts will aid in client acquisition, product promotion, and effectively communicating the benefits of GCL. Additionally, to enhance the promotion of green loans and their benefits to the borrowers (investors), bank officers should possess both theoretical and practical knowledge of common green measures, including energy efficiency and RE solutions enabling them to confidently discuss these topics during introductory or basic conversations with potential clients.

By addressing the identified limitations and implementing the recommended actions, Qatar can unlock the full potential of GCLs and significantly accelerate its transition towards a sustainable economy. GCLs can play a pivotal role in mobilizing financial resources towards RE projects, contributing meaningfully to achieving Qatar's ambitious climate change mitigation goals. Further research exploring the specific details of potential GCL programs and tracking the effectiveness of GCLs in promoting green investments would provide valuable insights for ongoing development and refinement of GCL implementation strategies in Qatar. Moreover, adopting clear taxonomies such as the GLP will help in differentiating between green and brown projects, ensuring the credibility and effectiveness of green credit lines. By realizing these recommendations, Qatar can bridge the gap with its competitors and leverage GCLs to achieve its ambitious clean energy goals.

NOTES

1. This chapter is based on outcomes from Workshop No. 4 of the Gulf Research Meeting (GRM) 2024, organized by the Gulf Research Center (GRC).
2. Qatar's baseline scenario is a projection of future GHG emissions assuming no additional mitigation measures are implemented beyond those already planned before the NDC submission. The 25% reduction target is measured against this projected emissions trajectory.
3. The ND-GAIN Country Indicator summarizes a country's vulnerability to: (1) climate change and other global challenges in combination with its readiness; (2) improve resilience.
4. A green lending market refers to the financial ecosystem specifically targeting environmentally sustainable projects, which includes products and services like green loans or bonds. It aims to channel funds into renewable energy, energy efficiency, and other green initiatives. By offering GCLs, local financial institutions can develop expertise in green financing and expand the market for environmental projects by providing specialized financial products (Shishlov et al., 2017).
5. Namely, Egyptian Pollution Abatement Project II, IFC's Commercializing Sustainable Energy Finance Program (CSEF) in Turkey – Credit line for leasing to three Turkish leasing companies, EBRD Green Economy Finance Facility Serbia – green credit line to UniCredit Bank Serbia.

6. According to the OECD, a clear national strategy for green finance is critical for mobilizing investments and ensuring that financial markets support sustainable development goals. The International Monetary Fund (IMF) emphasizes the importance of regulatory frameworks in ensuring financial stability and transparency, which are crucial for the success of financial instruments like GCLs (IMF, 2023). The World Bank highlights that the adoption of green building standards is a key indicator of a country's commitment to sustainable development and can drive significant environmental benefits (World Bank, 2023).
7. UAE Green Agenda 2015–2030 State of Green Finance in the UAE. The first national survey on contributions of financial institutions to the Green Economy.

REFERENCES

Almulla, Yousef, and Mark Howells. (2014). *Gulf Cooperation Council (GCC) Countries 2040 Energy Scenario for Electricity Generation and Water Desalination*. Master of Science Thesis, KTH Industrial and Engineering Management.

Al-Noaimi, Fatima, Tareq Al-Ansari, and Yusuf Bicer. (2023). "Toward a Long-Term Low Emission Development Strategy: The Case of Energy Transition in Qatar." *Global Challenges* 7(3): 2200229.

Al-Sarihi, Aisha. (2021). *Climate Action in the GCC: Current Status and Future Prospects*. JIME-IEEJ International Symposium, The Institute of Energy Economics, Japan.

Asian Development Bank (ADB). (2023). *Climate Change Action Plan, 2023–2030*. Manila: Asian Development Bank.

Aravamuthan, Vijay, Miguel Ruete, and Andres Dominguez. (2015). "Enhancing Private Sector Investment in Green Growth and Climate Change Resilience." Working Paper, Inter-American Development Bank.

Battiston, Stefano, Irene Monasterolo, Keywan Riahi, and Bas J. van Ruijven. (2021). "Accounting for Finance is Key for Climate Mitigation Pathways." *Science* 372(6545): 918–920.

Brown, Jessica, and Michael Jacobs. (2011). "Leveraging Private Investment: The Role of Public Sector Climate Finance." Overseas Development Institute.

Climate Bonds Initiative. (2020). *Green Bond Principles and Standards*. Available at: Climate Bonds Initiative https://www.climatebonds.net/our-expertise/climate-bonds-standard-and-certification-scheme/sector-criteria/electrical-utilities.

Corfee-Morlot, Jan, Valérie Marchal, Céline Kauffmann, Christopher Kennedy, Fiona Stewart, Christopher Kaminker, and Graeme Ang. (2012). "Towards a Green Investment Policy Framework: The Case of Low-Carbon, Climate-Resilient Infrastructure." OECD Environment Working Papers.

Enclude Limited. (2016). "*Enhancing Private Sector Investment in Green Growth and Climate Change Resilience*." Amsterdam: Enclude Limited.

Engineering Net Zero. (2022). *Gulf Cooperation Council Report*. Regional Energy Transition Report. London. https://www.atkinsrealis.com/en/media/download-center/report/engineering-net-zero-gcc-report

European Commission. (2020). *EU Taxonomy for Sustainable Activities*. https://finance.ec.europa.eu/sustainable-finance/tools-and-standards/eu-taxonomy-sustainable-activities_en

General Electric. (2021). *Pathways to Faster Decarbonization in the GCC's Power Sector: Accelerating the Energy Transition with a Combination of Renewables and Gas Power.* General Electric. https://www.ge.com/news/press-releases/ge-white-paper-highlights-pathways-to-faster-decarbonization-in-the-gccs-power

GFANZ. (2021). The Glasgow Financial Alliance for Net Zero. https://www.gfanzero.com/

Global Environment Facility. (2017). Introduction to green finance [Brochure]. https://documents1.worldbank.org/curated/en/405891487108066678/pdf/112831-WP-PUBLIC-Introduction-to-Green-Finance.pdf

International Energy Agency. (2023). Fossil fuels consumption subsidies 2022. IEA, Paris. https://www.iea.org/reports/fossil-fuels-consumption-subsidies-2022

International Energy Agency (IEA). (2021). *Energy Efficiency 2021.* https://www.iea.org/reports/energy-efficiency-2021

Lawrence Berkeley National Laboratory (LBNL). (2022). *The Future of Air Conditioning for Buildings.* https://eta-publications.lbl.gov/sites/default/files/future_of_efficiency_report_20220621.pdf

International Monetary Fund. (2023). *Gulf Cooperation Council Economic Prospects and Policy Priorities for the GCC Countries.* https://www.imf.org/en/publications/cr/issues/2023/12/14/gulf-cooperation-council-economic-prospects-and-policy-challenges-for-the-gcc-countries-542513

Loan Market Association (LMA). (2025). *Green Loan Principles.* Available at: LMA Green Loan Principles. https://www.lsta.org/content/green-loan-principles/

Organisation for Economic Co-operation and Development (OECD). (2016). "Climate Finance in 201–2014 and the USD 100 Billion Goal: A Report by the OECD in Collaboration with Climate Policy Initiative." OECD.

Organisation for Economic Co-operation and Development (OECD). (2020). *Green Financing: Challenges and Opportunities in Emerging Markets.* OECD.

State of Qatar, Ministry of Energy. (2024, May). *Qatar National Renewable Energy Strategy.* https://km.qa/RenewableEnergy/Documents/QNRES_Strategy_EN.pdf

Sakhrieh, Ahmad. (2016). "Energy Analysis for GCC Countries." In *Global Conference on Renewables and Energy Efficiency for Desert Regions*, 1–4. https://aurak.ac.ae/publications/Energy-Analysis-for-GCC-Countries.pdf

Shishlov, Igor, Tina Bajohr, Mariia Deheza, and Ian Cochran. (2017). *Using Credit Lines to Foster Green Lending: Opportunities and Challenges.* Paris: Institute for Climate Economics. https://www.i4ce.org/download/using-credit-lines-to-foster-green-lending-opportunities-and-challenges/

Smith, J., Mugnier, C., Shishlov, I., and Cochran, I. (2020). "Unlocking the Potential of Green Credit Lines: Lessons from Emerging Markets." *Journal of Sustainable Finance & Investment* 10(3): 257–273.

United Nations Environment Program (UNEP). (2019). *Global Trends in Renewable Energy Investment 2019.* https://www.unep.org/resources/report/global-trends-renewable-energy-investment-2019

United Nations Environment Program (UNEP) Finance Initiative. (2015). *The Principles for Positive Impact Finance: A Common Framework to Finance the Sustainable Development Goals.* UNEP Finance Initiative.

University of Notre Dame Global Adaptation Initiative. (2023). ND_GAIN Country Index. University of Notre Dame. https://gain.nd.edu/our-work/country-index/

Wogan, David, Shonali Pradhan, and Salman Albardi. (2017). *GCC Energy System Overview – 2017.* Riyadh: King Abdullah Petroleum Studies and Research Center.

World Bank. (2020). *Air Conditioning and Energy Demand in Hot Climates.* Washington, DC: World Bank.

World Bank. (2021). *World Development Report 2021: Data for Better Lives.* Washington, DC: World Bank.

World Bank (2023). *FY23 World Bank Climate-Related Financial Disclosures.* Washington, DC: World Bank.

8. Beyond rentierism: economic diversification, nation branding and public diplomacy in the United Arab Emirates

Omar Bortolazzi

8.1 INTRODUCTION

Over the past decade, the United Arab Emirates has become increasingly prominent, playing a major role in regional developments and at the international level. For many years the United Arab Emirates (UAE) systematically developed its military and security capabilities, positioning itself strategically to actively shape its own domestic as well as regional interests. Much academic attention has been focusing on the UAE's development of powerful surveillance and security capabilities in recent years. The surveillance and military dimensions can certainly be used to protect the nation from external or regional threats, but also for domestic purposes to maintain internal stability. However, this chapter argues that security and surveillance are one application of coercive measures; the United Arab Emirates is actively pursuing enduring strategies designed to cultivate narratives in harmony with the imperatives of its regime. Reprising from the theoretical analyses produced by Buzan which identifies five dimensions of security: political, military, economic, social, and environmental (Buzan, 1991a; Buzan et al., 1998)—this research aims to investigate the economic and diplomatic initiatives undertaken in recent years to support the UAE's economic diversification plans. In the last decade, the UAE has implemented a broad range of strategies to shift itself from an oil-reliant nation to elevate itself into an international brand. Economic diversification (private sector, real estate, construction, retail), tourism, and neoliberal policies made the UAE transition from natural resource extraction nation to post-industrial service economy. In turn, these post-rentier programs helped the leadership to maintain the stability of the governing system and the state over the need to implement participatory mechanisms. The country's economic diversification and distributive policies have ensured that the majority of the population has benefited from the growth of the country. This phenomenon has engendered a ubiquitous degree of endorsement for the adoption of a market-driven economic system, fostering additional economic expansion and diversification, and maintaining the *status quo*.

8.2 CONTEXT FOR ECONOMIC DIVERSIFICATION: RENTIER RESOURCES, HUMAN CAPITAL, AND DEVELOPMENT

The concept of "rent" (and "rentier," "rentierism") has deep historical roots in economics and political science, dating back to classical political economy, with theorists like Adam Smith[1] and David Ricardo.[2] Over time, the concept has evolved and been applied in various ways by different disciplines. In particular, political scientists and heterodox economists—such as those influenced by Marxist, institutionalist, or post-Keynesian thought—have developed distinct perspectives on rent and rentierism.

In classical economics, rent originally referred to the income derived from the ownership of land. David Ricardo, in his theory of differential rent, argued that landowners earn rent due to the scarcity of fertile land. Rent, in this context, was seen as unearned income, since it accrued not from productive activity but from the ownership of a naturally scarce resource. This concept was extended to other forms of unproductive income, including rents derived from monopolistic control over resources or assets.

As the field of political economy evolved, rent came to encompass a wider range of economic activities that generated income without direct productive contributions. This led to the modern understanding of "rentierism," where individuals or entities derive income from owning assets or resources rather than producing goods or services. In this context, "rentier income" refers to earnings from resources that are limited or monopolized, including land, natural resources, or capital assets.

In political science, rent and rentierism are closely associated with the analysis of state structures and their relationship with economic development. Political scientists who study rentier states focus on how governments derive income from external rents—primarily from natural resources like oil—and how this affects governance, social contracts, and state–society relations (Beblawi, 1987). The focus is less on the economic mechanics of rent and more on its implications for political stability, state legitimacy, and institutional development. For political scientists, the concept of rent is central to understanding how resource-rich states can maintain authoritarian regimes or weak democratic systems without relying on taxation. Rentier states, as described earlier, are often marked by their reliance on external rents rather than domestic economic activity, leading to a unique social contract where citizens are placated through state patronage rather than through democratic participation (Mahdavy, 1970). The rentier state model explains how resource wealth can create a passive populace, reduce the state's need for revenue from taxation, and undermine the development of accountable political institutions.

Heterodox economists, on the other hand, particularly those who challenge neoclassical economic theory, approach rent with a broader critique of capitalism. For them, rent is not just about unearned income from natural resources but also a broader category of income that arises from ownership or control over scarce assets, including intellectual property, capital, and even labor markets. They examine how rent-seeking behavior distorts markets, exacerbates inequality, and hinders productive investment. In heterodox economics, rentierism is often criticized for its role in fostering economic stagnation and inequality. Rent-seeking—attempts by individuals or corporations to increase their share of wealth without contributing to productivity—can lead to the concentration of wealth and the hollowing out of productive sectors of the economy. Authors such as Thorstein Veblen[3] and Joseph Schumpeter,[4] as well as more contemporary scholars, have discussed how rentier dynamics stifle innovation and reduce economic dynamism.

Brett Christophers in his book *Rentier Capitalism: Who Owns the Economy, and Who Pays for It?* (2020) provides a critical analysis of rentierism in contemporary capitalism. Christophers argues that the modern economy is increasingly dominated by rentiers—those who derive income from ownership and control of assets, rather than from productive activity. He broadens the concept of rentierism beyond natural resources, highlighting how rentier practices now permeate various sectors, including finance, real estate, infrastructure, and intellectual property. Christophers' key argument is that rentier capitalism, in which wealth is accumulated through the control of scarce assets, exacerbates inequality and redistributes income from the productive economy to asset owners. For instance, real estate investors or companies that hold patents are often able to extract significant rents without contributing to innovation or productivity growth. This aligns with the critiques posed by heterodox economists, who argue that rentierism distorts the economy by privileging asset owners over workers and innovators (Christophers, 2020). Christophers' analysis also reflects a broader trend in heterodox economics, where the focus is on how rentier practices contribute to systemic inequality. For example, the financialization of economies—where profits increasingly come from financial transactions rather than production—can be viewed as a form of rentierism. In this system, capitalists derive profits from the ownership of financial assets, contributing to the growing divide between capital and labor.

During the 1980s, political scientists developed a broad economic framework for understanding Middle Eastern states, centering on the concept of rent (Beblawi, 1987; Mahdavy, 1970). Rent, arising from the extraction and sale of natural resources, notably crude oil and gas reserves in the Middle East region, emerged as a pivotal source of wealth around which both the economic model and the governance structures of energy-rich nations were reconfigured. The unique case of the Gulf Cooperation Council (GCC) countries as rentier states has been central to this concept, given their possession of the largest share of global energy resources. Despite its capacity to generate substantial revenues for resource-endowed nations, the concept of rent has acquired a negative connotation, suggesting a dichotomy between an "allocative state" and a "productive state" (Ozyavuz and Schmid, 2015).[5] After four decades of this concept, it is evident that the historical, political, and economic dimension of the rentier state theory necessitates a comprehensive reevaluation and discussion.

In fact, there has been a growing debate about the applicability of the rentier state concept to the GCC countries. Some scholars argue that the concept may have become too general and imprecise to provide useful analytical insights. They suggest that the GCC countries have been able to diversify their economies and develop other sectors, challenging the notion that rentierism inevitably leads to economic stagnation (Springborg, 2013).[6] Furthermore, there is a recognition that the concept of rentier states needs to be revisited and revised in light of changing historical and political circumstances. The development of state institutions and the accumulation of fixed capital from oil rents have challenged the assumption that rents are consumables that cannot be accumulated into structural power (Springborg, 2013). Non-oil sectors are contributing to stabilizing the economies of the GCC and shaping future growth trajectories. While oil dependency causes fluctuations in growth rates, diversification (into non-oil sectors) is a key factor in creating stability and guiding future economic growth. Scholars have applied new institutionalist theories to analyze the political economies of rentier states (Elbadawi and Soto, 2012; North, 1994; Rodrik et al., 2022). This approach focuses on the role of institutions in shaping economic outcomes and emphasizes the importance of institutional development and governance in rentier states.

Since the 1970s, the United Arab Emirates and other nations in the Arabian Gulf have been developing policies and programs aimed to diversify their economic systems from being completely dependent on oil for growth and stability (Crystal, 1990; Davidson, 2009; Fasano and Zubair, 2003; Hvidt, 2013; Schilirò, 2013). Ewers argues that the Arabian Gulf countries have been reflecting the advice of economists who view over-reliance on one resource like oil as a "resource curse" (Ewers, 2016):[7] nations that are dependent on oil for revenues will produce negative economic outcomes that in the long term will not be sustainable. Therefore, a transition to a diversified economic model is desirable. In Ewers' analysis, the desirability of diversification is discussed in the context of the long-term negative outcomes of oil dependency. He highlights that Gulf states have made "concerted efforts to make the transition into less oil-dependent, and more diversified economies" (Ewers, 2016: 236). This transition is therefore desirable (1) for governments and elites: Diversification aims to address economic sustainability, particularly as oil revenues alone are insufficient to support future growth and the increasing demands of young and growing populations; Oil income is unreliable due to market volatility, and the Gulf countries are seeking to create competitive new economic sectors beyond oil; (2) for society (local populations): Diversification is necessary because oil economies have created labor market conditions, which rely heavily on expatriate labor, reduce incentives for local workforce development and human capital formation. Thus, diversification is desirable for the local population to create more inclusive economic opportunities that can be sustained beyond the oil era; (3) for future economic stability: the diversification of economic activities is critical to avoid the pitfalls of the "resource curse," where over-reliance on oil leads to poor long-term economic outcomes, which are not sustainable. Ewers points out that oil wealth has historically "crowded out human capital," which is essential for creating a diversified and sustainable economy (Ewers, 2016: 236).

According to the same author, even though a lot of investment has been made by Arab Gulf nations to diversify, they have not been very successful. "One reason, perhaps, is because oil abundance can crowd out human capital, a key requirement for economic development" (Ewers, 2016: 236). The measure of "success," in this context, appears to be tied to the creation of new, sustainable sources of economic growth; the development of local human capital; the reduction of labor market distortion; and, of course, economic diversification.

Nonetheless, there remains a notable dearth of knowledge concerning the dynamics of labor and human capital development within oil-based economies, and the extent to which they facilitate or impede the processes of diversification and structural transformation. In fact, the large amount of development from oil revenues taking place in the Gulf countries created numerous jobs and it attracted millions of migrant workers to their industries. During the first oil boom (1973–1986), the local labor forces were not able to meet the needs of the rapid modernization taking place in oil management, construction, technology, and other areas. As a result, expatriates came to constitute the predominant demographic in the workplace. The expertise provided by the expatriate labor force helped to achieve economic growth and development. Nevertheless, this phenomenon led to a deficiency in regional self-sufficiency for developing and maintaining a post-oil economic framework. Consequently, it fostered a substantial and enduring dependence on migrant labor. Of paramount importance is that the capacity to import foreign labor and expertise, coupled with the provision of well-remunerated public employment opportunities for the local populace, diminished the impetus for fostering indigenous, diversified human capital formation (Ewers, 2016: 237). Starting in the 1970s, the Gulf States have encountered a predicament characterized by an insufficient local population to support labor-intensive industrialization, but an abundance of capital to procure expertise in emerging sectors (Ewers, 2016: 237). During the same decade, Gulf States' goverments started to identify the most advantageous pathways for economic diversification, leading to different outcomes. Specifically, the United Arab Emirates (UAE) started formulating new strategies with the objective of transitioning from a pre-industrialized model centered on the extraction of natural resources to a post-industrial paradigm characterized by service-oriented and knowledge-based development (Ewers, 2016: 241). The UAE maintains its aspiration to draw in skilled foreign labor while simultaneously attempting to cultivate indigenous expertise in technology and knowledge domains to address the requisites of a post-industrial economic framework.

However, as emphasized by Gylfason (2001), human capital distinguishes itself from natural capital in that it possesses characteristics of being non-depletable.[8] Once acquired, it retains its relevance across a multitude of contexts and is inherently accessible (Gylfason, 2001). In order for a region to augment its reservoirs of human capital, it must enhance its educational and training infrastructures. These enhancements lead to heightened levels of labor productivity and foster technological knowledge acquisition, thus catalyzing the emergence of new avenues for competitive advantage. Numerous scholarly works underline the inverse correlation between the abundance of natural resources and the levels of investment and achievement in education (Gylfason, 2001; Stijns, 2006). One reason for this phenomenon lies in the fact that periods of resource booms often encourage a focus on short-term economic strategies, leading to insufficient allocations towards higher education as an integral component of long-term developmental endeavors (Birdsall et al., 2004). Furthermore, rentier states employ the mechanism of public sector employment as a pivotal instrument for the redistribution of oil-derived revenue, alleviation of unemployment, garnering political support, and upholding socio-political stability (Gelb et al., 1991). Within political economy research, there has been a predominant emphasis on the top-down, state-centric dynamics of demobilization in the prototypical rentier states located in the Gulf region. This perspective often cites the limited occurrence of street demonstrations or civil society organizations as indicative of the state's effectiveness. This "co-optation mechanism" has gained widespread notoriety as an explanatory framework for understanding political dynamics in oil-rich nations, particularly within the archetypal rentier states of the Gulf (Moritz, 2019).

According to Losman (2020), the rentier state usually becomes unstable over time. First of all, the rentier state gains revenue largely independent of their citizenry; they do not need to extract taxes from their populations.[9] In the absence of a need for citizens to contribute taxes, a social contract emerges wherein citizens place relatively fewer political demands on the government due to the state's provision of numerous services without imposing taxation. Additionally, in the context of rentier governments, there is a reduced necessity to establish mechanisms for financial accountability among their citizens, as the absence of taxes and the availability of social services and state-subsidized goods have effectively appeased the populace (Losman, 2020).

As governments do not rely heavily on tax collection, their primary economic role shifts towards the distribution of rents (Losman, 2020). According to Losman, this could potentially result in instability in two distinct ways: (1) when the government allocates wealth and economic privileges, there will inevitably be individuals who are dissatisfied with their share. Consequently, those who are discontented will have a clear and concrete target for directing their grievances: the system or the governing regime. Conversely, in economies grounded in an impersonal market, it becomes more challenging to assign blame to a specific aspect of the system; and (2) regimes operating under a rentier model struggle to justify their authority through citizen approval, such as through elections, transparency, or notable economic success. In such instances, rentier states often seek to garner support and legitimacy by appealing to moral and cultural foundations, such as invoking myths, traditions, or religious beliefs (Losman, 2020: 430; Shambayati, 1994: 307).

Nations endowed with abundant oil resources, whose fiscal sustenance hinges on rentier income, have the capacity to provide avenues for employment and substantial revenue generation also via their state-controlled oil enterprises (National Oil Companies). Nevertheless, as posited by Losman, these oil corporations frequently accord precedence to the pursuit of government objectives and interventions over the maximization of profit, thereby producing a unique configuration of operational performance and resource allocation. The National Oil Company then, "is often hamstrung because the political process can lead governments to have incoherent goals … that hamper its operations and increase its costs" (Losman, 2020: 430).

At any rate, to diversify an economy heavily reliant on the export of a single primary resource is a challenging endeavor. In the Gulf region, this challenge is further compounded by the complexities of labor market dynamics (Herb, 2019). Each of the Gulf monarchies maintains a dual labor market structure, consisting of one segment for their citizens and another for foreign nationals. Typically, citizens predominantly engage in public sector employment, while foreigners largely participate in the private sector (Herb, 2019). Within the public sector, the employment of citizens serves as a mechanism for distributing oil-derived revenues. Consequently, the comparatively elevated salaries provided to many Gulf nationals, particularly those in wealthier rentier states, exhibit a minimal correlation with labor productivity and market-driven wage levels for foreign labor (Herb, 2019). The private sector started, a few years ago, to hire citizens as a result of those government policies of Emiratization, Saudization, etc. These policies refer to the campaigns carried out throughout the Gulf to nationalize certain areas of employment. This stipulation by local governments is called Qatarization, Saudization, Omanization, Kuwaitization, and Emiratization. International companies in the region have to recruit a certain percentage of employees from the local workforce and experts predict that this percentage will increase in the future (Hornok, 2020).[10] Nevertheless, it is still unclear in the literature about the influence of localization on organizational effectiveness. The precise nature and magnitude of the benefits, if any, that accrue to multinational enterprises (MNEs) operating in the Middle East through the employment of nationals remain uncertain (Forstenlechner and Mellahi, 2011). A barrier to Emiratization is constituted by the fact that young Emiratis often prefer to work in the public sector.[11] The public sector is far more attractive for Emiratis as it provides superior employment conditions: remuneration, job security, hours of work, work content, and generous vacations. The attractions also include an opportunity to work in the native language, as well as an opportunity to practice *wasta*[12] to get a job (Zeffane and Kemp, 2020).

Furthermore, it is important to remember the enduring presence of the *kafala*[13] system across the Gulf region.[14] Rooted in the Bedouin societal tradition, this system assigns a *kafeel*, or sponsor, the responsibility of safeguarding migrant workers under their responsibility. The advent of the oil-based economy did not substantively alter this system of "permanent impermanence" (Ali, 2010: 64–65) which prescribes remuneration and entitlements for workers, encompassing expenses related to travel, basic salaries, leave, etc. In a similar vein, it is worth mentioning that control over land ownership falls within the authority of individual emirates rather than being a federal jurisdiction. The United Arab Emirates has deliberately implemented legal frameworks designed to safeguard its recently established federation against the potential influence of neocolonial forces (Guéraiche, 2017: 3).

In any case, a conspicuous commitment to achieving economic diversification is discernible in the contemporary Gulf region, particularly in the United Arab Emirates, where diversification efforts heavily rely on foreign labor. Dubai, in particular, has been a pioneer in implementing policies aimed at easing regulations and restrictions in this regard. None of the Gulf monarchies have succeeded in substantially diversifying their economies through the utilization of their own citizens as a labor force. The central question of Gulf diversification pertains to whether it will be the citizenry or foreign workers who will predominantly constitute the labor force within the diversified sectors of the economy. While the abundance of oil wealth has undeniably endowed Gulf economies with the financial means to establish competitive novel sources of economic growth, the ongoing challenge revolves around ensuring the sustainability of these endeavors, specifically in terms of nurturing a locally sourced labor force capable of sustaining non-oil industries.

Moreover, to conclude, it is important to highlight the political structure of the United Arab Emirates. The UAE is a federation of seven emirates, each governed by its own monarchy, with a federal supreme council consisting of the rulers of each emirate. The supreme council is the highest constitutional authority in the UAE and the primary body responsible for federal laws and policymaking, including fiscal policies and economic priorities. The President and Prime Minister of the UAE, positions held by the rulers of Abu Dhabi and Dubai respectively, play crucial roles in the decision-making process. The Federal Supreme Council, as the paramount decision-making body, has significant influence over national policy and economic decisions, including the distribution of oil revenues. The Council's decisions reflect a consensus among the emirates, ensuring that policies align with the broader national interests.

Individually, the rulers of each emirate wield substantial autonomy within their territories, particularly in Abu Dhabi and Dubai, which are the most economically significant. Abu Dhabi, holding the majority of the UAE's oil reserves, plays a dominant role in shaping policies related to oil revenue distribution. The emirate uses its revenues to fund large-scale infrastructure projects and social welfare programs both within Abu Dhabi and in the less affluent emirates.

The implementation of policies concerning the distribution of oil rents in the UAE is managed through several state-owned enterprises and government bodies, for example, the Abu Dhabi National Oil Company (ADNOC)[15] and Dubai Petroleum.[16] These entities are critical in the operational aspect of oil extraction and distribution of revenues. ADNOC, in particular, is a major player not only in oil production but also in the economic diversification efforts of the UAE (Cahil, 2021).

The Ministry of Finance clearly plays a crucial role in the allocation of federal funds and therefore in the distribution of oil revenues among the emirates. It ensures that the wealth generated from oil rents is invested in national projects and redistribution mechanisms that support the federation's economic goals. Entities like the Abu Dhabi Investment Authority (ADIA)[17] and Mubadala Development Company[18] manage a significant portion of the UAE's oil wealth, investing in both domestic and international projects. These investments are crucial for the UAE's strategy of economic diversification away from oil dependence.

In the UAE, therefore, the distribution of oil rents is intricately tied to its political structure, where the federal nature of governance allows for a concentration of decision-making power in the hands of a few key figures. This centralized control supports not only the strategic distribution of oil wealth but also the broader goal of economic diversification and development. The policy implementation is carried out through a network of national companies and financial bodies, ensuring that oil revenue benefits the country's economic development agenda. Thus, in the rentier state framework of the UAE, the effective decision-makers and policy implementers are closely linked to the ruling establishments, reflecting a blend of monarchical rule and strategic economic management.

In this respect, the rentier state model in the Gulf monarchies can indeed be considered unique due to its combination of high rent income per capita, political stability, effective reinvestment of rents into the economy, and comprehensive welfare provisions. These elements differentiate it substantially from the models seen, for example, in Venezuela and Nigeria, where political and economic instability, lower income from natural resources per capita, and less effective governance of resource wealth have led to significantly different outcomes.[19]

8.3 FROM RENTIERISM TO NON-TRADITIONAL SECURITY STRATEGIES

Traditionally, the significance of the Gulf region lay primarily in its energy resources.[20] However, recent events, particularly the Arab uprisings in 2011, have drawn a sharp increase in attention and focus to this region. Most of the Gulf States are now more active at the regional and international levels than in recent decades, primarily focusing on development and domestic issues. Since the inception of the Arab uprisings, the Gulf States have filled a vacuum of power in the region putting them at the center of attention. Until now, there has been a limited number of comparative studies conducted on the Gulf region that have offered comprehensive examinations of the security consequences arising from these evolving dynamics, particularly in relation to their effects on the security priorities of the Gulf States. An excellent starting point for addressing this gap is Buzan's (1991a) framework, which delineates five security dimensions: political, military, economic, social, and environmental, emphasizing the interconnectedness of these sectors and the importance of understanding cross-sectoral dynamics.

> Identifying security issues is easy for traditionalists, who, broadly speaking, equate security with military issues and the use of force. But it is more difficult when security is moved out of the military sector. There are intellectual and political dangers

> in simply tacking the word security onto an ever-wider range of issues. (Buzan et al., 1998: 1)

Buzan advances the need for a comprehensive approach to security studies that incorporates multiple sectors and levels of analysis. The author explores the concept of securitization and the distinction between securitizing actors and referent objects, arguing that security is a particular type of politics applicable to a wide range of issues, not just military ones. He proposes a constructivist method for distinguishing the process of securitization from that of politicization, which helps to understand who can securitize what and under what conditions.[21]

The Gulf States have also incorporated non-conventional security concerns, encompassing economic, social, and environmental dimensions, into their agenda (Woertz, 2013). With the attack against Aramco,[22] cyber security in the region received a wake-up call (Zetter, 2014). To mitigate potential threats and address vulnerabilities, the GCC states have instituted collaborative strategies and formulated new institutions, protocols, and strategies (Clarke, 2010; Green, 2015). The growing domestic demographic disparities have introduced a domestic security concern and presented new difficulties as Gulf States grapple with the implementation of nationalization initiatives aimed at diminishing their reliance on foreign labor and boosting the involvement of indigenous populations in the private sector.

The United Arab Emirates, in particular, has chosen to move away from a "pure" rentier state system by investing more in its people and industries, nation branding, tourism, and the implementation of "soft" and "smart power." The goal is to transition from state reliance for revenue to promoting economic growth through private enterprises and innovative technologies. This inclusivity extends to welcoming a substantial number of foreign individuals into the country, allowing for their integration, while simultaneously maintaining political stability, social order, and preserving traditions through the maintenance of the political status quo (Dobransky, 2011). Is the concept of a purely rentier economy valid, though? Scholarly perspectives on this matter are not unanimous. We could argue that a "pure" rentier system can be defined as an economic system or structure where a significant portion of income or wealth is derived from the ownership of assets that generate rental income, rather than from productive economic activities like manufacturing, services, or trade. This concept typically applies to individuals, corporations, or states that rely on rents, royalties, dividends, interest, or other forms of unearned income. Some key characteristics of a pure rentier system may include: (1) dependence on asset ownership; (2) minimal engagement in economic activities that produce new goods, services, or technologies. Economic activity is largely about managing and optimizing income from existing assets; (3) extraction of rent: the system extracts rent from other participants in the economy who need to utilize the assets owned by the rentiers. This can include everything from land and buildings to patents and natural resources; (4) wealth accumulation: wealth tends to accumulate among asset holders, reinforcing income inequality because those without significant assets have limited means to generate similar income; (5) economic inefficiency: such systems may lead to economic inefficiency and stagnation, as they can discourage productive investments and innovation when rent-seeking offers an easier return on investment; and (6) socio-economic stability or instability: depending on the broader economic and political context, a pure rentier system can contribute to socio-economic stability by providing a steady income to asset owners. However, it can also lead to instability by exacerbating wealth disparities and creating economic dependencies.

Does the UAE fully align with the defining characteristics that qualify a rentier state? Beblawi, the original proponent of Rentier State Theory (RST), acknowledges that "a purely rentier economy does not exist" (Beblawi, 1987: 384). Gray's theory of "late rentierism" effectively builds upon and adapts the fundamental elements of Beblawi and Luciani's initial RST framework, while maintaining its core principles (Gray, 2011).[23] The United Arab Emirates has historically been characterized as a rentier state due to its substantial reliance on revenue from oil and gas exports. Particularly before the 21st century, the UAE economy was heavily dependent on oil revenues. However, over the past few decades, the UAE, especially through its emirates like Dubai and Abu Dhabi, has been actively working to diversify its economy away from its dependence on oil revenues. This shift aims to transform the nation from a rentier state to a more diversified economy that includes the promotion of sectors such as tourism, infrastructures, real estate, aviation, and financial services. The UAE government has implemented policies to foster entrepreneurship and attract foreign investment, such as creating free zones, which offer tax breaks, custom duty benefits, and fewer restrictions on ownership. Through these efforts, the UAE has made significant progress in reducing its reliance on a pure rentier system. However, oil and gas still play a crucial role in its economy and government revenues, indicating that while the model has evolved, the transition is ongoing and not yet complete.

Economic diversification has been undertaken by the GCC in general, and the UAE in particular, since the 1990s (Ahmed, 2015). During the 1990s, Mohammed bin Zayed (MBZ) experienced a rising prominence and harbored more ambitious objectives for his nation. His aspirations included enhancing the UAE's self-reliance and securing foreign involvement in its security. He aimed to consolidate the country's global and regional influence to safeguard political and economic interests, forge enduring partnerships with friendly nations such as Saudi Arabia, and manage challenges, primarily from Iran and Islamist movements (Esfandiary, 2023: 6). Following the global economic crisis in 2007–2008, the UAE has managed to formulate a more targeted strategy, centered around its Vision 2021 plan. This plan is geared towards fostering a knowledge-based economy while also bolstering economic sustainability and diversification. However, upon examining the historical progression of the UAE, it becomes evident that the initial steps towards economic diversification were initiated through the visionary efforts of Sheikh Rashid bin Maktoum in Dubai. This was particularly noticeable with the creation of the port conglomerate known as the Dubai Port Authority. Guéraiche highlights that the UAE's significant entry into the globalized economy occurred in 2006 when it sought to acquire six ports in the United States, marking a substantial milestone in its global economic engagement. The UAE's acquisition of these ports in the US expanded its influence on the global market. Guéraiche also observes that the UAE's growing integration into the global economy played a pivotal role in the economic challenges it encountered as a consequence of the repercussions of the Wall Street crisis (Guéraiche, 2017). During this period, DP World, a prominent symbol of the country's globalization efforts, experienced substantial setbacks due to the recession (Esfandiary, 2023: 6). Nonetheless, cities like Dubai have succeeded in gradually establishing supplementary industries to generate domestic revenue for the nation. Thus, while the Emirate of Abu Dhabi primarily concentrated on oil and gas activities, the economy centered in Dubai exhibited a broader commitment to diversification by actively promoting sectors including construction, tourism, and financial investment (Ghanem, 1992). Ahmed explains how the contributions of the non-oil sectors in the country have been able to develop and contribute (until 2015) to an estimated 67.3% of the nation's domestic GDP. For example, financial corporation contribution to the GDP grew from 6.3% in 2008 to 7% in 2012, and governmental services grew from 4.6% to 5.5% during the same period (Ahmed, 2015). Additionally, it has been projected that the travel and tourism industry will contribute about 280.6 billion United Arab Emirati dirham to the UAE's GDP by 2028.[24] This upsurge in tourism sector activity is anticipated to facilitate the nation's pursuit of economic diversification, opening the way for enhanced economic sustainability within the country. Necessarily, the development towards an economic diversification must be seen as comprehensive. According to Hvidt,

> [...] the apparent developmental success of Dubai may be understood as the outcome of conscious policies conducted by a "late-late" developing state in order to "catch up" with the "developed world". The development can be seen as an outcome of a broad range of economic, institutional, political and cultural factors that function in interaction; that is, this development lends itself to a multi-clausal explanation. (Hvidt, 2009: 418)

This comprehensive diversification strategy seems to reiterate the fundamental principles that were initially put into practice during the UAE's foundational phase in the 1970s. To establish stability, the UAE adopted an interventionist-redistributive model, which was made possible by its substantial oil revenues. As a consequence of the substantial oil revenues generated since the 1970s, this developmental strategy made it possible to create a comprehensive welfare system for the population of the Emirates. As a result, the UAE has upheld its political and social stability by directing these significant oil revenues towards the advancement of social and economic infrastructure, as well as the delivery of social services, healthcare, and education (Schilirò, 2013; Shihab, 2001; Yousef, 2004). Simultaneously, as far as foreign policy is concerned, the UAE followed a strategy of progressive assertiveness. As explained by Esfandiary, assertiveness denotes a nation's growing inclination towards making assertive foreign policy choices and showcasing a clear readiness to actively engage in diverse global arenas to advance its own objectives, even when such actions may not align with the interests of its allies and friendly nations (Esfandiary, 2023: 7). The ultimate goal is self-sufficiency through a "calculated, long term strategy [...] to equip a state with the necessary means — economic, intellectual, military, policy" (Esfandiary, 2023: 7).

This view on the UAE's necessity to transition from oil dependency to diversification is most certainly justified by the urgency of economic sustainability and resilience. Furthermore, this model seems to be consistent with Buzan's need to refine and widen the concept of security and to focus greater attention on non-military elements: "There are two opposing schools of thought in security studies which conceptualize security differently: wideners and traditionalists. While traditionalists define security by equating it with military issues and the use of force, wideners accept it more than military power" (Buzan et al., 1998: vii). This concept is also in line with the UAE's strategies to uphold both domestic and regional security by employing both conventional and non-conventional methods and policies—including massive programs of nation branding and a sophisticated utilization of "soft" and "smart power" (non-military objects). Would exploring this logic of security help us to find out what differentiates security from that which is purely political? Is a non-traditional approach to security helpful in understanding to what extent "soft power" can help a post-rentier state to maintain the political status quo?

8.4 UAE'S PUBLIC DIPLOMACY: "SOFT POWER" AND NATION BRANDING

Historically, the concept of power in international relations has been conventionally defined and evaluated in quantifiable "hard" terms, often encompassing military and economic capabilities. Hard power is wielded through coercion, involving the utilization of force, the threat of force, or economic sanctions. In contrast to the coercive nature of "hard power," "soft power" pertains to the application of persuasion as a means to attain foreign policy goals. "Soft power" does not refer to the traditional foreign policy tools of carrot and stick, "seeking instead to achieve influence by building networks, communicating compelling narratives, establishing international rules, and drawing on the resources that make a country naturally attractive to the world."[25] Joseph Nye introduced the concept as early as 1990 in his work *Bound to Lead: The Changing Nature of American Power.* He described "soft power" as the ability to appeal to and persuade others using the attractiveness of a country's culture, political ideals, and policies. In 2004, Nye further elaborates on the concept in his *Soft Power: The Means to Success in World Politics*, where he delved deeper into the idea of persuasion through co-optation instead of coercion (Ulrichsen, 2017: 161). States should "set the agenda and attract others in world politics, and not only to force them to change by threatening military force or economic sanctions. This is 'soft power' — getting others to want the outcomes that you want co-opts people rather than coerces them" (Nye, 2004: 5). In a similar direction, other scholars have started to focus on the notion of "state branding" (Van Ham, 2002: 2) and "nation branding" (Anholt, 2006b). "Soft power" is integral to the branding process, as the appeal of a nation's culture, political values, and policies constitutes the essence of "soft power." In the 21st century, nation branding has emerged as a prominent dimension of "soft power," with numerous countries actively adopting and employing it to bolster their economies and enhance their international image. According to Anholt, a nation's brand combines the people's perception of a particular country incorporating seven key domains of national competence: tourism promotion, brand export, government policies (both domestic and foreign), the population's reputation, cultural heritage, the power to attract investment, and a skilled workforce (Anholt, 2006b). Simon Anholt considers a nation brand as "the most valuable asset: it is national identity made robust, tangible, communicable, and – at its best – made useful" (Anholt, 2013). Successful branding necessitates the cooperation of policymakers, the business sector, and the local community. Anholt contends that a nation's global standing can be effectively enhanced through a discreet approach, dedicated individuals leading the effort, and effective coordination among government entities, the private sector, and the broader citizenry (Anholt, 2013). Branding within subsidiary entities has grown in importance, a trend predominantly driven by the forces of globalization. In this context, products, services, and assets converge with global markets and cultural elements within a worldwide community. A city brand that effectively portrays a powerful and positive image engages in competition with other cities, aiming to secure the trust and respect of consumers, investors, and tourists. It is favorable image that grants a vital competitive international primacy. "Clichés and stereotypes—positive or negative, truthful or false—fundamentally shape our behavior toward other places, their people, and their products" (Anholt, 2007: 1). Consequently,

> if the purpose of public diplomacy is simply to promote government policies, it is likely to be superfluous or futile, depending on the good name of the country or its government at that particular time. If the country is in favour, then unless the policy is patently wrong-headed, it is likely to be well received and simply needs to be communicated. Little art or skill are required to do this. If on the other hand the country suffers from a poor or weak reputation, then almost no amount of promotional skill or expenditure can cause the policy to be received with enthusiasm, and it will either be ignored or taken as further proof of whatever evil is currently ascribed to the country. This is why I have often defined brand image as the context in which messages are received, not the messages themselves. (Anholt, 2007: 4)

The UAE began implementing its branding strategy in the 1980s, and it became more assertive in the 1990s, with the Department of Tourism and Commerce Marketing taking the lead in positioning and marketing the nation as a global financial hub. This effort resulted in the transformation of Dubai, from a dormant desert region into a prominent metropolis in the Middle East, driven by the UAE's economic expansion and city branding. While Dubai's initial rapid growth was fueled by oil, it now constitutes only 6% of the country's GDP (Balakrishnan, 2008). Dubai has prioritized the development of service-oriented industries and tourism as part of its strategy to supplant oil as the primary revenue source for the state (Al-Sharabani, 2007). Likewise, the leadership in Abu Dhabi recognized the significance of fostering a favorable perception of the city as a viable complement to Dubai. This effort was aligned with the objectives of Vision2030 for economic diversification and transformation, and it evolved into a structured branding initiative aimed at attaining global recognition. The Office of the Abu Dhabi Brand was established in the late 2000s, introducing the slogan "Travelers welcome" as Abu Dhabi's initial branding message. This slogan was enthusiastically embraced through various local policies and marketing initiatives. Abu Dhabi's new image stands in stark contrast to that of Dubai. It positions itself as a cultural hub with renowned museums, such as the Louvre (another strategic endeavor in cultural diplomacy), and a sun-soaked resort that hosts international events like Formula One. This distinction becomes especially evident when compared to Dubai, renowned for its extravagant ventures that have earned it the reputation of being a "city of superlatives" (Beauregard, 2003). A successful nation-branding strategy involves identifying a clear focal point to create a lasting impression in the consumer's mind, ensuring its lasting presence in their memory (Anholt, 2009; Zeineddine and Nicolescu, 2017). "It is an attempt to tick the boxes of Anholt's hexagon-figure for rendering the nation branding process successful" (Zeineddine and Nicolescu, 2017: 578).

This strategic approach holds significant importance, not only in developing economic and human capital and establishing the state but also in guiding nation-building initiatives through public policies and diplomatic efforts. Consequently, alongside traditional instruments for the UAE's expression of "soft power," such as foreign aid, a range of government-managed initiatives are employed to nurture the interconnection of nation-building, nation branding, and public diplomacy. As demonstrated by the creation of the UAE Soft Power Council in May 2017, the UAE places a strong emphasis on nation branding and the projection of "soft power" as integral components of its public diplomacy strategy. In conjunction with public diplomacy initiatives, nation-branding campaigns are utilized as instruments of "soft power" in the UAE's foreign policy. As the UAE continues to protect its strategic interests abroad and address structural deficiencies, the strategic use of "soft power" tools has the potential to facilitate the projection of "smart power"—a skillful combination of both "hard" and "soft power" mechanisms to advance the nation's overarching goals.

8.5 SMART-SECURITIZING THE NATION

The common thread that links the various stages of Nye's theory of "soft power" is "attraction": the ability to seduce through cultural production, education, innovation, technology, lifestyle—in short, a discourse (and a strategy) based on a cultural, social, and political model that attracts and seduces others, leading them to want to be like you and reversing Machiavelli's advice to the Prince: "it is much safer to be feared than loved" (Calculli, 2017). Scholars have long equated Gulf states' political stability strategies (specifically in reference to Saudi Arabia and the UAE) with the capacity to build a strong national narrative. Derichs and Demmelhuber (2017: 191) argue that Gulf monarchies whose "power translates into state power" remain strongly engaged in "a still ongoing process of nation building," striving to construct a nation "coterminous with the state to perpetuate rule" (Uniacke, 2021). To attain this synergy, Morgenthau had already advanced the theory that governments should mold the required public sentiment to garner support for their established policies, long before the advent of digital media (Morgenthau, 1965; Jones, 2019: 1390). In the same vein, Halliday underlines the importance of the creation of particular identities and ideologies to maintain the support of society and state–society relations (Halliday, 2005: 37). This is where "soft power" comes into play, serving to enable and ease the process of engagement within state–society relations on a domestic level, and to readjust power dynamics on both regional and global scales. Relying exclusively on the state's coercive machinery is insufficient for comprehending the notable shifts in power dynamics occurring both within the Arab region and globally. Through successful public diplomacy initiatives, the UAE has enhanced its foreign policy influence and is now capable of exerting substantial regional and international leverage. This has been possible through the concurrent interconnection and interaction of the five dimensions of power outlined by Buzan:

> Military security concerns the two-level interplay of the armed offensive and defensive capabilities of states, and states' perceptions of each other's intentions. Political security concerns the organizational stability of states, systems of government, and the ideologies that give them legitimacy. Economic security concerns access to the resources, finance and markets necessary to sustain acceptable levels of welfare and state power. Societal security concerns the ability of societies to reproduce their traditional patterns of language, culture, association, and religious and national identity and custom within acceptable conditions for evolution. Environmental security concerns the maintenance of the local and the planetary biosphere as the essential support system on which all other human enterprises depend. (Buzan, 1991a: 433)

These five categories do not function in isolation from one another. They are all intricately interconnected, forming a cohesive and interdependent framework (Buzan, 1991a: 433). Additionally, with the media and communication digital transformation, a segment of nation branding and "soft power" shaping has been directly entrusted to the general populace, including citizens, tourists, and expatriates. Individuals are no longer regarded as passive recipients of the nation's image but as active participants in shaping it, "volunteering, contributing to the community, and displaying," for example, "tolerance and respect for others" (Jones, 2017: 63). Buzan's approach once more proves effective in unpacking the concept of security, aiming to gain a deeper understanding of its intricacies and the requisites for addressing it. "Soft power," nation branding, and public diplomacy all play a role in this strategic vision.

> The "national" security problem turns out to be a systemic security problem in which individuals, states and the system all play a part, and in which economic, societal and environmental factors are as important as political and military ones. From this integrative perspective, the levels and sectors appear more useful as viewing platforms from which one can observe the problem from different angles, than as self-contained areas for policy or analysis. (Buzan, 1991b: 8)

Among the five dimensions, societal security is arguably the most captivating to explore, particularly in relation to economic dimensions. Although it is challenging to disentangle it from the political realm, societal threats revolve around questions of identity and the equilibrium (or its absence) within a specific state (Stone, 2009). In contrast to its previous subordination to the state as described in Buzan's *People, States, and Fear*, the societal dimension is proposed by Waever et al. as a domain associated with the state, but also given a new meaning as an object of security in its own right (McSweeney, 1996). As mentioned above, "[s]ocietal security concerns the ability of a society to persist in its essential character under changing conditions" (Stanger, 1993: 839–840). Within the framework of the UAE's post-traditional form of economic "liberal" developmentalism, social security emerges as a product of the discourse on national security, economic modernization with Western influences, and the consolidation of identity. Nonetheless, the process of modernization has brought about a conflict between the attenuation of native cultural ideals and the values associated with modernization, which are oftentimes synonymous with Westernization.[26] Identity, however, is not an inherent aspect of society; instead, it emerges through a process of negotiation involving individuals and interest groups (McSweeney, 1996). As observed by McSweeney, "an identity is a consequence of a political process, and it is that process, not the label symbolizing it, which constitutes the reality that needs explication" (McSweeney, 1996: 91). How is this identity thesis compatible with Buzan's security theory? The idea of a powerful state is founded on the prerequisite of society being under the authority of the state. The responsibility of shaping societal identity—identified by Buzan as the state's role in fostering social cohesion necessary for achieving strength and eligibility for membership in a security community—is a shared responsibility between the state and society.

Accumulating broad domestic support, and simultaneously constructing a national image emphasizing capitalism, tourism, and tolerance, have enabled the UAE to establish a solid regime. This regime not only boasts extensive control and military security but also possesses the capabilities to oversee the economy, society, and political affairs (Uniacke, 2021). As Bryant points out, communicative technology serves as a conduit where "the commanding heights will go to those who understand information and communications technology in technical, social, economic, political, and security-related dimensions" (Bryant, 2012: 20). In this context, Emirati citizens play a role in the diversification and nation-branding process. This collaboration and interaction between the state and society align with Asef Bayat's notion of "reimagined civil society": a civil society structured in accordance with the principles of "individual, identity, freedom, competition, and free market" (Bayat, 2017: 178).

8.6 CONCLUSION

The evolving dynamics in the Gulf region have been demonstrated to hold significant security implications. These implications span across various dimensions, including political, military, economic, social, and environmental sectors. Over the past decade, the United Arab Emirates has emerged as a significant player on both regional and international stages. Its deliberate efforts in building military and security capabilities have allowed it to secure its national interests and maintain internal stability. However, I attempted to demonstrate how traditional security and surveillance are just one facet of the UAE's multifaceted approach to achieving its objectives.

Drawing upon the comprehensive framework of security dimensions outlined by Buzan, encompassing political, military, economic, social, and environmental aspects, this chapter has explored the economic and diplomatic initiatives pursued by the UAE to drive its economic diversification plans. These endeavors have been instrumental in transforming the UAE from an oil-dependent nation into a global brand with a thriving post-industrial service economy. Key strategies, such as promoting the private sector, real estate, construction, retail, and tourism, have not only fueled economic growth but have also reinforced the stability of the country's governing system. One of the notable achievements of the UAE's economic diversification and distribution policies is their capacity to benefit a substantial portion of the population, resulting in broad support for the adoption of a market-driven economic system. This broad-based support has further facilitated economic expansion and diversification. The cumulative effect of these endeavors has substantially bolstered the United Arab Emirates' strategic positioning, both within the region and on the global stage. The intricate interplay between various dimensions of security and economic development in the UAE's pursuit of its national and regional interests played a pivotal role in aligning the UAE's diverse foreign policy objectives. Many of the UAE's regional investment strategies were driven by simultaneous political, military, diplomatic, symbolic, and economic necessities. The military, economic, cultural, and diplomatic dimensions mutually reinforced each other, thereby solidifying and extending the UAE's influence.

NOTES

1. Adam Smith did not specifically focus on the concepts of "rentierism," "rent," or a "rentier economy" as they are understood in contemporary economics. However, his discussions on rent can be found in his *The Wealth of Nations* ([1776] 2012), where he addresses the concept of economic rent, particularly in relation to land ownership.
2. David Ricardo is more directly associated with the development of the theory of economic rent, which laid the groundwork for modern discussions on rentierism and rentier economies. In his most important work on this subject Ricardo (1817), presents his famous *theory of rent*, which is now known as *Ricardian rent*.
3. In *The Theory of the Leisure Class* ([1899] 1994), Veblen describes a class of individuals (the leisure class) who engage in conspicuous consumption and

live off of wealth or rents rather than through productive labor. This rentier class, according to Veblen, derives income not from contributing to the economy but by owning capital, property, or other rent-producing assets.

4. In *Capitalism, Socialism, and Democracy* (1942), Schumpeter discusses the idea of "creative destruction," which refers to the constant process of innovation that leads to the demise of old industries and the rise of new ones. In this context, rentier behavior is often seen as contrary to innovation because rentiers seek to preserve the status quo and extract profits without contributing to the dynamic, competitive processes that Schumpeter sees as vital to capitalism.
5. The allocative state is primarily focused on the allocation of resources within the economy. It plays a central role in redistributing resources and wealth to ensure that they are distributed fairly and equitably among the population. In a productive state, the government takes on an entrepreneurial role. It invests in industries, infrastructure, and technology to stimulate economic activity and increase productivity.
6. In terms of economic growth rates, the record of GCC countries has been varied. While periods of economic downturn have occurred, particularly during oil price slumps, several GCC countries have undertaken significant efforts to diversify their economies and reduce reliance on oil revenues. For example, the UAE and Saudi Arabia have invested heavily in non-oil sectors such as tourism, financial services, and infrastructure. Despite these efforts, however, the dependence on hydrocarbons remains substantial, and the extent to which these diversification strategies have fundamentally transformed their economies still remains a topic of debate among scholars. According to the IMF, the long-term growth rates in the region have seen fluctuations, but countries like Qatar and the UAE have generally maintained steady growth through prudent fiscal policies and strategic diversification initiatives (IMF Report, 2023). To provide an accurate and up-to-date assessment of economic growth trends in the GCC, recent figures show that the region's economic performance is closely linked to oil production, yet non-hydrocarbon sectors have been playing an increasingly significant role in sustaining growth. For 2023, GDP growth in the GCC was projected to slow to around 2.5%, a sharp decline from the exceptional 7.3% in 2022, largely due to lower oil earnings and production cuts under OPEC+ agreements. Hydrocarbon GDP was expected to decline by 1.3% to 3.9%, depending on the country, while non-hydrocarbon sectors continued to grow, with forecasts of 3.9% in 2023 across the region (IMF Report, 2023; World Bank Press Release, 2023). Saudi Arabia and the UAE, in particular, have maintained strong non-oil GDP growth rates, driven by sectors such as retail, construction, tourism, and other services. Saudi Arabia's non-hydrocarbon GDP grew by 4.5% in the first half of 2023, and the UAE posted 5.9% growth over the same period (IMF Report, 2023; World Bank Press Release, 2024). This shows that while growth rates in the GCC have fluctuated due to oil dependency, non-oil sectors have increasingly

contributed to stabilizing their economies, and diversification efforts continue to shape their future growth trajectories.

7. The resource curse theory suggests that countries rich in natural resources, such as oil, may experience negative economic and political consequences. This theory highlights the challenges of managing resource wealth and the potential for corruption, rent-seeking behavior, and political instability in rentier states. The term "resource curse" was coined by Richard Auty (1993) in *Sustaining Development in Mineral Economies: The Resource Curse Thesis*. See also Auty (2012) and Ross (2012).
8. In Gylfason's (2001) analysis, "non-depletable" refers to the idea that once knowledge, skills, and education are acquired, they are not easily exhausted or "used up" in the same way that natural resources like oil, minerals, or timber can be. Human capital is seen as renewable and can be applied across various industries or contexts over time. This concept has clearly practical limitations with individuals' lifespans and skill degradation over time. In fact, people can forget or lose skills if they don't maintain or practice them.
9. Value Added Tax on goods and services has since been introduced in Saudi Arabia and the United Arab Emirates, beginning January 1, 2018.
10. On November 29, 2010 the Ministry of Labour released Ministerial Resolution 1187 of 2010 (MR 1187), which represents a strong effort to increase the participation of UAE nationals in private sector professional roles through Emiratization. MR 1187 provides a "carrot-and-stick" approach; while providing incentives to organizations which comply and participate, it also provides for severe penalties for non-compliance. In essence, Emiratization is a strategy that seeks to use the country's human resources in the most favorable way in the economic process, through the transfer of skills and knowledge from expatriates to UAE nationals (citizens).
11. https://gulfnews.com/uae/many-emiratis-prefer-public-sector-1.61971
12. The term *wasta* refers to a social mechanism prevalent in Arab cultures, where personal networks and relationships are used to gain access to resources, services, or advantages that may otherwise be difficult to obtain through formal channels. It is often associated with social capital and is used to bypass bureaucratic processes, relying on interpersonal connections and influence. While *wasta* can facilitate transactions, it is frequently critiqued as a form of corruption, nepotism, or favoritism, undermining meritocracy and institutional fairness (Cunningham and Sarayrah, 1993; Hutchings and Weir, 2006).
13. The *kafala* system, originating from Islamic jurisprudence, is a sponsorship framework predominantly—but not exclusively—used in Gulf Cooperation Council (GCC) countries, regulating the relationship between foreign workers and their employers. Under this system, migrant workers' legal residency and employment status are contingent upon their sponsoring employer (*kafeel*), who has significant control over their mobility, including the ability to approve job changes or exit permits. While it facilitates labor migration, the *kafala* system has been widely criticized for enabling exploitative labor conditions and restricting workers' rights.

14. Several Gulf Cooperation Council (GCC) states have shown interest in reforming the *kafala* system. For instance, Qatar has made significant changes to its *kafala* system in recent years, particularly in the lead up to the 2022 FIFA World Cup. Similarly, Saudi Arabia has also announced plans to reform its *kafala* system to improve the conditions for foreign workers. However, the extent and effectiveness of these reforms vary and are subject to ongoing debate and scrutiny. In January 2016, the United Arab Emirates initiated policy adjustments aimed at facilitating enhanced labor mobility for some worker categories. Individuals categorized as "highly skilled" are granted the prerogative to conclude a fixed-term employment contract without being subject to the customary employment restriction, provided they adhere to the stipulated contractual notice period, which amounts to a minimum of one month, or alternatively, if the employer voluntarily waives the notice requirement (https://www.migrant-rights.org/campaign/end-the-kafala-system/).
15. https://www.weforum.org/organizations/abu-dhabi-national-oil-company-adnoc/
16. https://www.dubaipetroleum.ae/
17. https://www.adia.ae/
18. https://www.mubadala.com/
19. Venezuela's oil industry has suffered from political interference, underinvestment, and sanctions. Nigeria's oil sector is plagued by corruption and inefficiency. These factors contribute to less stable rent incomes compared to the Gulf monarchies. In both Venezuela and Nigeria, efforts at diversification have been less successful and inconsistent. Economic and political instability have made it difficult to attract the necessary investment for diversification. Venezuela, in particular, has become more oil-dependent over the years.
20. The first significant oil discovery in the Gulf region occurred in 1908 in Persia (modern-day Iran) by the Anglo-Persian Oil Company (Yergin, 1991). This event marked the beginning of the Gulf's association with vast energy resources. The expansion of oil discoveries in the Gulf region began in Bahrain, where oil was first found in 1932. This made Bahrain the earliest of the Arab Gulf states to achieve significant oil production. Shortly thereafter, in 1938, Saudi Arabia struck oil in commercial quantities, a development that would eventually position the kingdom as one of the leading global oil producers. Around the same period, Kuwait and Qatar also discovered oil, with Kuwait in 1938 and Qatar in 1939, further embedding the region's significance within the global energy landscape (Crystal, 1990). Oil discoveries in the United Arab Emirates occurred later, starting in the 1950s and 1960s, with a particularly notable find in Abu Dhabi in 1958 (Davidson, 2005).
21. The concept of national security has undergone a transformative evolution over time, with its understanding influenced by theoretical interpretations in international relations, historical events, and prevailing trends. In general, the policy and academic discourse on national security emphasizes key aspects such as stability, safety, protection, and the absence of fear, threats, and conflicts. Furthermore, security can be defined in relation to individual values,

encompassing elements such as physical safety, economic prosperity, autonomy, and psychological well-being (Retter et al., 2020).

22. On September 14, 2019, a drone strike targeted the oil processing facilities located in eastern Saudi Arabia, specifically at Abqaiq and Khurais. These facilities were under the operation of Saudi Aramco, the state-owned oil company of Saudi Arabia. The attack occurred as part of the broader Houthi–Saudi Arabian conflict, which was an outgrowth of the Yemeni Civil War, and within the context of the Persian Gulf crisis spanning from 2019 to 2021.
23. "Late rentierism," as defined by Matthew Gray, refers to the adaptation of rentier state theory (RST) to the contemporary socio-political realities of the Arab Gulf states. It describes how these states, while retaining the fundamental aspects of a rentier state, including centralization of power and reliance on external rents (primarily from hydrocarbons), have evolved to address new challenges. These include globalization, development pressures, and demographic growth. Consequently, the state has become more entrepreneurial and responsive, particularly in the economic sphere, yet remains resistant to democratic reforms (Gray, 2011).
24. https://www.statista.com/topics/4643/tourism-industry-of-the-uae/#topicHeader__wrapper
25. https://softpower30.com/what-is-soft-power/
26. Understanding the basis of the UAE's identity is associated with a more comprehensive understanding of the underlying cultural developments that have taken place in the UAE, and which culminated in the contemporary Bedouin culture with its traditions that now caters to a globalized audience. The ethnographic mapping of the UAE shows a diverse region composed of groups from various ethnic backgrounds that have emerged due to political and commercial development in the region throughout the protectorate years of the Trucial States. Due to the social dynamics between these immigrants and the indigenous Bedouin people, the UAE developed a diverse cultural landscape in which the cultural ideals of these various groups co-existed. The Federal Union, however, proved to be a pivotal point that delineated the preponderance of Bedouin ideals, which over time were tailored to propagate the deep-rooted Bedouin heritage of the UAE, which is the most compatible with the nationalist Emirati identity that the leadership was trying to implement. The establishment of different economic, cultural, and political institutions served to be the modus operandi in which these traditions were emphasized and prioritized. This, however, concurrently came with the suppression of other traditions that were deemed incompatible with this Bedouin narrative. Ultimately, this has created an "imagined community" in the UAE that is tied together by a sense of social solidarity originating from a set of traditions that do not encompass the entire diversity of the cultural landscape of the region.

BIBLIOGRAPHY

Ahmed, Ahmed Zain Elabdin (2015). "The Role of Diversification Strategies in the Economic Development for Oil-dependent Countries: The Case of UAE." *International Journal of Business and Economic Development* 3, no. 1: 47–57.

Al-Sharabani, A. (2007). "Modernizing the United Arab Emirates." *The McKinsey Quarterly* 3, no. 1: 45–52.

Ali, Syed (2010). *Dubai. The Gilded Cage.* New Haven, CT: Yale University Press.

Anholt, Simon (2006a). "The Anholt-GMI City Brands Index: How the World Sees the World's Cities." *Place Branding* 2: 18–31.

Anholt, Simon (2006b). "Why Brand? Some Practical Considerations for Nation Branding." *Place Branding* 2, no. 2: 97–107.

Anholt, Simon (2007). *Competitive Identity: A New Model for the Brand Management of Nations, Cities and Regions.* London: Palgrave Macmillan.

Anholt, Simon (2009). "Should Place Brands Be Simple?" *Place Branding and Public Diplomacy* 5, no. 2: 91–96.

Anholt, Simon (2013). "Beyond the Nation Brand: The Role of Image and Identity in International Relations." *Exchange: The Journal of Public Diplomacy* 2, no. 1: article 1.

Auty, Richard (1993). *Sustaining Development in Mineral Economies: The Resource Curse Thesis.* London: Routledge.

Auty, Richard (2012). "The Oil Curse." In *Handbook of Oil Politics*, edited by Robert E. Looney, 337–348. Abingdon: Routledge.

Balakrishnan, Melodena Stephens (2008). "Dubai – A Star in the East: A Case Study in Strategic Destination Branding." *Journal of Place Management and Development* 1, no. 1: 62–91.

Bayat, Asef (2017). *Revolution Without Revolutionaries: Making Sense of the Arab Spring.* Stanford, CA: Stanford University Press.

Beauregard, Robert A. (2003). "City of Superlatives." *City and Community* 2, no. 3: 183–199.

Beblawi, Hazem (1987). "The Rentier State in the Arab World." *Arab Studies Quarterly* 9, no. 4: 383–398.

Birdsall, Nancy, Pinckney, Thomas, and Sabot, Richard (2004). "Natural Resources, Human Capital and Growth." In *Resource Abundance and Economic Development*, edited by Richard M. Auty, 57–75. Oxford: Oxford Academic.

Bryant, Elizabeth (2012). "The Iron Fist vs. the Microchip." *Journal of Strategic Security* 5, no. 2: 1–26.

Buzan, Barry (1991a). "New Patterns of Global Security in the Twenty-First Century." *International Affairs (Royal Institute of International Affairs 1944–)* 67, no. 3: 431–451.

Buzan, Barry (1991b). *People, States and Fear: An Agenda for International Security Studies in the Post-Cold War Era* (2nd ed.). Hemel Hempstead: Harvester.

Buzan, Barry, Waever, Ole, and de Wilde, Jaap (1998). *Security. A New Framework for Analysis.* Boulder, CO and London: Lynne Rienner.

Cahil, Ben (2021). "Everything at Once: Transformation of Abu Dhabi's Oil Policy." The Arab Gulf States Institute in Washington. Issue Paper 1.

Calculli, Marina (2017). "La violenza invisibile del soft power: per una critica di Joseph Nye." *Il manifesto*, May 25.

Christophers, Brett (2020). *Rentier Capitalism: Who Owns the Economy, and Who Pays for It?* London: Verso.

Clarke, Richard A. (2010). *Cyber War: The Next Threat to National Security and What to Do About It.* New York: Harper Collins.

Crystal, Jill (1990). *Oil and Politics in the Gulf: Rulers and Merchants in Kuwait and Qatar.* Cambridge: Cambridge University Press.

Cunningham, Robert B. and Sarayrah, Yasin K. (1993). *Wasta. The Hidden Force in Middle Eastern Society.* Westport, CT: Praeger.

Davidson, Christopher M. (2005). *The United Arab Emirates: A Study in Survival.* Boulder, CO: Lynne Rienner.

Davidson, Christopher M. (2009). *Abu Dhabi: Oil and Beyond.* New York: Columbia University Press.

Derichs, Claudia and Demmelhuber, Thomas (2017). "Monarchies and Republics, State and Regime, Durability and Fragility in View of the Arab Spring." *Journal of Arabian Studies* 4, no. 2: 180–194.

Dobransky, Steve (2011). "The United Arab Emirates and the Black Pearl Model of Economic Development." *International Journal on World Peace* 28, no. 2: 45–83.

Elbadawi, Ibrahim and Soto, Raimundo (2012). "Resource Rents, Political Institutions and Economic Growth." Working Paper Series, Work 678. Cairo: Economic Research Forum.

Esfandiary, Dina (2023). *New Order in the Gulf. The Rise of the UAE.* London, New York and Dublin: Bloomsbury I.B. Tauris.

Ewers, Michael C. (2016). "Oil, Human Capital and Diversification: The Challenge of Transition in the UAE and the Arab Gulf State." *The Geographical Journal* 182, no. 3: 236–250.

Fasano, Ugo and Zubair, Iqbal (2003). *GCC Countries. From Oil Dependence to Diversification.* Washington: International Monetary Fund Publication Services.

Forstenlechner, Ingo and Mellahi, Kamel (2011). "Gaining Legitimacy Through Hiring Local Workforce at a Premium: The Case of MNEs in the United Arab Emirates." *Journal of World Business* 46, no. 4: 455–461.

Gelb, A., Knight, J. B., and Sabot, R. H. (1991). "Public Sector Employment, Rent Seeking and Economic Growth." *The Economic Journal* 101, no. 408: 1186–1199.

Ghanem, Shihab M. A. (1992). *Industrialization in the United Arab Emirates.* Aldershot, UK and Brookfield, VT: Avebury.

Gray, Matthew (2011). "A Theory of 'Late Rentierism' in the Arab States of the Gulf." Scholarly Paper, Doha: Georgetown University Center for International and Regional Studies.

Green, James A. (2015). *Cyber Warfare: A Multidisciplinary Analysis.* Abingdon: Routledge.

Guéraiche, William (2017). *The UAE: Geopolitics, Modernity and Tradition.* London and New York: I.B. Tauris.

Gylfason, Thorvaldur (2001). "Nature, Power and Growth." *Scottish Journal of Political Economy* 48, no. 5: 558–588.

Halliday, Fred (2005). *The Middle East in International Relations: Power, Politics and Ideology.* Cambridge: Cambridge University Press.

Herb, Michael (2019). "Labor Markets and Economic Diversification in the Gulf Rentiers." In *The Politics of Rentier States in the Gulf. The Project on Middle East Political Science*, 8–12. POMEPS Studies 33.

Hornok, Judith (2020). *The Arab Business Code.* Abingdon and New York: Routledge.

Hutchings, Kate and Weir, David (2006). "Guanxi and Wasta: A Comparison." *Thunderbird International Business Review* 48, no. 1: 141–156. doi:10.1002/tie.20090.

Hvidt, Martin (2009). "The Dubai Model: An Outline of Key Development-Process Elements in Dubai." *International Journal of Middle East Studies* 41, no. 3: 397–418.

Hvidt, Martin (2013). "Economic Diversification in GCC Countries: Past Records and Future Trends." LSE Online Documents on Economics 5525, London School of Economics and Political Science, LSE Library. Available at https://eprints.lse.ac.uk/55252/.

International Monetary Fund Report (2023). Gulf Cooperation Council: Economic Prospects and Policy Challenges for the GCC Countries, IMF Country Report No. 23/413, December 5. Washington, DC: International Monetary Fund. doi:10.5089/9798400263279.002.A001. Available at https://www.elibrary.imf.org/downloadpdf/journals/002/2023/413/article-A000-en.pdf.

Jones, Calvert W. (2017). *Bedouins into Bourgeois: Remaking Citizens for Globalization.* Cambridge: Cambridge University Press.

Jones, Marc Owen (2019). "Propaganda, Fake News, and Fake Trends: The Weaponization of Twitter Bots in the Gulf Crisis." *International Journal of Communication* 13: 1389–1415.

Losman, Donald L. (2020). "The Rentier State and National Oil Companies: An Economic and Political Perspective." *The Middle East Journal* 64, no. 3: 427–445.

Mahdavy, Hossein (1970). "Patterns and Problems of Economic Development in Rentier States: The Case of Iran." In *Studies in the Economic History of the Middle East*, edited by Michael A. Cook, 428–467. London: Routledge.

McSweeney, Bill (1996). "Review: Identity and Security: Buzan and the Copenhagen School." *Review of International Studies* 22, no. 1: 81–93.

Morgenthau, Hans J. (1965). *Politics Among Nations: The Struggle for Power and Peace.* New York: Knopf.

Moritz, Jessie (2019). "Oil and Societal Quiescence: Rethinking Causal Mechanisms in Rentier State Theory. The Politics of Rentier States in the Gulf." POMEPS Studies 33.

North, Douglass (1994). "Economic Performance Through Time." *American Economic Review* 84, no. 3: 359–368.

Nye, Joseph S. (1990). *Bound to Lead: The Changing Nature of American Power.* New York: Basic Books.

Nye, Joseph S. (2004). *Soft Power: The Means to Success in World Politics.* New York: Public Affairs.

Ozyavuz, Anais and Schmid, Dorothee (2015). "Persistence and Evolutions of the Rentier State Model in Gulf Countries." Institut Francais des Relations Internationales (IFRI), Paris and Brussels.

Retter, Lucia, Frinking Erik, Hoorens, Stijn, Lynch, Alice, Nederveen, Fook, and Phillips, William (2020). *Relationships Between the Economy and National Security: Analysis and Considerations for Economic Security Policy in the Netherlands.* Santa Monica, CA: RAND Corporation.

Ricardo, David (1817). *On the Principles of Political Economy and Taxation.* London: John Murray.

Rodrik, Dani, Subramanian, Arvind, and Trebbi, Francesco (2002). "Institutions Rule: The Primacy of Institutions over Integration and Geography in Economic Development." Working Paper 02/189, Washington, DC: International Monetary Fund.

Ross, Michael (2012). *The Oil Curse: How Oil Wealth Shapes the Development of Nations*. Princeton: Princeton University Press.

Schilirò, Daniele (2013). "Diversification and Development of the UAE's Economy." Munich Personal RePEc Archive, MPRA Paper No. 84584.

Schumpeter, Joseph A. (1942). *Capitalism, Socialism, and Democracy*. New York: Harper & Row.

Shambayati, Hootan (1994). "The Rentier State, Interest Groups, and the Paradox of Autonomy: State and Business in Turkey and Iran." *Comparative Politics* 26, no. 3: 307–331.

Shihab, Mohamed (2001). "Economic Development in the UAE." In *United Arab Emirates: A New Perspective*, edited by Ibrahim Alabed and Peter Hellyer, 249–259. London: Trident Press.

Smith, Adam ([1776] 2012). *The Wealth of Nations*. Wordsworth Classics of World Literature. Ware, UK: Wordsworth Editions.

Springborg, Robert (2013). "Review: GCC Countries as 'Rentier States' Revisited." *Middle East Journal* 67, no. 2: 301–309.

Stanger, Allison K. (1993). "Review of *Identity, Migration and the New Security Agenda in Europe* by Ole Wæver, Barry Buzan, Morten Kelstrup and Pierre Lemaitre." *Slavic Review* 54, no. 3: 839–840.

Stijns, Jean-Philippe (2006). "Natural Resource Abundance and Human Capital Accumulation." *World Development* 34, no. 6: 1060–1083.

Stone, Marianne (2009). "Security According to Buzan: A Comprehensive Security Analysis." Security Discussion Papers Series, no. 1. Groupe d'Etudes et d'Expertise "Sécurité et Technologies" GEEST.

Ulrichsen, Kristian C. (2017). *The United Arab Emirates. Power, Politics and Policymaking*. Abingdon and New York: Routledge.

Uniacke, Robert (2021). "Authoritarianism in the Information Age: State Branding, Depoliticizing and 'De-civilizing' of Online Civil Society in Saudi Arabia and the United Arab Emirates." *British Journal of Middle Eastern Studies* 48, no. 5: 979–999.

Van Ham, Peter (2002). "The Rise of the Brand State: The Postmodern Politics of Image and Reputation." *Foreign Affairs* 80, no. 5: 2–6.

Veblen, Thorstein ([1899] 1994). *The Theory of the Leisure Class*. New York: Penguin Books.

Woertz, Eckart (2013). *Oil for Food: The Global Food Crisis and the Middle East*. Oxford: Oxford University Press.

World Bank Press Release (2023). *GCC Economic Growth Expected to Slow to 2.5% in 2023*. Available at: https://www.worldbank.org/en/news/press-release/2023/05/17/gcc-economic-growth-expected-to-slow-to-2-5-in-2023.

World Bank Press Release (2024). *New GCC Economic Update Finds Improved Quality of Education is Critical for Sustained Economic Growth*. Available at: https://www.worldbank.org/en/news/press-release/2024/05/29/new-gcc-economic-update-finds-improved-quality-of-education-is-critical-for-sustained-economic-growth.

Yergin, Daniel (1991). *The Prize: The Epic Quest for Oil, Money, and Power*. New York: Simon & Schuster.

Yousef, Tarik (2004). "Development, Growth and Policy Reform in the Middle East and North Africa." *Journal of Economic Perspectives* 18, no. 3 (2004): 91–115.

Zeffane, Rachid and Kemp, Linzi (2020). "Emiratization: Benefits and Challenges of Strategic and Radical Change in the United Arab Emirates." In *Case Studies in*

Work, Employment and Human Resource Management, edited by Tony Dundon and Adrian Wilkinson, 245–253. Cheltenham, UK and Northampton, MA, USA: Edward Elgar Publishing.

Zeineddine, Cornelia and Nicolescu, Luminița (2017). "Theory and Practice: Nation Branding in the Middle East." *Strategic Conference Proceedings*, 573–584.

Zetter, Kim (2014). *Countdown to Zero Day: Stuxnet and the Launch of the World's First Digital Weapon*. New York: Broadway Books.

9. Hunger, stability and alliances diversification: the food security in the Gulf and opportunities to cooperate with Argentina

Joel Foyth

9.1 INTRODUCTION

"Hunger makes me think a lot. When there is flour and everything, I sleep peacefully and comfortably. When there is no flour, you can't sleep", said Ali, a displaced Yemeni in Mokha camp (Khorsandi, 2022). However, only a few kilometres separate it from Qatar, one of the ten countries with the highest GDP per capita in the world, highlighting the differences in the Middle East and North Africa (MENA). Despite these contrasts, food security is one of the challenges common to the entire MENA, which faces major difficulties: little arable land, water scarcity, extreme weather, political crises, and a growing population demanding more and more food.

In addition, food insecurity significantly impacts the region's political stability. During the Arab Spring of 2011, many Arabs faced severe socio-economic crises. The Gulf monarchies managed to get through this process with relative stability but became involved in conflicts in their neighbouring countries. Today, the socio-economic indices of food security are in worse condition, and the possibility of an *Arab Spring 2.0* remains.

This chapter analyses food security in the Arab Gulf states of the Gulf Cooperation Council (GCC) and the MENA region. First, food security will be defined, and a brief summary of global trends will be presented. Then, food security in the GCC will be examined, focusing on recent external shocks and the situation in neighbouring countries, whose instability indirectly impacts its stability. Finally, prospects for collaboration with new international partners will be explored, focusing on Latin America and Argentina, a significant food exporter whose connection with the Arab world has yet to reach its full potential.

9.2 WHAT IS FOOD SECURITY?

The Food and Agriculture Organization (FAO)'s World Food Summit in 1996 defined food security as "when all people, at all times, have physical, social, and economic access to sufficient, safe, and nutritious food that meets their daily energy needs and dietary preferences for an active and healthy life" (FAO 2011, 2).

According to this definition, food security has four dimensions: food availability (consistently having enough food available); food access (having enough resources to obtain appropriate and nutritious food); food use/utilization (appropriate use of food based on basic nutrition knowledge); and the stability of these three dimensions over time (Ben Hassen and El Bilali 2019).

Many people may not go hungry, but rather be food insecure, meaning they must lower the quality or quantity of food they consume to survive. This can also contribute to other health issues, such as obesity. Nutritious food is typically more expensive than processed or flour- and fat-based foods. Thus, as average salaries fall, less healthy items are consumed. Both malnutrition and obesity can be signs of food insecurity.

In 2013, the FAO developed the Food Insecurity Experience Scale to assess various levels of food insecurity. Three main levels of food insecurity were identified: (1) mild insecurity (some concern about acquiring food); (2) moderate insecurity (lower quality of food intake or skipping meals); (3) severe insecurity (going more than one day without food or drink).

9.3 GLOBAL TRENDS IN FOOD SECURITY

Food security is a top priority for the United Nations (UN), and at least three agencies are working to achieve this goal: the FAO, which currently has 191 member countries; the World Food Programme (WFP), which provides food in times of crisis to more than 120 countries; and the International Fund for Agricultural Development (IFAD), a financial organization founded in 1978 that has provided more than USD 23.2 billion for projects related to rural development. Goal 2 of the Sustainable Development Agenda, 'Zero Hunger', explicitly tackles this problem and it is also indirectly included in the other SDGs: social and economic progress is impossible without ensuring that everyone has access to the food they require (Ben Hassen and El Bilali 2019).

In addition, globalization and the use of agricultural machinery, no-till farming, fertilizers, irrigation systems, and biotechnology have improved food production. According to Cascante, global output of food now is more than enough to meet global needs, and "the food supply covers the demand of the 8 billion people, even for a larger consumption than necessary" (2024, 2).

However, the prospect for global food security appears dismal. According to the FAO, IFAD, WHO, UNICEF, and WFP (2023) report *The State of Food Security and Nutrition in the World*, a progressive decline in food supplies and security has been noted since the second decade of the 21st century, which has become more pronounced after 2020. How is that possible? The problem lies not in production, but in the availability, access, and quality of food. To explain these inequalities, FAO et al. (2023), Cascante (2024), and García Juanatey (2023) provide some reasons:

1. The expansion of market forces in food access has improved commercial and productive efficiency, but also has negative effects on rural communities and the poorest segments of society who are unable to access the market as sellers or consumers.
2. The rise of transnational corporations who have gained control of key sections of the global food production chain but pursue goals that do not necessarily align with the global food security agenda.
3. Protectionism: the United States and the European Union, for example, have safeguarded domestic producers. Many developing economies – normally specialized in agricultural industries, and commodities sellers – cannot compete with those subsidized goods.
4. A highly concentrated market in which two or three countries control the supply of some basic products.
5. The use of food as financial assets which, in the face of excessive speculation, can generate unexpected price increases.
6. Climate change, as well as changes to the phosphorus and nitrogen cycles and biodiversity loss, pose the greatest threat to the world's poorest countries.

However, two big crises exacerbated global food insecurity: the COVID-19 pandemic and the Russia–Ukraine war.

SARS-COV-2 spread quickly over the world due to the high level of global interconnection. Although the entire world was united in the face of a common threat, quarantines, isolations, and border restrictions fragmented the planet. The fall of economic activity caused the most significant worldwide recession of the century, while disruptions in global supply chains resulted in goods shortages and difficulties accessing them.

On the other side, the conflict between Russia and Ukraine had terrible consequences (Al-Saidi 2023; Woertz 2022a). Any war on this scale causes significant disruption in the global economy. But Ukraine and Russia are also major agricultural producers. Ukraine's soil, known as *Chernozem* or 'black soil', is exceptionally productive because of its high humus, potassium, phosphorus, and microelement content. Russia is the world's largest wheat producer, accounting for over 30% of global production, alongside Ukraine. Ukraine is the world's largest producer of sunflower oil, with Russia coming in second, accounting for 60% of global production.

The disruptions surrounding the conflict, along with the fact that a substantial portion of Russian and Ukrainian grains were unable to be shipped for an extended period, drove up grain prices. Russia is also a major fertilizer provider, and disruptions in its supply caused rises in agricultural production costs in other nations.

According to the FAO et al. (2023) report, the pandemic increased the number of people suffering from hunger by 90 million between 2019 and 2020. Although the recovery in 2021 was significant, it varied by region, leading to an additional increase of 38 million people between 2021 and 2022. In 2022, it is estimated that 691 to 783 million suffered hunger, 122 million more than in 2019. The rise in food, agricultural input, and energy prices hampered the recovery of employment and incomes for the most disadvantaged.

The relative absence of changes in worldwide hunger between 2021 and 2022 hides significant regional and subregional disparities. The hunger increase has continued in Western Asia, the Caribbean, and all African subregions. On the Asian continent, improvements were seen in all subregions except Western Asia, where the prevalence of malnutrition rose from 10.2% in 2021 to 10.8% in 2022.

On the other side, the global prevalence of extreme food insecurity fell marginally from 11.7% in 2021 to 11.3% in 2022, which translates to 27 million fewer individuals. However, the number of people suffering from extreme food insecurity reached 900 million in 2022, up 180 million from 2019 figures. Facing that situation, the report summarizes:

> It is projected that almost 600 million people will be chronically undernourished in 2030, pointing to the immense challenge of achieving the SDG target to eradicate hunger. This is about 119 million more than in a scenario in which neither the pandemic nor the war in Ukraine had occurred, and around 23 million more than if the war in Ukraine had not happened (FAO et al. 2023, 7) (see Figure 9.1).

9.4 FOOD SECURITY IN THE GCC

According to the data in the FAO et al. (2023) report on the MENA, the number of undernourished people has doubled since 2010, from 25.2 million to 51.2 million, and the prevalence of serious food insecurity has increased from 9% in 2015 to 11.1% in 2022. Before COVID-19, Al-Fawwaz and Ahmed

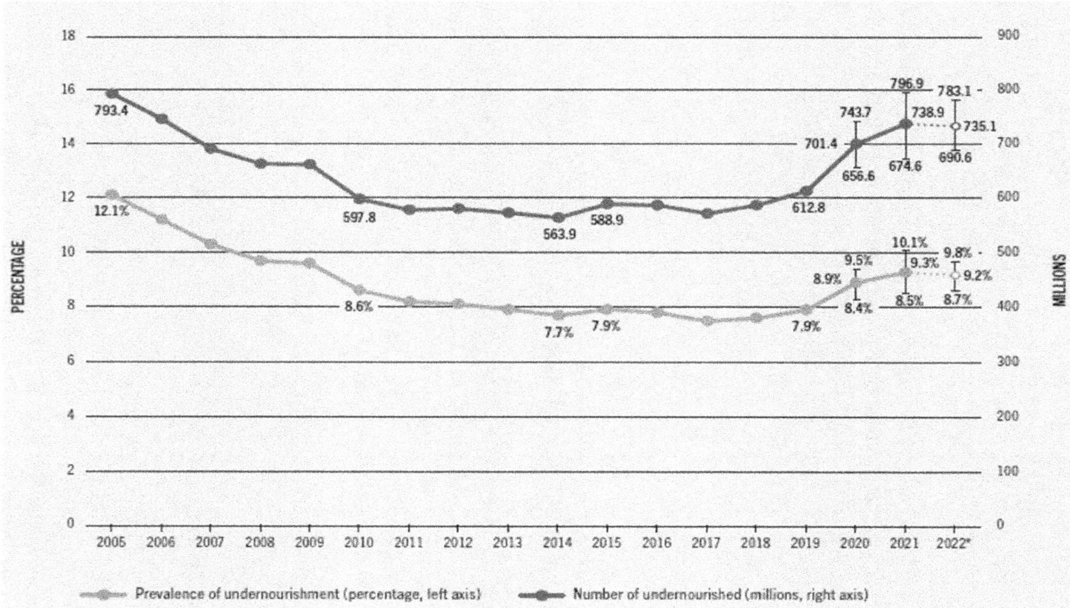

Source: FAO et al. (2023).

Figure 9.1 *Global hunger remained virtually unchanged from 2021 to 2022 but is still far above pre-COVID-19 pandemic levels*

(2016) described some of the factors that contributed to this critical situation in the MENA:

1. The region has few rivers, which are shared by multiple countries, resulting in tensions over their use.
2. Low rainfall combined with severe temperatures causes quick evaporation, making agricultural cultivation problematic.
3. The advance of desertification.
4. Low investment in agri-food technology.
5. Dependence on food imports, which are subject to fluctuations in world prices.

A serious global food crisis erupted between 2007 and 2008, increasing global food prices. There is still a debate about the causes, but there is a general consensus about some reasons that generated it: poor harvests in many parts of the world due to weather; low levels of food storage; increased demand from China and India; worldwide population expansion; increased biodiesel consumption; and global economic shifts. At that moment, food-exporting countries imposed withholdings on their products, reducing their exports, in order to mitigate the impact of the increase in global prices on their own markets. In that situation, the MENA was entirely exposed. As a result, a large number of social conflicts broke out in the region. This was the 'first signal' of the region's vulnerability, and food security was given prominence on the regional agenda, considering the political and social implications (Al-Fawwaz and Ahmed, 2016; Kamal 2018; Woertz 2022b).

Within MENA, the GCC countries have a comparatively low population density and represent approximately 30% of global oil and 20% of gas reserves, becoming one of the wealthiest regions in the world (Ben Hassen and El Bilali 2019). These countries' economic strength distinguishes them from their neighbours, and enables them to finance their food imports. According to the Global Food Security Index (Economist Impact 2022), the Gulf monarchies have the highest levels of regional food security: the United Arab Emirates (1), Israel (2), Qatar (3), Oman (4), Bahrain (5), Saudi Arabia (6), Jordan (7), Turkey (8), and Kuwait (9).

However, as Ben Hassen and El Bilali (2019) point out, this does not imply self-sufficiency. Gulf countries rely significantly on food imports and have little control over their food supply chain. During the 2007–2008 food crisis, GCC countries experienced significant inflationary pressure due to the increase of global food prices.

More than 95% of the Gulf's territory is vulnerable to desertification, which limits agricultural development (Elmi 2017). In addition, it is the region of the globe with the least amount of water resources, accounting for about 1% of the world's freshwater resources, and approximately 85–90% going to support its – inefficient – agricultural production. According to estimates, climate change could cause temperatures to rise by 2 degrees in the next 15 to 20 years and up to 4 degrees by the end of the century, resulting in a 20–30% decline in water availability by 2050 (Fabani 2016).

The GCC countries took the initiative to face this problem. Saudi Arabia established an extensive programme of subsidies and financing for wheat growing, and by 1984 it became self-sufficient. However, it was expensive and required extensive irrigation and fertilizer systems, resulting in soil degradation (Ben Hassen and El Bilali 2019; Fabani 2016).

As a result, the Arab Gulf states changed their strategy to allow food imports (Kamal 2018). However, this creates concerns in contractionary periods of international trade, and it is dependent on the stability of international trade logistics. There are at least three main routes to supply Gulf demand: the Suez Canal, the Strait of Bab al-Mandab, and the Strait of Hormuz. The conflict in Yemen, the rivalry between Saudi Arabia and Iran, and the overall instability in the region make it particularly vulnerable to possible cuts. Even still, about 80–90% of the food consumed in the Gulf is imported (Elmi 2017).

In addition to the failed attempt to expand domestic agriculture and implement an open policy on food imports, the GCC countries made significant foreign investments in agriculture following 2007–2008 (Elmi 2017). Since then, the Arab monarchies have signed 67 land purchase deals, acquiring 4.36 million hectares of cropland around the world, in many developing countries. Likewise, Arab agricultural firms, such as Al Dahra or Hassan Food, launched their investments in agricultural companies (Fabani 2016).

However, these initiatives were criticized in the receiving countries due to their environmental consequences, the displacement of native communities, and the 'extractivist behaviour', since they were carried out in nations with major food insecurity challenges. As Kamal (2018) indicates, these measures raised dependence on the international market, because these countries many times put limits on food exports based on their own food security.

The Arab Gulf countries have also implemented a food reserve and stockpile strategy. However, this is costly and risky, since grains can be attacked by pests in silos and their preservation requires certain temperature and humidity levels that are difficult to guarantee in the Gulf's severe temperatures and demand additional energy costs. Nonetheless, it has proven a valuable technique. In 2018, Oman announced intentions to build a bulk agricultural port in Salalah capable of storing 60,000 tons of grain (Ben Hassen and El Bilali 2019).

The GCC has gradually acknowledged its reliance on foreign markets and focused on managing it. In this regard, the Arab monarchies in the Gulf have made a reasonably effective transition into modern value chains in food processing, distribution, and trade, proposing deals with large agricultural exporters and establishing food marketing and distribution corporations. For example, the Saudi Agricultural and Livestock Investment Company partnered with Bunge to acquire a majority position in the privatized Canadian Wheat Board. Similarly, the Gulf's entrepreneurs have a significant impact in other MENA nations through huge companies such as Americana in Kuwait and Savola in Saudi Arabia. This was complemented by a more flexible and adaptable connection with the foreign market, including diversifying suppliers, streamlining health measures, and facilitating import flows (Woertz 2022b).

9.5 THE IMPACT OF COVID-19 AND THE WAR IN UKRAINE

The SARS-COV-2 pandemic's impact on food security was transmitted by the resulting deep worldwide economic crisis. The GCC was heavily hurt by the decline in international activity and trade, which resulted in a collapse in oil prices and a sharp drop in tourists. However, Woertz (2020) demonstrates that in terms of food, these countries were able to handle the situation differently than during the 2007–2008 global food crisis. Social distancing policies had a higher impact on conventional food value chains, which are dominated by small and medium-sized firms that are labour-intensive. However, the Arab Gulf's modern food value chains, which are dominated by supermarkets and capital-intensive processing plants, were less susceptible to these shocks.

Nevertheless, the GCC states face other challenges. These countries have one of the highest numbers per capita of persons with diabetes and obesity, both of which are risk factors for infection. Sedentary lifestyles and excessive consumption of goods high in sugars, fats, and carbs demonstrated nutritional weaknesses.

Food accessibility issues were linked to the most disadvantaged sectors: immigrant workers. They represent significant percentages of the population: the UAE (88%), Qatar (76%), Kuwait (74%), Bahrain (51%), Oman (41%), and Saudi Arabia (32%). Many of these immigrant workers have transitory and often low-wage positions. These populations were the most affected by the COVID-19 pandemic because they had difficulties in accessing the healthcare system, and their income was diminished as a result of the unexpected halt in economic activity. The economic crisis posed a significant challenge by reducing their income and forcing them to choose between staying in the Gulf – with reduced salaries or no pay at all – or returning to their countries with little savings.

However, GCC countries took the lead in vaccination campaigns, soon obtaining the coverage required for herd immunity. The UAE led with 98%, followed by Qatar (94%), Kuwait (76%), Saudi Arabia (74%), Bahrain (70%), and Oman (68%) (Paredes Rodríguez 2023). However, just as the initial shock had subsided, the crisis started in Eastern Europe. The drop in Russian gas and hydrocarbon sales, combined with the closing of the Black Sea port of Odesa, from which cereals were shipped, anticipated the region's challenges.

According to Paredes Rodríguez (2023), the Ukraine war created a contradictory scenario for the GCC countries. They benefited from a rise in hydrocarbon prices, which reversed the pandemic's fall and reached USD 117.72 per barrel by June. For example, Saudi Arabia raised $110 billion, compared to $49 billion in 2020. This offered monetary resources to solve the crisis, but it also highlighted the lack of economic diversification and the heavy reliance on the international market for food security.

Elmi (2017) shows that there is a direct relationship between energy and agricultural pricing because the fertilizers industry, the usage of machinery, and the transportation of agricultural products require a significant quantity of fuel. Price increases in one of these items are generally followed by increases in the others. Although the GCC countries gained more resources from its exports, inflation increased significantly as food costs rose. Similarly, it was not easy to diversify suppliers. Russian and Ukrainian wheat is cheaper because of its lower quality, and the surge in oil prices led to increased international freight costs, making products from other regions still more expensive (Paredes Rodríguez 2023).

9.6 THE IMPACT OF COVID-19 AND THE WAR IN UKRAINE ON THE REST OF THE MENA

The GCC cannot ignore what is going on in its neighbouring countries. In 2011, the Arab Spring emerged in protest at poor economic conditions, corruption, and a lack of freedom. The Gulf was mostly stable until demonstrations started in Bahrain. This crisis was rapidly contained by Saudi and Emirati soldiers, but for more than a decade, the GCC states remained involved in regional conflicts in Yemen, Syria, and Libya, investing enormous amounts of money in different military factions.

From 2020 to 2022, the other countries of MENA experienced these shocks in different ways than the GCC. Robert Mardini, the director-general of the International Committee of the Red Cross stated:

> There is an urgent and rapidly deteriorating global food security situation, especially in parts of Africa and the Middle East. Armed conflict, political instability, climate shocks, and the secondary impacts of the COVID-19 pandemic have weakened capacities to withstand and recover from shocks. The knock-on-effects of the armed conflict in Ukraine have made an already critical situation even worse. (International Committee of the Red Cross 2022)

The emergence of the virus and the isolation measures created enormous challenges, as important economic activities are carried out in sectors with a large concentration of people, such as in the well-known bazaars with typical street hawking. Furthermore, previous economic weakness limited the stimuli that states could undertake in the face of massive budget deficits, income declines, and high debt levels – especially in countries like Lebanon or Egypt. As a result, the regional economy declined by 5.7%, reaching 13% in conflict-affected countries. According to Paredes Rodríguez (2023), 14 million extra poor people have been added to the current 115, excluding the GCC.

The vaccination programmes against COVID-19 in the MENA countries other than the GCC were slower. By the end of 2022, rates of vaccination were still well below the necessary 70%: Iran 68%, Turkey 63%, Morocco 64%, Tunisia 52%, Jordan 44%, Lebanon 43%, Egypt 39%, and the PA 35%. The worst performances were in Iraq with 18%, Libya 17%, Syria 10%, and Yemen 2%. This revealed a new division in the region: between middle-income and impoverished countries. There were significant differences between countries like Egypt or Morocco and those in conflict, such as Syria or Yemen. In the latter case, the sharp global economic recession dealt a final blow to millions of people who were already facing food problems. In response to the economic crisis, many governments reduced the resources that were available to foreign humanitarian aid organizations, forcing them to limit their food assistance programmes.

These countries were already struggling to recover from the pandemic's consequences when the Ukraine crisis began. Tunisia, Egypt, Syria, Turkey, Jordan, and Lebanon have not only seen substantial increases in food prices but also in energy costs, exacerbating the social and economic crises. The food supply cut caused a significant catastrophe, given the countries' reliance on these imports. When the percentages are broken down by the amount of wheat imported from Russia and Ukraine, the dependence is clear: Egypt imports the most from Russia, accounting for 60.4%, followed by the United Arab Emirates (46.8%), and Yemen (26.7%). Lebanon imports 80.4% from Ukraine, followed by Tunisia (48.6%) and Morocco (14.6%) (Arab Reform Initiative 2022) (see Figure 9.2).

Egypt, Lebanon, Turkey, and Tunisia all reported poverty rates of 32.5%, 74%, 14%, and 17.2%, respectively, in 2019.

Cooking oil consumption increased by 36% in Yemen and 39% in Syria. Wheat flour increased by 47% in Lebanon, 15% in Libya, and 14% in Palestine. Egypt saw 14.9% annual inflation, leading to price increases of 29% for vegetables, 66% for cereals, 28% for bread, 24% for fish, and 22% for meat. In Egypt, there is still potential for action to subsidize some commodities, but in nations like Lebanon, the cost of the basic basket has increased by 351%

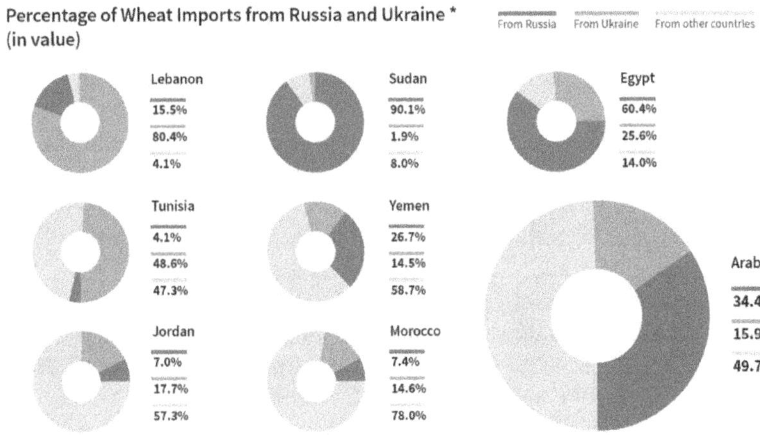

Source: Arab Reform Initiative (2022).

Figure 9.2 Dependence of Arab countries on wheat imported from Russia and Ukraine

annually. Syria and Yemen have also had huge increases of 97% and 81%, respectively.

This sparked considerable social frustration, resulting in a return of protests similar to those seen during the Arab Spring. Poor global crops caused the FAO food price index to reach its highest level in 50 years in 2011. Food prices reached a new high in March 2022, but this time it was aggravated by increases in a wide range of products, including fertilizers, fuel, and transportation. Egypt is a key example: it is the most populated Arab country, with a considerable proportion of its population facing economic difficulties, and it is the world's largest wheat importer (Al-Saidi 2023). Bread and other wheat derivatives contribute for 40% of the population's caloric income, with wheat imports accounting for 60% of the total consumed.

Bread has a significant political impact. That is, it is intentionally subsidized to prevent societal unrest and revolts like those seen in the 1970s, 2008, and 2011. It was no coincidence that the people at Tahrir Square chanted as a mantra the phrases "bread, dignity, and freedom" (*kheb, karama, hurriya*) (Paredes Rodríguez 2023, 215).

Lebanon, Syria, Libya, and Yemen are on the brink of humanitarian disaster. In Yemen, the overall value of food imports exceeds that of all exports, and the World Food Programme provides emergency food assistance to 11 million people (Welsh 2022). According to the FAO-WFP joint forecast for 2022, 17.4

million Yemenis were predicted to face acute food insecurity, 5.6 million to be in the emergency phase, and 31,000 to be in the highest food insecurity emergency. In addition, roughly 2.2 million children under the age of five and 1.3 million pregnant and lactating women were estimated to suffer from acute malnutrition in 2022.

9.7 THE TROUBLED FOOD INSECURITY IN THE MENA

Faced with this dismal panorama, the Arab Barometer report says:

> Still, those suffering from food insecurity express a higher desire to emigrate. And finally, food insecurity has devastating effects on present and future outlooks, with food insecure citizens – particularly youth – likely to say both that their lives are better than their parents and their children's lives will be better than their own. (Al-Shami 2022, 12)

This dilemma affects the entire area, as it has become the primary importer of grains, particularly wheat, and no country is self-sufficient in food production. Despite the potential for integration, fragmenting pressures exist, and governments prioritize their interest and their sovereignty over multilateralism (Woertz 2022b).

Rivalries prevail in the region. In the Gulf, the rivalry between the Arab monarchies – especially Saudi Arabia – and Iran has shaped the geopolitics of the entire MENA. Since 2011, Riyadh and Tehran have engaged in a *death match*, intervening in the conflicts that emerged after the Arab Spring failure, and funding various armed groups to strengthen their power and wear down their adversaries. At the same time, the GCC has been fractured by the conflict with Qatar, which has been accused of supporting the Muslim Brotherhood. As a result, Amirahmadi asserts that a dark geopolitics has emerged:

> The new geopolitics of the Middle East will be characterized by failed states, political chaos, popular revolt, religious extremism, inter-state conflict, foreign rivalries, and military interventions. Countries of the region will be left plundered, their social systems twisted and dehumanized, their environments ruined, and their cities and towns vacated by citizens migrating to safer places. In such a dark scenario, a condition of despair will prevail and extremist groups and their rivals, struggling for self-preservation, will scar the Middle Eastern landscape. (2015, 93)

This chaotic scenario harms food security in the region. The 2019 FAO report shows that all food indices have deteriorated since 2011. Although environmental variables present a significant difficulty in resolving this issue, violence and regional fragmentation have further exacerbated the situation (see Figures 9.3 and 9.4).

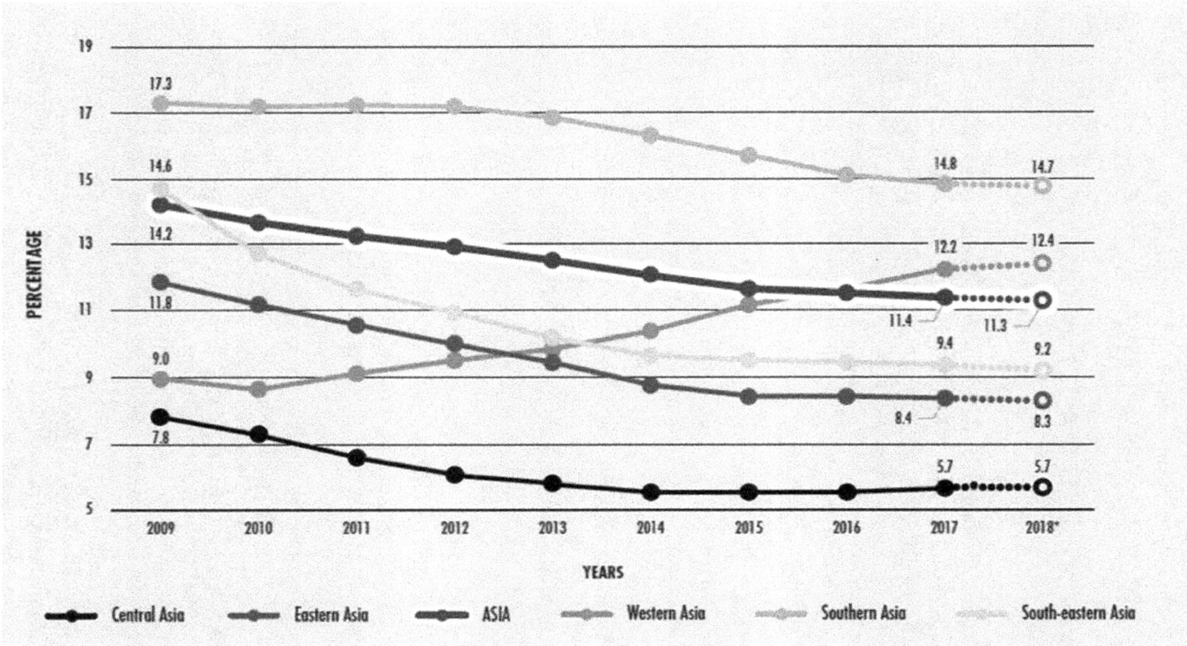

Source: FAO et al. (2019).

Figure 9.3 *Progress in the level of malnutrition in Asia*

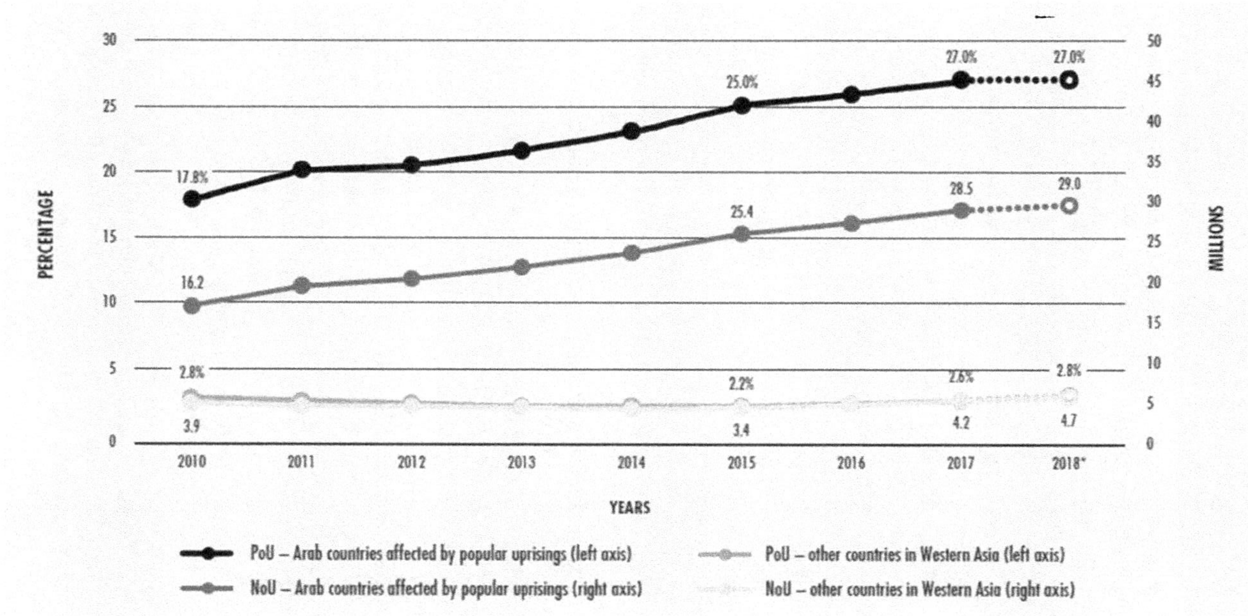

Source: FAO et al. (2019).

Figure 9.4 *Prevalence of malnutrition in West Asian countries*

9.8 THE GULF AND LATIN AMERICA: OPPORTUNITIES IN THE MIDDLE OF THE CRISIS

Due to geographical distance and cultural differences, relationships between Latin American countries and the Gulf states have generally been cordial yet distant. Both regions have prioritized their relationship with traditional global power, such as Europe, the United States, and increasingly China. However, in the last years a new political vision has emerged in the GCC countries' leadership – especially in Saudi Arabia, the UAE, and Qatar – with a more autonomist perspective, that considers it important to diversify partners, and also perceive their countries as future leaders of a more multipolar world. Within this framework, COVID-19 and the war in Ukraine exposed the potential for a shared agenda with Latin America, centred on food security, the energy market, and productive and technical development.

In this analysis, the focus will be on cooperation potential with Argentina, Latin America's third-largest economy. It is a bi-oceanic country with an Exclusive Economic Zone of 2,809,237 km^2 rich in maritime resources. It has a significant mining industry and is part of the 'lithium triangle' shared with Bolivia and Chile, which has over half of the world's reserves. This will be crucial for the development of renewable energy batteries (Barría 2019). In turn, the extraction of Vaca Muerta, a significant formation of unconventional hydrocarbons, is expected to produce 27 billion barrels of oil and 802 trillion cubic feet of gas, making it the fourth country with non-conventional oil reserves and the second of gas (Mirazón 2018).

However, Argentina is a major player in the agricultural industry. The core zone of the country, constituted by the provinces of Santa Fe, Buenos Aires, and Córdoba, has one of the richest soils in the world and is located in the Guaraní Aquifer. It is the second country in the world in terms of per capita water resources. Argentina has a 'surplus' of production since it can feed its population while also exporting enormous quantities. According to the FAO, Argentina is one of seven countries that are responsible for around 55% of total food exports worldwide (United Nations – Argentina 2021).

According to a study conducted by the Rosario Stock Exchange (Bolsa de Comercio de Rosario 2020), in 2020, Argentina was the world's third-largest producer of cereals and oilseeds; the first exporter of soybean oil and flour; the third exporter of corn flour and oil; the third exporter of soybeans; the third exporter of sunflower oil and pellets; the second exporter of sorghum; the third corn exporter; the sixth exporter of wheat and derivatives – the seventh of net wheat; the fifth barley exporter; the fifth producer and major exporter of biodiesel; the fifth global producer of milk powder; the sixth of cheese; the ninth in raw milk production; the twelfth in skimmed milk powder production; and the sixth producer and the fifth exporter of beef.

Argentina is also developing an important innovation ecosystem in the AgTech, BioTech, and AgrifoodTech sectors, where diverse start-ups create and apply innovative technological solutions in the agri-food chain. These new technologies use 'blockchain', artificial intelligence, IoT, and biotechnology to collect and analyse data from the field, genetics, transactions, and climate phenomena, thereby improving production, efficiency, sustainability, and profitability. They are still in their early phases, but Argentina has significant prospects to make a technological leap and establish itself as a regional and worldwide reference point.

The challenges and complementarities between Argentina and the Arab Gulf states are clear. They are 'emerging' countries, producing commodities, but have reached a certain level of diversification and technological development. However, they are vulnerable to external shocks, still with inequalities and lack of economic development. There are also clearly defined complementary needs. Argentina requires markets to export food and agro-industrial products with added value and internationalize the agri-food tech companies. The GCC can serve as a distribution base for Argentine products throughout the Arab world. For its part, the Gulf must continue to diversify its partners to ensure food supply and prevent potential supply disruptions in the international market.

However, some barriers prevent this link from deepening: long distances, which make international trade more expensive; language and cultural differences; quality standards, such as Halal certification, which is costly for small Argentine and Latin American businesses; and the lack of an assertive trade policy. The First South America–Arab Countries Summit in 2005 witnessed Mercosur and the GCC sign an agreement to begin a trade liberalization process, but it was gradually diluted without making significant progress (Mercociudades 2005).

A strategic alliance between the GCC and Latin America might grow from this relationship, based on investments, food security, the energy market, and technological development. Noronha (2022) shows that trade between the two regions has been expanding rapidly. The primary exports from Latin America were gold, meat, iron ore, cereals, sugar, and coffee. For its part, the GCC exported plastic polymers, aluminium, ammonia, oil, and fertilizers to Latin America. Latin America has had a notable surplus of trade, with US$17.2 billion in exports in 2019, compared to the GCC's average yearly export of US$2,500–3,500 between 2016 and 2020. Even if there are plenty of chances to increase bilateral trade, the actual numbers are still far lower than they could be. In 2020, the GCC's imports from Latin America made up 3.2% of its total imports, while its exports to the region made up less than 1%. The trade between Argentina and the Arab world reflects the same trend. The principal Arab trading partners of the Argentine economy are Saudi Arabia, Egypt, and the UAE. None of them are among the top 15 trading partners, despite the fact that generally the commercial balance is in favour of Argentina's economy.

A small and lopsided trade balance could be seen as a barrier to strengthening the relationship. But this emphasizes how crucial political activity is to building and expanding the connection. Certainly, one of the most pressing needs is to advance the establishment of a free trade agreement between Mercosur and the GCC. The GCC has signed these agreements with other regions that put Latin American products at a disadvantage. This type of agreement becomes an imperative need to create the general framework to advance on the deepening of the link.

"Several steps must be taken, starting with fundamentals such as increasing Latam's diplomatic and business presence in the GCC, as well as facilitating migration and increasing flight connections" Noronha (2022, 16) points out, emphasizing the importance of political will in moving forward with deepening the link. In addition, different kinds of sectoral agreements can be created to address certain needs within the context of a general trade agreement. To maintain long-term supplies over a period of ten or twenty years, the GCC countries could, for instance, negotiate with Argentina and other Latin American countries to purchase basic agricultural commodities, such as wheat or corn, and agree on future prices and quantities. These agreements would be similar to *forward contracts*. One could also take comparable actions while buying processed food items. Argentina will greatly benefit from this, as agro-food small and medium-sized enterprises (SMEs) play a major role in the country's economy. These economic players as well as the main Arab supermarket chains like Tamimi, Danube, Lulu, etc. should be parties to such agreements. The rationale behind settling on a long-term food supply agreement lowers uncertainty about shortages and abrupt price swings.

Expanding commercial relations with Argentina and other Latin American nations might potentially exacerbate the trade deficit for the GCC. However, the latter can obtain global gains by linking with other areas. Investing is certainly one of them. Argentina needs to invest heavily in order to upgrade its infrastructure, advance technologically, and achieve financial stability. The GCC nations could seize this chance to diversify their interests in Argentine firms by buying logistics or agriculture firms, for instance. Furthermore, Argentina is experiencing a protracted financial crisis that has led to a significant currency crisis. The GCC countries can utilize the granting of credits to get out of this crisis as a negotiating chip to strengthen their position in bilateral commerce.

In this scenario, the Gulf would diversify its food suppliers, while Argentina would extend its market and potentially gain inputs, technologies, and investments. Argentina might build collaborative agricultural development cooperation initiatives with the GCC, which would help neighbouring countries. Egypt, Syria, Iraq, Yemen, or Jordan might increase agricultural production while maximizing the use of natural resources by integrating agricultural technologies and considerable Argentine agricultural expertise. In this approach, the demand for food imports could be reduced.

Some of the GCC monarchies and Argentina have already carried out important cooperation programmes in developing countries. Important agricultural production-related organizations exist in Argentina, such as the CREA network and the Argentine No-Till Farmers Association (AAPRESID), both of which have completed cooperative projects aimed at transferring technology and know-how to support agricultural production in Sub-Saharan Africa. Similarly, Argentine organizations like the Rosario Stock Exchange and the National Institute of Agricultural Technologies (INTA) play a significant role in advancing and developing digital agriculture technologies. These kinds of organizations can be invited to consider cooperative initiatives aimed at technology transfer and agricultural technological advancement in the MENA region. Implementing triangle cooperation initiatives among Argentina, the GCC, and the MENA's Arab nations can prove to be beneficial for this region.

Without a doubt, there is a wide variety of topics on a shared agenda between both regions, which require significant work to achieve them.

9.9 CONCLUSION: WHAT CAN THE GCC DO?

Food security will remain a challenge for the Arab Gulf states and the whole of the MENA. However, the GCC can take steps to alleviate this issue. Al-Saidi summarizes this vision: "Alongside more regional frameworks for collaboration on food security, future action to mitigate such food crises should include the strengthening of local sustainable agriculture, storage capacities, and grain procurement strategies from international suppliers" (2023, 1).

First and foremost, consumption patterns must improve, as there is a significant degree of food waste in the Gulf countries – heavily influenced by subsidy programmes. On the other hand, some specific agricultural production can be developed. In the course of this initiative, investment in digital technology in the AgTech, BioTech, AgrifoodTech, and other similar industries is critical. In the MENA, Israel has encouraged the formation of hundreds of agri-food start-ups, resulting in significant agricultural production even in arid circumstances. The UAE have started along this path. It launched its National Food Security Strategy in 2018, intending to be the world's first food-secure country by 2051. One of the initiatives has been the establishment of the Food Tech Valley in Dubai, which aims to be the world's first metropolis dedicated to agricultural technology and triple food production in the UAE. This cluster is divided into four groups: agrotechnology and engineering, a food innovation centre, research and development centres, and a smart food logistics centre (Das Augustine 2023).

At least three significant technologies have already started to grow (Government of Dubai n.d). One of these is vertical agriculture, which implies growing in a vertical structure that may stack several layers of crops, similar to floors, and use LED illumination in greenhouses with climate control and sprinkling irrigation. The technique is tailored to the particular requirements of each crop, resulting in harvests throughout the year. Emirati enterprises in this industry include Badia Farms, Dubai Industrial City, and Pure Harvest Smart Farms.

Another sector has been hydroponic cultivation, which involves placing plant roots directly into a nutrient solution rather than soil. This 'closed loop' system collects and recirculates water rather than letting it drain. This technology uses 70% less water, eliminates the need for toxic chemicals, and allows for a longer harvest season.

Third, the Desert Control company created Liquid NanoClay technology, which blends clay and water nanoparticles and, when mixed with desert sand, helps the land to retain moisture, transforming it into fruitful soil. This reduced the demand for irrigation by 45% while also absorbing carbon dioxide emissions (Eco Inventos 2022).

The growth of these high-tech companies provides advantages in terms of sustainability, food security, and technological development, improving also the economic diversification process. However, there is debate over the overall economic and environmental balance. Vertical farms, for example, demand major investments in air conditioning and LED lighting, signifying a higher energy cost than traditional agriculture. Many of these Gulf companies still rely heavily on the conventional energy infrastructure, which is subsidized and based on hydrocarbons, raising concerns about their long-term sustainability. However, this local production incurs lower international freight costs. Without a doubt, the long-term sustainability of these industries remains unknown, but they are sectors that should be fostered and incorporated into a worldwide environmental and productivity strategy (Gerretsen 2020).

But the key point is that the GCC will need to change its international positioning. Because of its economic and political strength, it has emerged as the most prominent MENA subregion. However, it has acted in the region from a security perspective, intervening in – and sadly exacerbating – regional conflicts and investing billions in military groups. The GCC countries must change their approach and collaborate to improve their neighbours' food security, which will minimize the likelihood of conflict and provide an opportunity to display constructive regional leadership. With its excellent port, logistics, commercial, and financial infrastructure, the GCC has the potential to become a hub for food trade, ensuring supplies to the entire MENA region and Asia.

On the other hand, nearby nations such as Egypt, Morocco, Jordan, Syria, and Iraq have better natural conditions. This regional policy aims to support GCC neighbours in developing their food production sectors through finance and cooperation programmes for agricultural development. Similarly, these are suitable markets for Gulf-based AgTech and AgrifoodTech companies to expand into. Establishing some regional food production chains is critical for maintaining a buffer against the fluctuations of the worldwide market. It is crucial to keep in mind that, in Europe, the Common Agricultural Policy of 1962 was one of the pillars of integration in the formation of the European Union. Similarly, this regional agricultural-food policy has the potential to bridge the MENA's fierce rivalries. This is an opportunity for the GCC nations to be the leaders of this movement.

However, this new international insertion entails a strengthening of the engagement with other actors outside the region. According to Woertz (2022b), a reinvigorated *food diplomacy* must be developed that includes strong coordinated action with the region in international forums as well as negotiations with other regional blocs to ensure and strengthen agricultural product supply. Building a strategic partnership with Latin America is critical here since they were previously secondary partners but can now provide food, technology, and training to help the MENA region boost its productive capacities.

When seeking international partners, the Arab Gulf states have prioritized strategic-military connections and the main global powers. However, food security has provided an ideal chance to strengthen ties with Latin America. The most recent international shocks since 2020 have demonstrated that the region remains vulnerable, but can find new partners with whom to collaborate. Food security, the energy market, and agricultural technical progress might serve as the foundation for this new regional approach.

There is little doubt that the following years will be defined by global uncertainties, including increased climate change, the persistence of the conflict in Ukraine and regional tensions in the MENA, and the potential appearance of new disruptive phenomena, such as COVID-19. Faced with this, the future not only holds risks but also opportunities to reshape the Gulf's international role and change its productive pattern. Without a doubt, the future remains uncertain, but the GCC can make the necessary decisions to lead a positive role in the MENA.

REFERENCES

Al-Fawwaz, Abdulrahman and Ahmed, Abdullah. (2016). "The reality of food security in the Arab world". *International Journal of Asian Social Science*, Vol. 6, (4): 251–261. https://doi.org/10.18488/journal.1/2016.6.4/1.4.251.261

Al-Saidi, Mohammad. (2023). "Caught off guard and beaten: The Ukraine war and food security in the Middle East". *Frontiers in Nutrition*, Vol. 10: 1–15. https://doi.org/10.3389/fnut.2023.983346

Al-Shami, Salma. (2022). "Food insecurity and its discontents in the Middle East and North Africa". *Arab Barometer Wave II*. Princeton: Arab Barometer. https://www.arabbarometer.org/report/food-insecurity-and-its-discontents-in-the-middle-east-and-north-africa/

Amirahmadi, Hooshang. (2015). "Dark geopolitics of the Middle East". *The Cairo Review of Global Affairs*, Vol. 18: 86–94. https://www.thecairoreview.com/essays/dark-geopolitics-of-the-middle-east/

Arab Reform Initiative. (2022). "The impact of the Ukraine war on the Arab region: Food insecurity in an already vulnerable context". *ARI*, March 11. https://www.arab-reform.net/publication/the-impact-of-the-ukraine-war-on-the-arab-region-food-insecurity-in-an-already-vulnerable-context/

Barría, Cecilia. (2019). "El triángulo del litio: 3 obstáculos que enfrentan Argentina, Bolivia y Chile para escapar de la 'maldición de los recursos naturales'". *BBC*, June 19. https://www.bbc.com/mundo/noticias-48666235

Ben Hassen, Tarek and El Bilali, Hamid. (2019). "Food security in the Gulf Cooperation Council countries: Challenges and prospects". *Journal of Food Security*, Vol. 7, (5): 159–169.

Bolsa de Comercio de Rosario. (2020). *Comercialización de Granos – Programa de Formación*. Rosario, Argentina: Bolsa de Comercio de Rosario.

Cascante, Kattya. (2024). "La (in)seguridad alimentaria del siglo XXI: Una mirada crítica de la globalización". *GATE Center*. Working paper no. 7. https://gatecenter.org/la-in-seguridad-alimentaria-del-siglo-xxi-una-mirada-critica-de-la-globalizacion/

Das Augustine, Babu. (2023). "Dubai's Food Tech Valley and ReFarm to build a hi-tech gigafarm". *The National News*, December 6. https://www.thenationalnews.com/business/technology/2023/12/06/dubais-food-tech-valley-and-refarm-to-build-a-hi-tech-gigafarm/

Eco Inventos. (2022). "Innovación que convierte la arena del desierto en suelos fértiles en solo 7 horas". June 2. https://ecoinventos.com/liquid-nanoclay/#google_vignette

Economist Impact. (2022). "Global Food Security Index 2022". https://impact.economist.com/sustainability/project/food-security-index

Elmi, Abdirasbid A. (2017). "Food security in the Arab Gulf Cooperation Council States". In *Sustainable Agriculture Reviews*. Vol 25, edited by Eric Lichtfouse, 89–114. Cham: Springer. https://doi.org/10.1007/978-3-319-58679-3_3

Fabani, Ornela. (2016). "Cambio climático, agua y seguridad alimentaria: América Latina en la mira de las monarquías del Golfo". In *Anuario del Instituto de Relaciones Internacionales*, edited by Norberto E. Consansi. La Plata: Departamento de Medio Oriente, Instituto de Relaciones Internacionales. http://hdl.handle.net/11336/62521

Food and Agriculture Organization (FAO). (2011). *Seguridad Alimentaria Nutricional, Conceptos Básicos*. 3rd Edition, February.

FAO, IFAD, UNICEF, WFP and WHO. (2019). *The State of Food Security and Nutrition in the World 2019. Safeguarding against Economic Slowdowns and*

Downturns. Rome, FAO. https://www.wfp.org/publications/2019-state-food-security-and-nutrition-world-sofi-safeguarding-against-economic

FAO, IFAD, UNICEF, WFP and WHO. (2023). *The State of Food Security and Nutrition in the World 2023. Urbanization, Agrifood Systems Transformation and Healthy Diets across the Rural–Urban Continuum*. Rome, FAO. https://doi.org/10.4060/cc3017en

García Juanatey, Ana. (2023). "El deterioro de la seguridad alimentaria global". In *Bienes y derechos básicos en tiempos de crisis una mirada desde lo urbano*, edited by Marta Galceran-Vercher, 19–24. Barcelona: CIDOB Report 10. https://www.cidob.org/publicaciones/deterioro-seguridad-alimentaria-global-urbana-contexto-post-ucrania

Gerretsen, Isabelle. (2020). "Farming tech fit for the desert". *DW*, July 22. https://www.dw.com/en/united-arab-emirates-vertical-farming/a-54252631

Government of Dubai. (n.d) "Innovación e inversión en agrotecnología". *Invest in Dubai*. https://www.investindubai.gov.ae/es/insights-and-resources/news-insights/food-agriculture-guide/innovation-investment-agritech#:~:text=Badia%20Farms%20fue%20la%20primera,y%20hierbas%20para%20restaurantes%20locales

International Committee of the Red Cross. (2022). "Deteriorating hunger situation an urgent crisis for millions caught in armed conflict". July 12. https://www.icrc.org/en/document/deteriorating-hunger-situation-urgent-crisis-millions-caught-conflict

Kamal, Abid. (2018). "The status of food security in the Gulf Cooperation Council (GCC) countries". *JIGYASA*, Vol. 11, (3): 121–130.

Khorsandi, Peyvand. (2022) "Yemen: Millions at risk as Ukraine war effect rocks region Peyvand Khorsandi Peyvand". Worlf Food Program. March 14. https://www.wfp.org/stories/yemen-millions-risk-ukraine-war-effect-rocks-region

Mercociudades. (2005). "El Mercosur selló un acuerdo comercial con los países Árabes". May 18. https://mercociudades.org/el-mercosur-sello-un-acuerdo-comercial-con-los-paises-arabes/

Mirazón, Ezequiel. (2018). "Vaca Muerta: el atractivo de invertir en no convencionales". *PWC Argentina*. https://www.pwc.com.ar/es/publicaciones/vaca-muerta-invertir-en-energia-no-convencional.html

Noronha, Melanie. (2022). "Cultivating ties: Deepening trade and investment between Latin America and the GCC". *Economist Impact*, March 16. https://impact.economist.com/new-globalisation/cultivating-ties-deepening-trade-and-investment-between-latin-america-and-gcc

Paredes Rodríguez, Ruben. (2023). "La pandemia de COVID-19 y la Guerra de Ucrania: implicancias socio-económicas en la región del MENA". In *¿Y ahora adónde vamos? Nuevos desafíos en el Medio Oriente*, edited by Ornela Fabani and Ignacio Rullansky, 205–218. La Plata: Universidad Nacional de La Plata. Facultad de Ciencias Jurídicas y Sociales.

United Nations – Argentina. (2021). "Análisis conjunto del sistema de Naciones Unidas 2021: los efectos de la pandemia por covid-19 en la Argentina". UN Buenos Aires. https://argentina.un.org/es/145708-an%C3%A1lisis-conjunto-del-sistema-de-naciones-unidas-2021-los-efectos-de-la-pandemia-por-covid

Welsh, Caitlin. (2022). "The impact of Russia's invasion of Ukraine in the Middle East and North Africa". *Center for Strategic & International Studies*, May 18. https://www.csis.org/analysis/impact-russias-invasion-ukraine-middle-east-and-north-africa

Woertz, Eckart. (2020). "Wither the self-sufficiency illusion? Food security in Arab Gulf States and the impact of COVID-19". *Food Security*, Vol. 12: 757–760. https://doi.org/10.1007/s12571-020-01081-4

Woertz, Eckart. (2022a). "Geopolítica de los alimentos: la guerra en Ucrania impacta en la seguridad alimentaria de Oriente Medio" in Opinión CIDOB No. 718: 1–4. https://www.cidob.org/publicaciones/geopolitica-alimentos-guerra-ucrania-impacta-seguridad-alimentaria-oriente-medio

Woertz, Eckart. (2022b). "The Russian war against Ukraine: Middle East food security at risk". Hamburg: German Institute for Global and Area Studies (GIGA) - Leibniz-Institut für Globale und Regionale Studien, Institut für Nahost-Studien. https://nbn-resolving.org/urn:nbn:de:0168-ssoar-81596-5

10. Leveraging cultural and creative industries for sustainable economic diversification in Qatar

Maha Alshebani and Zariyah Zein

10.1 INTRODUCTION

Qatar has rapidly restructured its economy within a single generation and currently boasts one of the highest GDP per capita globally (United States Department of State, 2023). In the midst of worldwide economic changes and breakthroughs in technology, Qatar finds itself at a crucial point, actively speeding up the process of transitioning to an economy that is diverse and built on knowledge. The strategic change is embodied in the Third Qatar National Development Strategy (NDS3) 2024–2030, which acts as a blueprint to guide the country in achieving the Qatar National Vision 2030 (General Secretariat for Development Planning, 2008).

Central to this vision is the development of Cultural and Creative Industries (CCIs), which hold significant potential for contributing to economic diversification and national growth. The cultural and creative sector in Qatar encompasses a wide range of activities, including arts, design, media, and heritage conservation. Promoting innovation in non-oil sectors creates new revenue streams and jobs, fostering long-term growth and stability as well as enriching the cultural understanding of the nation, stimulating innovation, and attracting international tourism and investment (Al-Sulaiti et al., 2024). National examples, such as Katara Cultural Village, Qatar Museums, Doha Film Institute, and the M7 Creative Hub, will be analyzed throughout this chapter to provide an overall understanding of the vibrant cultural and creative sector in Qatar, thus providing the drive necessary to diversify economic benefits and enhance the country's global standing.

Despite the promising potential, Qatar's CCIs face several challenges that hinder the development of their full potential. Understanding these challenges and identifying opportunities for growth is crucial for leveraging Qatar's rich cultural heritage and burgeoning art scene to achieve national economic growth. This chapter aims to explore how Qatar can effectively utilize its cultural and creative resources to foster economic diversification. The research will delve into the current state of CCIs in Qatar, examine the key challenges, and provide strategic recommendations for enhancing the sector's contribution to the economy.

In addressing these challenges, this chapter will contribute to the broader discourse on economic diversification in Qatar, providing insights that can inform policy decisions and strategic initiatives. Ultimately, the goal is to highlight the critical role that CCIs can play in shaping a sustainable and prosperous future for Qatar, aligned with its national vision and aspirations.

10.2 LITERATURE REVIEW

As stated by the Department for Culture, Media and Sport (DCMS) in the UK in 1998, CCIs encompass cultural industries, creative arts, and creative services (DCMS, 1998). CCIs are recognized as a fusion of creative and intellectual assets that possess both corporate value and meet market demands (Santoro, Bresciani, & Papa, 2020). Consequently, the creative economy emerged as a key component of economic diversification strategies (Al Naimi, 2022).

10.2.1 Economic Dimensions and Contributions

Over the past few years, research on CCI and its economic impact has become an area of great interest to researchers and policymakers (Towse & Navarrete Hernández, 2020). Of late, research in the area has emphasized the economic potential of the industries, focusing on the processes involved in bringing output from the industry to market, and the challenges people within the industry face. The creative industry is very unique yet unpredictable, most relevantly due to the demand for artistic products changing based on individual tastes and culture trends (Caves, 2000). However, as Caves (2000) notes, creative and cultural industries play a vital role in the economy. Recent reports estimate that these industries contribute 3.1% to global GDP and 6.2% to employment, with the value of cultural goods and services exports doubling to $389.1 billion (UNCTAD, 2024; UNESCO, 2022a). The challenges identified by Caves (2000) including the unpredictability of the sector, the commercial incentives over genuine creativity, and steep hierarchies and biases within the art world remain relevant, but new dimensions such as digital distribution and the impact of social media have introduced additional complexities and opportunities for artists.

10.2.2 An Overview of Qatar's Cultural Creative Industries

As Qatar moves towards reaching its vision of 2030 of fostering a capable and educated population with strong morals in line with the country's direction, through prioritizing most relevantly social and economic development, investment in CCI cultivates a society empowered with a strong sense of cultural heritage and national identity, contributing to a sustainable creative economy. Al-Hammadi and Alkaabi (2021) assert that Qatar is actively constructing national heritage narratives as a means to shape a modern national identity, one that reflects the country's diverse population, including both citizens and residents in alignment with the goals of Qatar National Vision 2030. Qatar has made substantial investments in cultural infrastructure, establishing landmark institutions such as the Museum of Islamic Art, the Katara Cultural Village, and the National Museum of Qatar, which opened in 2019. The latter stands out for its striking architectural design and was constructed at a reported cost of $434 million (Öztürkkal & Togan-Eğrican, 2019). These venues not only preserve and showcase Qatari heritage but also provide investment into spaces capable of hosting international exhibitions and events, thereby positioning Qatar as a global cultural hub.

Initiatives such as the Doha Film Institute (DFI) further underscore the country's commitment to nurturing creative talent and fostering a vibrant cultural scene. The DFI has been instrumental in supporting local filmmakers, offering funding, training, and mentorship, and promoting Qatari cinema on the international stage. Through initiatives such as the Ajyal Film Festival, the DFI provides a platform for emerging filmmakers from around the world to showcase their work, facilitating cultural exchange and enhancing Qatar's global cultural presence.

Additionally, the Qatari government has launched several initiatives aimed at supporting the growth of CCIs. Programs such as the M7 innovation hub in Msheireb, along with its affiliated business incubator Scale7, provide vital platforms for creative entrepreneurs to develop, launch, and showcase their work. As a state-of-the-art facility, M7 offers a range of resources including co-working spaces, workshops, and exhibition areas designed to foster innovation, collaboration, and professional growth among artists and designers. Scale7, Qatar's first fashion and design business incubator, aims to accelerate the growth of startups in the creative industries by providing mentorship, networking opportunities, and access to investment (M7, 2024). These initiatives are part of a broader strategy to integrate CCIs into the national economic framework, recognizing their potential to drive innovation and economic diversification. By embedding CCIs within the economic agenda, Qatar aims to create a dynamic environment where creativity and commerce intersect, generating new economic opportunities and enhancing the country's cultural landscape.

From a social perspective, leveraging the economic impact of the cultural sector is crucial for Qatar to preserve its cultural identity amid globalization and modernization. The sector offers a dynamic platform to celebrate Qatari heritage through a contemporary lens while also creating space for non-Qatari residents to share their narratives and lived experiences in the country. This inclusive approach was evident in events such as the "Pop Up" showcase held from 26 to 30 November 2024 at the M7 creative hub in Msheireb. The event featured a curated group of regional fashion designers from across the Gulf, alongside guest designers from Morocco, invited in recognition of the Qatar–Morocco 2024 Year of Culture program (Years of Culture, 2024).

According to Qatar's Planning and Statistics Authority, the nation invested 2.9 billion Qatari Riyals in cultural commodities in 2021, contributing substantially to the national GDP (Planning and Statistics Authority, 2022). This investment underscores Qatar's commitment to the development of the cultural sector, reflecting the country's direction in preserving the creative and cultural industries, which are seen as a vital component of the country's diversification strategy. The cultural sector not only enriches the national economy but also plays a crucial role in job creation, tourism, and the promotion of Qatar's international image. Cultural events and institutions attract tourists, fostering a vibrant tourism sector that complements the traditional economic pillars of oil and gas. Additionally, the promotion of Qatari culture on the global stage enhances the country's soft power, building international relationships and fostering cultural diplomacy.

10.2.3 Theoretical Frameworks

The growth of Creative and Cultural Industries (CCIs) in Qatar is centered around diversifying the economy towards a more knowledge-based model. CCIs are widely acknowledged for their significant contributions to economic growth, creativity, and cultural diversity. However, they face numerous challenges that can hinder their progress and long-term sustainability. Research in this field highlights the importance of fostering a tolerant and open environment that embraces diversity, as this is essential for the development, dissemination, implementation, and enhancement of creative ideas (UNESCO & UNDP, 2013).

This research is grounded in five main theories, which have provided a comprehensive understanding of the sector. The researchers adopted a top-down approach to analyze the sector, utilizing the following theories:

10.2.3.1 Institutional theory

Institutional theory examines the impact of institutional structures—such as rules, regulations, and conventions—on the behavior and growth of CCIs. According to North, institutions play a crucial role in shaping the norms that govern how organizations operate and develop. In the context of CCIs, institutional structures can either facilitate or impede growth (North, 1990).

Application in Qatar's CCIs

- *Relevant institutions*: Key institutions influencing CCIs in Qatar include the Ministry of Culture, Qatar Museums, and the Qatar Development Bank. These entities set policies, provide funding, and regulate the sector.
- *Impact on growth*: Supportive regulations can encourage innovation and investment, while bureaucratic hurdles can deter creative entrepreneurs.
- *Potential changes*: Streamlining regulatory processes, providing legal and administrative support, and establishing clear intellectual property rights guidelines can enhance the growth of CCIs in Qatar.

10.2.3.2 Human capital theory

Human capital theory emphasizes the economic value of an individual's knowledge, skills, and abilities. This aligns with Qatar's vision of investing in both infrastructure and people to drive economic production and growth (Al-Sada, Disli, & Koc, 2022).

Application in Qatar's CCIs

- *Investment in people*: Qatar is investing in educational institutions and training programs to develop a skilled workforce for CCIs. For example, the Doha Film Institute offers training and mentorship programs for local filmmakers.
- *Economic production and growth*: By developing human capital, Qatar aims to create a workforce capable of driving innovation and economic diversification (Qatar Development Bank [QDB], n.d.).
- *Skill acquisition*: Programs like Scale7 provide mentorship and networking opportunities for creative entrepreneurs, helping them acquire the skills needed to succeed in the industry (Qatar Development Bank [QDB], n.d.).

10.2.3.3 Social capital theory

Social capital theory highlights the importance of social networks, relationships, and trust in promoting cooperation and economic transactions. CCIs serve as a platform for bringing people together to share and engage, fostering collaboration and creativity (Hauge, Pinheiro, & Zyzak, 2018).

Application in Qatar's CCIs

- *Role of CCIs in social interaction*: CCIs in Qatar, such as the Katara Cultural Village, host events and exhibitions that foster community engagement.
- *Enhancing collaboration*: Social networks facilitate collaboration and knowledge sharing, leading to the development of new ideas and projects (Dalle Nogare & Murzyn-Kupisz, 2022).
- *Building trust*: Trust within the creative community can lead to more efficient transactions and partnerships. Initiatives like mentorship programs and collaborative projects help strengthen these networks (Gloor, 2006).

10.2.3.4 Market development theory

Market development theory explains the expansion of markets and the factors contributing to their growth. It provides a structured approach to examining the challenges and opportunities associated with engaging audiences and ensuring the long-term viability of CCIs (Kotler & Keller, 2012).

Application in Qatar's CCIs

- *Expanding markets*: Qatar's CCIs face challenges such as low audience engagement and limited international recognition. Strategies like targeted marketing campaigns and digital platforms can address these issues.
- *Engaging audiences*: Understanding audience preferences through data analytics and market research is crucial for effective engagement.
- *Long-term viability*: Building an online presence and collaborating with influencers can enhance the sector's visibility and sustainability (Gloor, 2006).

10.2.3.5 Theory of cultural production

The theory of cultural production analyzes the processes involved in the creation, dissemination, and consumption of cultural goods and services. Understanding these processes helps identify obstacles and opportunities within the cultural production cycle (Bourdieu, 1993).

Application in Qatar's CCIs

- *Production processes*: High production costs and limited access to resources can hinder the growth of creative enterprises.
- *Dissemination and use*: Effective dissemination strategies, such as leveraging digital platforms and international collaborations, are crucial for reaching audiences.
- *Enhancing creative outputs*: Addressing obstacles like funding gaps and regulatory hurdles can create an environment that supports the creation and amplification of creative outputs (Ministry of Culture, Qatar, 2021).

10.3 METHODOLOGY

This chapter used a qualitative research methodology to investigate the current situation and opportunities of Cultural and Creative Industries (CCIs) in Qatar. The research methodology aims to achieve a comprehensive understanding of the sector's contribution to sustainable economic diversification. This will be accomplished by conducting a literature review and conducting in-depth semi-structured interviews with key players (see Table 10.1).

Table 10.1 Overview research methodology

Component	Details
Philosophical stance	Interpretivism
Research approach	Inductive
Research type	Qualitative
Research design	Exploratory
Research context	Cultural and Creative Industries (CCIs) in Qatar
Interview protocol	Five stakeholders from the cultural and creative industry were interviewed using purposeful sampling to provide more insights about practices and challenges of the creative and cultural industry
Data collection method	Interview
Data analysis methods	Thematic analysis manually

Source: Compiled by authors.

10.3.1 Data Collection

In qualitative research, selecting the right participants is crucial for obtaining credible and transferable results (DiCicco-Bloom & Crabtree, 2006). Non-probabilistic sampling approaches, such as purposive sampling was used to ensure that the information gathered is relevant and insightful (Saunders, Lewis, & Thornhill, 2009). For this study, purposive sampling was employed to select participants from within the cultural and creative industry in Doha. Participants included creatives and executives who were interviewed face-to-face in semi-structured sessions lasting between 40 to 60 minutes. The sample size of fewer than five participants is justified by the nature of small-sample research, which benefits from in-depth exploratory studies (Saunders, Lewis, & Thornhill, 2009). Both primary and secondary data were collected for this research, in order to fully understand CCIs in Doha.

10.3.1.1 Secondary data

Secondary data was collected from a number of sources:

1. Official government documents: these documents provided an insight into the creative and cultural industry. Essential publications such as Qatar National Vision 2030, annual reports from respective ministries, and policy papers are a few of the essential publications used.
2. Economic reports: these documents provide up-to-date data and analysis on the economic effects and possibilities of CCIs in Qatar and around the world.
3. Academic papers: These papers provided a deep dive into the theoretical elements of CCI as well as insight into the development of the sector.

10.3.1.2 Primary data

Qualitative data collection methods like in-depth interviews, focus groups, and observations were considered. However, the in-depth interview technique was chosen as the most suitable due to its ability to capture rich, detailed information directly from respondents (Creswell & Poth, 2016).

To adequately prepare for the interview, ten semi-structured interview questions were compiled (see Appendix). Five semi-structured interviews were conducted with key individuals from within the sector, to truly grasp the challenges and opportunities. The participants consisted of three males and two females, aged between 35 and 65, who now occupy executive-level positions and make significant contributions to the Creative Industries in Qatar. The semi-structured interview style offers freedom, enabling participants to openly articulate their experiences and viewpoints while ensuring comprehensive exploration of important issues. The interview questions seek to elicit thorough opinions regarding several topics, such as legal and legislative frameworks, audience involvement, societal attitudes, and market development.

10.3.2 Questionnaire Development

The interview questionnaire was developed based on the literature review (Creswell & Poth, 2016). Participants were assured that subject identifiers were eliminated, and that anonymity would be kept, to assure that responses reflected personal opinions and experiences of the participants from the CCI in Qatar and not the associations they represented. Interviews were semi-structured, allowing open-ended responses to gather detailed information about events, processes, and issues related to CCI in Qatar.

Participants were initially contacted via email and professional networks inviting them for one-to-one interviews about CCI. Ethical considerations were thoroughly addressed, ensuring participants' consent and understanding of the study's purpose. Interviews were audio-recorded when permitted, and detailed notes were taken.

10.3.3 Data Analysis

The process of analyzing qualitative data requires organization to assist in the theme identification which helps in understanding the concerns, perception, and recommendation of the participants.

- *Data organization*: The transcriptions undergo meticulous inspection and organization to enhance analysis. This stage involves dividing the data into manageable chunks, based on the interview questions and over all main topics.
- *Theme identification*: Thematic analysis is employed to code the data and uncover recurring themes and patterns across the interviews. The transcripts were thoroughly reviewed on numerous occasions to guarantee a comprehensive comprehension of the material.

Finally, an extensive analysis of the data was conducted to comprehensively comprehend the underlying concerns, perceptions, and recommendations expressed by the participants. This stage entails establishing connections between the findings and the wider body of literature and theoretical frameworks that were examined in the literature review.

10.4 RESULTS AND DISCUSSION

This section presents the findings from interviews with key stakeholders in Qatar's CCIs, including executive-level contributors, entrepreneurs, and artists. The data presented highlight the current challenges that are hindering the development of the CCI in Qatar including the lack of audience engagement and interest in the sector, the difficulties faced upon entry into the sector, the overall societal perceptions towards the sector, and finally, the global perception of Qatar in terms of its contribution internationally to the cultural creative sector.

10.4.1 Audience Engagement

One of the most pressing challenges that was identified during our research into the CCIs in Qatar is the difficulty in engaging audiences from the Qatari society effectively. Specifically, the challenge emerges in terms of audiences acknowledging and attending cultural events and supporting creative initiatives, which in turn results in the growth and success of such initiatives. It is clear that Qatar has invested vastly in cultural infrastructure and numerous initiatives to promote creative activities over the past few years. Yet our participants have observed that "many creative enterprises struggle with visibility and reaching broader audiences" (Participant #1, personal communication, May 2024). Additionally, Participant #1 noted, "We have world-class museums and cultural venues, but attracting a consistent local audience remains a challenge. People need to feel connected to the cultural offerings, and that requires targeted engagement strategies."

This disconnect between the creative output and audience engagement has been an issue for the creative industry; many creative businesses lack the necessary marketing capabilities and resources to effectively promote their products and services (Al-Shamsi, 2021). The limited understanding of market dynamics within the CCIs further complicates efforts to cultivate a loyal customer base (Pitts & Price, 2020). "Effective audience engagement is crucial for building sustainable creative enterprises, but without robust frameworks and strategies, many creative businesses find it challenging to connect with their target audiences. This disconnect can lead to low visibility for creative products and services, ultimately hindering the growth of the sector" (Margoni et al., 2021).

10.4.2 High Barriers to Entry

The research has found that the Creative and Cultural Industries (CCIs) in Qatar face significant barriers to entry, primarily due to bureaucratic processes and the high costs associated with starting and sustaining creative businesses. These bureaucratic hurdles can be particularly burdensome for small and medium-sized enterprises (SMEs) within the CCIs. Participant #4, a creative entrepreneur, commented: "Navigating the bureaucratic processes is incredibly time-consuming and can be discouraging, especially for smaller businesses without the resources to handle it. We need more streamlined processes to help us focus on creativity rather than paperwork" (Al-Mutawa & Alsudairi, 2020). The nature of doing business within the CCIs is unique, creative business may be stifled or even deterred from starting if the regulatory environment is seen as both time-consuming and difficult to navigate.

Additionally, participants have highlighted that financing CCIs is seen as more difficult than traditional business. Researchers have supported this claim, indicating that traditional financing options are often inadequate for creative businesses due to their perceived high risk and intangible assets. Al-Mutawa and Alsudairi (2020) note that there is a pressing need for innovative financing solutions tailored to the specific requirements of the creative sector. These solutions could include grants, low-interest loans, and investment funds specifically designed to support creative entrepreneurs.

Moreover, the high cost of entry into the sector is another formidable barrier (Hagoort & Kooyman, 2010). Starting and sustaining a creative business often requires substantial initial investment, which can be prohibitive for many aspiring entrepreneurs. This financial burden includes costs associated with setting up physical spaces, purchasing equipment and materials, marketing, and navigating the complex regulatory landscape. An interviewee from the creative sector highlighted this challenge, stating,

> t]he financial challenges faced by people in the industry that I find myself in are more or less based on not understanding how expensive print can be. Or the preparation work that goes into it—preparing the documents, preparing the content, etc. The barriers of entry into the sector are very high and often make it difficult to start, despite the eagerness to produce authentic cultural content.

This quote underscores the multifaceted nature of the financial hurdles in the CCIs. Beyond the direct costs of production and operation, creative entrepreneurs must also contend with expenses related to regulatory compliance, legal fees, and administrative processes.

10.4.3 Changing Social Perceptions Towards CCIs

Participant #4 highlighted how, in many societies, including Qatar, traditional professions such as engineering, medicine, and finance are often valued more highly than careers in the arts and creative industries. Additionally, Participant #5 shared, "Parents often discourage their children from pursuing creative careers because they don't see it as a stable or prestigious path. This mindset needs to change if we want to develop a strong creative workforce." This cultural bias can deter individuals from pursuing careers in the creative sector, leading to a talent gap that hampers the growth of CCIs.

Bowell (2015) notes that changing these perceptions is crucial for encouraging more people to enter creative fields and for society to value and support CCIs. There is a need for greater public awareness about the economic and social contributions of the creative industries. Ball, Pollard, and Stanley (2010) stated that work within the cultural and creative industry lacks clear definition, which results in failure of recognition of creative work as stable employment due to the assumption that creative work is primarily a hobby or a leisurely pleasure.

10.4.4 International Recognition of Qatar as a Cultural Hub

The Qatar National Vision 2030 has four main goals, which it prioritizes to pave the way for Qatar to strategically advance. The main pillars are: Human Development, Social Development, Economic Development, and Environmental Development. Focusing specifically on the Social Development pillar, Qatar has specifically and most relevantly prioritized the development of a society which is capable of playing a significant role towards the development of Qatar's place on an international platform (Government Communications Office, 2024).

Participant #2 (age 65), reminisced about the global perception of Qatar 15–20 years ago, noting that when visiting countries abroad, there was little knowledge of the small state in the Gulf called Qatar. The participant emphasized that the global shift happened primarily when Qatar was granted the chance to host the 2022 FIFA World Cup in 2010.

During the 2022 FIFA World Cup in Qatar, it was evident how the country had strategically utilized the mega sporting event to promote its culture to the influx of international audiences attending and watching. The most obvious cultural example was the mascot La'eeb, who was designed to animate a piece of cultural dress relevant to Qatari culture, the Ghutra which was later commercialized in a strategy that designed the headwear to be worn by international guests and children, sharing a part of Qatari identity with all visitors (Savage & Borg, 2022).

To examine a key resource on Qatar's global political stance, Mehran Kamrava (2015) describes Qatar as a "little giant," noting that despite its small geographic size, it has made substantial advancements and become influential in diplomatic, cultural, and economic sectors. Kamrava (2015) highlights that the nation's soft power initiatives, particularly in the realm of the creative cultural industries and its cultural diplomacy strategies, have played a crucial role in enhancing Qatar's visibility in diplomatic, international public, and commercial arenas.

Participant #2 concluded the discussion of Qatar's place on a global level by stating that: "Qatar's success during the WC was primarily due to the cultural creative industries contributions, a goal that was being worked towards for over a decade. Now that it has passed, what comes next? How do we ensure that the international relations built are sustainable?"

10.4.5 Strategic Recommendations

10.4.5.1 Audience engagement

To enhance audience engagement in Qatar's Creative and Cultural Industries (CCIs), it is crucial to conduct thorough audience research to understand the preferences, behaviors, and needs of potential consumers. Segmenting audiences based on demographics, cultural interests, and engagement levels will allow for tailored marketing and engagement strategies that can effectively reach specific target groups. Based on these insights, the development and implementation of targeted marketing campaigns using both traditional media, such as newspapers, TV, and radio, as well as digital platforms, including social media, websites, and email marketing, to reach diverse audience segments can be advanced (Qatar Development Bank, 2022).

Furthermore, Al-Shamsi builds on this approach, by specifically highlighting the significant contributions resulting from tailored collaborations with local influencers and celebrities, emphasizing that it can further enhance the reach and impact of these campaigns locally (Al-Shamsi, 2021). Building a robust online presence through websites, social media channels, and online marketplaces dedicated to Qatari creative products, such as virtual galleries and online exhibitions, can attract and engage a global audience. Employing search engine optimization (SEO) strategies can improve the discoverability of creative content (UNESCO, 2021). Collaborating with schools, universities, and community organizations can help integrate these events into society (Bowell, 2015). Additionally, implementing visitor feedback mechanisms can help continuously improve the overall experience and ensure that offerings align with audience expectations (McKinsey & Company, 2022). Although geographically small, Qatar hosts a diverse population, encompassing a broad spectrum of international cultures, languages, and identities. Consequently, fostering institutional and personal connections, along with engaging in dialogue with international audiences, is crucial for Qatar's success in developing its Cultural Creative Industries (CCI). Moreover, Participant #1 states that "there is a need for comprehensive audience research to understand the preferences and behaviors of potential consumers. Developing targeted marketing campaigns and leveraging digital platforms can enhance visibility and engagement" (van Ham, 2008). Therefore, organizing more cultural events and exhibitions and enhancing online presence can help attract and retain a sustainable audience, thus creating a vibrant cultural ecosystem, inclusive of all diverse groups of the population based in Qatar and fostering cultural exchange and dialogue.

10.4.5.2 High barriers of entry

To address the high barriers of entry into Qatar's Creative and Cultural Industries (CCIs), a multifaceted approach is required, focusing on simplifying regulatory processes, providing targeted financial support, and enhancing business training and support systems.

According to the Creative Economy report by the British Council (n.d.), providing access to legal advisors and administrative support can help creative entrepreneurs navigate regulatory and legal requirements, including intellectual property rights, contract negotiations, and other legal matters. Collaboration between government entities and industry leaders is vital to promote the value of creative professions. Developing policy initiatives and regular consultations and feedback mechanisms between regulatory authorities and the creative sector can help ensure that policies are supportive and responsive to the evolving needs of CCIs. Establishing advisory boards or councils that include representatives from the creative industries can provide valuable insights and recommendations for policy improvements (UNESCO, 2021).

In terms of simplifying regulatory processes, it is essential to establish a centralized online platform where creative entrepreneurs can access all necessary information and complete required processes for business registration, licensing, and compliance. This platform should offer clear, step-by-step guidelines to simplify navigation through bureaucratic procedures. The design hub M7 and its business incubator Scale7, previously mentioned, has taken the initial steps by providing workshops to learn about such requirements. However, to reach a broader audience, further development should be readily available to a larger audience, perhaps by the umbrella organization Qatar Museums, which M7 falls under and their respective online platforms (Scale7, n.d.). Qatar Museums has ongoing and direct access to Qatar's creatives who may be at different levels of growth and career development. Therefore, the notion of working as a bridge between them and governmental agencies can potentially provide a solution.

In terms of providing targeted financial support, introducing financial products specifically designed for the creative sector can significantly lower the financial barriers to entry. Grants, low-interest loans, and investment funds tailored to the unique needs of creative enterprises should be developed to cover the costs of setting up physical spaces, purchasing equipment, and marketing.

In terms of enhancing business training and support systems, offering workshops and training programs focused on financial literacy and business management tailored to the creative sector can help entrepreneurs better manage their finances, plan their budgets, and navigate funding opportunities. Collaboration with educational institutions is crucial to integrate arts-focused curricula that include practical business skills. This can prepare students for careers in the creative sector and ensure a steady supply of skilled professionals.

Additionally, establishing mentorship programs that connect new entrepreneurs with experienced industry professionals can provide valuable guidance on business strategy, regulatory compliance, and financial management. Participant #2 emphasized the importance of utilizing Qatar's existing contributors to the CCI by stating that:

> We need to give the teachers the support to pass the message to the amateurs. Why is there no grant for the professionals to have the opportunity to pass on their capabilities and skills? We need to understand how to use grants and to value the buried brains that we have hidden in Qatari households who witnessed the CCI shift that happened since Qatar was established.

By addressing the high cost of entry through targeted financial support, comprehensive business training, and mentorship programs in the CCI sector, Qatar can create a more attainable and accessible creative economy. This approach will enable a broader range of individuals to contribute to the CCIs, fostering innovation and driving economic diversification.

10.4.5.3 Changing social perceptions towards CCIs

Emphasizing the role of CCIs in shaping national identity and preserving cultural heritage will foster a broader appreciation for the creative sector (Al-Shamsi, 2021). In Qatar, CCIs play a vital role in reflecting the nation's unique cultural narratives and historical experiences. Therefore, by preserving traditional art forms, practices, and heritage sites, these industries help maintain a tangible connection to the past while also enabling contemporary cultural expressions to flourish. This dual role not only reinforces a sense of national pride and continuity but also promotes cultural diversity and inclusion within the society (Al-Shamsi, 2021). Moreover, highlighting the contributions of CCIs to national identity can enhance social cohesion by bringing together diverse communities through shared cultural experiences. Events such as festivals, exhibitions, and performances provide platforms for different cultural groups to showcase their heritage, fostering mutual understanding and respect. This inclusivity strengthens society and builds a more cohesive and resilient society. Participant #2 builds on this notion by stating that "Culture influences our daily life, our upbringing and how we perceive ourselves. Culture ensures a sense of belonging; it builds loyalty and strong national identity resulting in sustainable societal contribution and unity."

Public awareness campaigns and educational programs that underscore the economic and social contributions of CCIs are essential for changing public perceptions and garnering wider support. Organizing industry events, conferences, and networking sessions can foster collaboration and knowledge sharing among creative entrepreneurs, investors, and policymakers. Showcasing the achievements and potential of the creative sector through media, public exhibitions, and educational curricula can inspire a new generation to value and participate in the cultural economy. These events provide valuable opportunities for learning and partnership development, further supporting growth in the sector and a broader appreciation for CCIs which will ultimately lead to greater investment, innovation, and sustainability in the sector.

Furthermore, providing comprehensive career guidance and counseling in schools and universities is another critical step. These programs should emphasize the diverse opportunities available within CCIs, highlighting how creative careers can contribute to both personal fulfillment and economic success. Organizing career fairs, mentorship programs, and internships can give students first-hand experience in the creative sector, helping them understand and navigate potential career paths. Collaborations with industry professionals can offer students valuable insights and networking opportunities, further encouraging them to pursue careers in CCIs (Bowell, 2015). Partnerships with international arts institutions can bring global perspectives and best practices to local education, enriching the learning experience and expanding opportunities for students. Encouraging participation in arts-related extracurricular activities can further foster early interest and skill development, laying a solid foundation for future careers in CCIs.

An additional approach would be recognizing and celebrating achievements in the creative sector through awards, scholarships, and public acknowledgments that can elevate the status of creative professions and inspire more individuals to pursue such careers. Establishing national awards for excellence in various creative fields can attract international attention and investment, showcasing Qatar's commitment to nurturing and promoting creative talent. This recognition helps build a culture that values and supports creative endeavors, driving the growth of CCIs (World Economic Forum, 2025).

By integrating these strategies, Qatar can harness the full potential of its creative and cultural industries to strengthen national identity, preserve cultural heritage, and promote economic and social development.

10.4.5.4 International recognition of Qatar as a cultural hub

The international recognition of Qatar's cultural and creative industries' capabilities can elevate the nation's global standing. Initiatives like Qatar Museums, their projects and affiliates, demonstrate how cultural and creative industries can be leveraged to enhance diplomatic relations and cultural exchanges. These efforts not only eventually enhance economic income from cultural tourism and international investment but also sustainably establish Qatar as a hub of cultural excellence and international dialogue on the global stage.

Participant #1 acknowledged the sustainable capabilities of Qatar as an international cultural hub by stating that "[c]ultural exchange programs act as a clear and direct vehicle to build direct ties between Qatar and its diplomatic partners." This statement is supported by Qatar Museums' ongoing annual initiative, the Years of Culture (YoC). The YoC was launched in 2012 as an annual program where Qatar collaborates with one of its diplomatic partners for a full calendar year to share and learn about each other's cultural and artistic heritage (Years of Culture, 2024).

During this period, both Qatar and the partner country organize various events, festivals, and exchange programs to foster mutual understanding and cross-cultural dialogue, a vital component of establishing Qatar as a diverse cultural hub (M7, 2024). This project is a key example of the capabilities of a cultural and creative industries-focused initiative that targets collaboration based on the exchange of knowledge and culture that will inevitably build sustainable diplomatic relations that work to enhance the nation's image to foreign audiences and potential investors.

Participant #2 emphasized the importance of the cultural and creative sector by stating that it is the key to open the gates for foreign investment and economic diversification. The participant stated that Qatar does not need fast cash or a direct cheque but instead aims to obtain opportunity and a stronger standing on the global stage (Interview with participant #2, April 2024). The participant clearly stated that the "the work being done is not to benefit specific members of the Qatari society, but instead Qatar as a whole, as a nation".

Additionally, Sangchumnong in this research found that the cultural and creative industries have vastly developed in the last decade, resulting in the softening of boundaries around the sector in terms of building skills and capabilities which allow contributors of the CCI to smoothly be incorporated into the wider economy; most relevantly, the capacity to contribute to the tourism sector (Sangchumnong, 2019).

According to Participant #3, the CCI is a significant contributor to Qatar's international recognition in the sense that it boosts the nation's cultural appeal in terms of attracting tourists. The participant emphasized that "[c]ultural attractions and investments draw visitors, which thereby generates revenue and promotes Qatar's cultural heritage to a global audience. Which in turn, stimulates local businesses, from hospitality to retail, creating a multiplier effect throughout the local economy" (Interview with participant #3, April 2024).

By the utilization of such approaches which offer international opportunities, alongside recommendations mentioned throughout this research to enhance human capabilities and accessibility within the cultural and creative industries, Qatar has a clear path to successfully achieve the QNV2030 goal of developing a society capable of significantly playing a role in developing Qatar's international standing (General Secretariat for Development Planning, 2008). Thus, contributing drastically to the development of the cultural creative industries and in turn, the sector's contribution to diversifying the economy of the nation.

10.5 CONCLUSION

This chapter has explored the significant potential of Qatar's Creative and Cultural Industries (CCIs) to contribute to the country's economic diversification and cultural enrichment as outlined in the Qatar National Vision 2030. Through comprehensive analysis, it has been shown that Qatar has made substantial investments in cultural infrastructure and initiatives to promote creative activities. Despite these efforts, critical challenges remain that hinder the full realization of the sector's potential.

While this chapter provides a comprehensive overview of the current state of Qatar's CCIs and offers strategic recommendations, there is a need for future research to delve deeper into specific areas. Future studies could explore the impact of digital technologies on the CCIs in Qatar, the role of international collaborations in enhancing global competitiveness, and the effectiveness of current educational reforms in nurturing creative talent. Additionally, longitudinal studies to track the progress and impact of implemented strategies over time would provide valuable insights into the long-term development of the sector.

In conclusion, by addressing the identified challenges and implementing the comprehensive strategies proposed in this research, Qatar can create a robust framework to support the growth and sustainability of its creative and cultural industries. These initiatives will help engage audiences more effectively, simplify bureaucratic processes, change social perceptions towards creative careers, and ultimately foster a vibrant and sustainable creative economy recognized globally. This multifaceted approach not only drives economic diversification and cultural enrichment but also strengthens national identity and cultural heritage, positioning Qatar as a global hub for creative and cultural excellence.

BIBLIOGRAPHY

Al-Hammadi, M. I., & Alkaabi, I. M. (2021). *Socio-economic development, globalization and the need for heritage policy in Qatar: Case study.* QSpace Institutional Repository. 10.4236/jss.2021.93028https://doi.org/10.4236/jss.2021.93028

Al-Mutawa, M. M., & Alsudairi, M. (2020). Challenges facing cultural and creative industries in the Gulf Cooperation Council (GCC) countries. *Arabian Journal of Business and Management Review (Oman Chapter)*, *9*(8), 1–13.

Al Naimi, S. M. (2022). Economic diversification trends in the Gulf: The case of Saudi Arabia. *Circular Economy and Sustainability*, *2*, 221–230. https://doi.org/10.1007/s43615-021-00106-0

Al-Sada, M., Disli, M., & Koc, M. (2022). Building human sustainable capital via education: The case of Qatar. *Art, Networks & Development, 3*(1), Article 5030. Qatar University. Retrieved December 01, 2025, from https://journals.qu.edu.qa/index.php/ANDD/article/view/5030/3143

Al-Shamsi, S. A. H. (2021). Creative economy development in the United Arab Emirates: Current status and challenges. *International Journal of Innovation, Creativity and Change, 16*(1), 1–15.

Al-Sulaiti, A., Hamouda, A. M., Al-Yafei, H., & Abdella, G. M. (2024). Innovation-based strategic roadmap for economic sustainability and diversity in hydrocarbon-driven economies: The Qatar perspective. *Sustainability, 16*(9), 3770. https://doi.org/10.3390/su16093770

Ball, L., Pollard, E., & Stanley, N. (2010). *Creative graduates creative futures.* CGCF Higher Education.

Bourdieu, P. (1993). *The field of cultural production: Essays on art and literature.* Cambridge: Polity Press.

Bowell, I. (2015). Beyond the gate: Community arts participation enhances teaching and learning. *Curriculum Matters, 11*, 31–51. https://doi.org/10.18296/cm.0003

British Council. (n.d.). *Creative economy.* Retrieved May 23, 2024, from https://arts.britishcouncil.org/what-we-do/creative-economy.

Caves, R. E. (2000). *Creative industries: Contracts between art and commerce.* Harvard University Press.

Creswell, J. W., & Poth, C. N. (2016). *Qualitative inquiry and research design: Choosing among five approaches* (4th ed.). Sage Publications.

Dalle Nogare, C., & Murzyn-Kupisz, M. (2022). Do museums foster innovation through engagement with the cultural and creative industries? In M. Heinecke & C. C. Essers (Eds.), *Arts, entrepreneurship, and innovation* (pp. 153–186). Springer Nature Switzerland. https://doi.org/10.1007/978-3-030-98304-8_7

Department for Culture, Media and Sport. (1998, April 9). *Creative industries mapping documents 1998.* GOV.UK. https://www.gov.uk/government/publications/creative-industries-mapping-documents-1998

DiCicco-Bloom, B., & Crabtree, B. F. (2006). The qualitative research interview. *Medical Education, 40*(4), 314–321. https://doi.org/10.1111/j.1365-2929.2006.02418.x

General Secretariat for Development Planning. (2008). *Qatar National Vision 2030.* State of Qatar. https://www.npc.qa/en/QNV/Documents/QNV2030_English_v2.pdf

Gloor, P. A. (2006). *Swarm creativity: Competitive advantage through collaborative innovation networks.* Oxford University Press.

Government Communications Office. (2024). *Qatar National Vision 2030* [Strategic framework]. Government Communications Office. https://www.gco.gov.qa/en/state-of-qatar/qatar-national-vision-2030/

Hagoort, G., & Kooyman, R. (2010). *Study on the entrepreneurial dimension of cultural and creative industries.* HKU, Utrecht School of the Arts.

Hauge, E. S., Pinheiro, R. M., & Zyzak, B. (2018). Knowledge bases and regional development: Collaborations between higher education and cultural creative industries. *International Journal of Cultural Policy, 24*(4), 485–503. https://doi.org/10.1080/10286632.2016.1218858

Kamrava, M. (2015). *Qatar: Small state, big politics* (e-book ed.). Cornell University Press.

Kotler, P., & Keller, K. L. (2012). *Marketing management* (14th ed.). Prentice Hall.

M7. (2024). *Home of creatives.* Qatar Museums. https://m7.org.qa/en/

Margoni, T., Senftleben, M., Antal, D., Bodó, B., van Gompel, S., Handke, C., Kretschmer, M., & Poort, J. (2021). *Ensuring the visibility and accessibility of European creative content on the world market: The need for copyright data improvement in the light of new technologies*. Institute for Information Law, University of Amsterdam; KU Leuven; Centre for IT & IP Law. https://doi.org/10.2139/ssrn.3785272

McKinsey & Company. (2022). *Achieving growth with leadership mindsets: Putting customer feedback to work*. McKinsey & Company. https://www.mckinsey.com/capabilities/growth-marketing-and-sales/our-insights/achieving-growth-putting-leadership-mindsets-and-behaviors-into-action

Ministry of Culture. (2021). *Cultural strategy of the State of Qatar*. Ministry of Culture. https://www.moc.gov.qa/en/

North, D. C. (1990). *Institutions, institutional change and economic performance*. Cambridge University Press.

Öztürkkal, B., & Togan-Eğrican, A. (2019). Art investment: Hedging or safe haven through financial crises. *Journal of Cultural Economics*, *44*(3), 481–529. https://doi.org/10.1007/s10824-019-09371-2

Pitts, S. E., & Price, S. M. (2020). *Understanding audience engagement in the contemporary arts*. Routledge. https://doi.org/10.4324/9780429342455

Planning and Statistics Authority. (2022). Qatar statistical yearbook 2022. Doha, Qatar: Planning and Statistics Authority. https://www.psa.gov.qa/en/statistics/Statistical%20Releases/General/QSY/QSY_2022.pdf

Qatar Development Bank. (2022). *GEM Qatar national report 2021: Monitoring entrepreneurship in a post-pandemic context* [Statistical report]. Global Entrepreneurship Monitor. https://www.qdb.qa/-/media/qdbapp/publications-pdf/qatar_gem_2021_en.pdf

Qatar Development Bank. (n.d.). *Scale7: Empowering creative visionaries* [About page]. Scale7. Retrieved June 23, 2025, from https://scale7.qdb.qa/en/about.

Sangchumnong (2019) Development of a sustainable tourist destination based on the creative economy: a case study of Klong Kone Mangrove Community, Thailland, *Kasetsart Journal of Social Sciences*, *49*(3), 642–649.

Santoro, G., Bresciani, S., & Papa, A. (2020). Collaborative modes with Cultural and Creative Industries and innovation performance: The moderating role of heterogeneous sources of knowledge and absorptive capacity. *Technovation*, *92–93*, Article 102003. https://doi.org/10.1016/j.technovation.2018.06.003

Saunders, M., Lewis, P., & Thornhill, A. (2009). *Research methods for business students* (5th ed.). Pearson Education.

Savage, W., & Borg, S. (2022). *What is the World Cup 2022 mascot? Explaining name, meaning and story behind Qatar's La'eeb*. Sporting News United Kingdom. https://www.sportingnews.com/uk/football/news/world-cup-2022-mascot-qatar-laeeb-explain-name-meaning-story/ojkmuozds4e8vkjyitzif3cz

Scale7. (n.d.). *First fashion & design business incubator in Qatar* [About page]. Qatar Development Bank. Retrieved May 1, 2024, from https://scale7.qdb.qa/en/.

State of Qatar. (2024). *Third Qatar national development strategy 2024–2030*.

Throsby, D. (2010). The economics of cultural policy. Cambridge University Press.

Towse, R., & Navarrete Hernández, T. (Eds.). (2020). *Handbook of cultural economics* (3rd ed.). Edward Elgar Publishing. https://doi.org/10.4337/9781788975803

UNESCO. (2021). *Cultural and creative industries in the face of COVID-19: An economic impact outlook*. UNESCO. https://unesdoc.unesco.org/ark:/48223/pf0000377863

UNESCO. (2022a). *Re|shaping policies for creativity: Addressing culture as a global public good.* UNESCO Publishing. https://unesdoc.unesco.org/ark:/48223/pf0000381945

UNESCO. (2022b, February 10). *Share of employment in cultural and creative industries as a percentage of total employment worldwide in 2020, by region.* Statista. https://www.statista.com/statistics/1290367/global-share-of-culture-employment-by-region/

United Nations Conference on Trade and Development. (2024). *Creative economy outlook 2024: Trends, challenges and opportunities.* UNCTAD. https://unctad.org/system/files/official-document/ditctsce2024d2_ch01_en.pdf

United Nations Educational, Scientific and Cultural Organization (UNESCO) & United Nations Development Programme (UNDP). (2013). *Creative economy report, 2013 (special edition): Widening local development pathways* [Special edition]. UNESCO. https://unesdoc.unesco.org/ark:/48223/pf0000224698

United States Department of State. (2023, December 7). *2022 investment climate statements: Qatar.* https://www.state.gov/reports/2022-investment-climate-statements/qatar/

van Ham, P. (2008). Place branding: The state of the art. *The Annals of the American Academy of Political and Social Science*, *616*(1), 126–149. https://doi.org/10.1177/0002716207312274

World Economic Forum. (2025, January 19). *Reskilling revolution: Preparing 1 billion people for tomorrow's economy.* World Economic Forum. https://www.weforum.org/stories/2025/01/reskilling-revolution-preparing-1-billion-people-for-tomorrow-s-economy-2c69a13e66/

Years of Culture. (2024, November 26–30). *M7 pop-up – not your average label [Event description].* Qatar–Morocco 2024 Year of Culture. https://yearsofculture.qa/editions/qatar-morocco/events/m7-pop-up-not-your-average-label

APPENDIX

Final Interview Questions

Introduction

- Can you describe your role and experience in relation to the cultural and creative industries within Qatar?
- In your view, what is the significance of CCIs in the economic diversification efforts of Qatar?

Challenges and Opportunities

- What are the main challenges facing the cultural creative sector in Qatar in terms of economic contribution and growth?
- In your opinion, how do you think current policy and regulatory frameworks impact the development of CCIs in Qatar?
- What changes would you recommend in policy or regulatory frameworks, to better support CCIs?
- Can you discuss any successful models or initiatives within Qatar that have effectively supported the growth of CCIs and why you think it was impactful?

Financial Support and Social Perceptions

- What are the specific financial challenges faced by entrepreneurs and businesses within CCIs in Qatar?
- In your opinion, what strategies could be employed to improve audience engagement for CCI products and services in Qatar?
- How do you think social perceptions of the cultural creative sector impact its development and growth in Qatar?

Future Recommendations

- How can Qatar utilize its rich culture and blooming art scene to successfully achieve national economic growth through the cultural creative sector?
- How can Qatar better leverage their cultural heritage and contemporary creativity to strengthen their position in the global creative economy

Index